EDUCATIONAL THERAPY

Volume 3

Educational Programs

MARSHALL B. ROSENBERG,
EDITOR

BERNIE STRAUB PUBLISHING CO., INC. & SPECIAL & CHILD PUBLICATIONS

© 1973 BERNIE STRAUB PUBLISHING CO., INC. &
SPECIAL CHILD PUBLICATIONS
4535 Union Bay Place N.E.
Seattle, Washington 98105

Standard Book Number: 0-87562-026-4
Library of Congress Catalog Card Number: 67-8807

Printed in the United States of America

CONTENTS

PREFACE

The critics of our educational system have been vociferous in recent days. I like the way Postman and Weingartner summarize these criticisms:

> *If* [the institution we call school] *is irrelevant, as Marshall McLuhan says; if it shields children from reality, as Norbert Wiener says; if it educates for obsolescence, as John Gardner says; if it does not develop intelligence, as Jerome Bruner says; if it is based on fear, as John Holt says; if it avoids the promotion of significant learnings, as Carl Rogers says; if it induces alienation, as Paul Goodman says; if it punishes creativity and independence, as Edgar Friedenberg says; if, in short, it is not doing what needs to be done, it can be changed; it* must *be changed.*[1]

The present book is an attempt to bring together what several persons are doing to improve our educational system. The articles were chosen on the basis of the following criteria: first, that programs discussed are innovative; second, that the programs discussed have gone past the theoretical level and have been tried in a real life setting; and third, that the programs are practical and within the capability of implementation in public schools. In other words, the book attempts to expose educational programs that are innovative, operational, and practical. This is not a book reporting research findings; when evaluative information was available it has been included but it has not been our purpose to determine whether the programs reported were successful. The purpose is to expose new ideas being tried to improve education, not to expose proven ideas.

[1]Postman, N. and Weingartner, C. TEACHING AS A SUBVERSIVE ACTIVITY. New York: Delacorte Press, 1969.

Although each program described in the book seems to direct itself primarily toward working with students or teachers or the school as a part of the total community, each level is involved to some degree in every program. The final chapter differs from the others in that it is not a description of an operational program but a report of a conference on educational change, which is included here to indicate directions which might guide future innovations in education.

Marshall B. Rosenberg

MOTIVATING THE DISABLED LEARNER

Robert J. Stout, Ed.D.
Director, Diagnostic and Special Learning Center
Colorado Springs Public Schools
Colorado Springs, Colorado

Larry Bussey, M.A.
Coordinator, Special Service Projects
Colorado Springs Public Schools
Colorado Springs, Colorado

This chapter describes the program of the Diagnostic and Special Learning Center of School District #11 of Colorado Springs, Colorado, where remedial instruction is provided for children whose academic achievement level is "below expectation." This report focuses on a "trail analysis" technique for discovering the variables that promote or interfere with learning. "Trailing" includes examination of motivational variables both outside and within the remedial setting, as well as those within the pupil in "physical, social-emotional, and psycho-educational" aspects. Approaches for enhancing motivation are then described, and the chapter closes with a discussion of the evaluation procedures employed thus far and some conclusions about results.

M. B. R.

12

MOTIVATING THE DISABLED LEARNER

Introduction

The problem of motivating the reluctant and disabled learner is rather extensive. A number of variables can exert favorable or unfavorable influences upon the youngster's behavior. Academic progress can be hindered when seemingly small but significant variables apparent within the particular remedial or clinical setting are considered as capable of significantly influencing behavior. The Diagnostic and Special Learning Center of School District #11 of Colorado Springs, Colorado, attempts to discover and to deal with motivational variables outside the remedial setting, within the remedial setting, and within the youngster himself in physical, social-emotional and psycho-educational aspects. The purpose of this article is to report on variables that seem either to promote or to interfere with the fullest utilization of the remedial instruction. Some of the variables may be unique to this Center's particular structure and mode of operation, and may not be observed in a different type of setting. Therefore, it may be helpful to give a brief description of the Center's structure and function.

The Diagnostic and Special Learning Center was designed to diagnose and to remediate learning disabilities of children from schools eligible under Title I of the Elementary and Secondary Education Act. The staff is comprised of a combination director-school psychologist, audiologist, nurse, social worker, test consultant, three teachers and a secretary. All professional staff members except teachers are primarily responsible for collecting data relevant for diagnostic purposes. However, teachers often assist with some cases. For example, if some aspect of the diagnosis is not entirely clear, the youngster is placed with a Center teacher for a week or two for diagnostic teaching. The teacher aims at clarification of what seems to control the child's behavior, how he copes with it, and how he responds to various types and levels of instructional media.

The diagnostic workup is aimed at providing remedial information. After the diagnostic information is assembled and evaluated, the teacher builds a model of how the child interacts with his environment on psychomotor, perceptual, and psycholinguistic levels—the areas of learning disabilities. In addition, the teacher then designs a program for improving the weak academic tool areas such as reading, writing, spelling, arithmetic, and language. The rationale is that the learning disability is interfering with normal learning of one or more of the basic academic skills mentioned above.

A typical Center youngster arrives and departs from the Center by school bus. He receives 90 minutes of remediation daily Monday through Thursday. Fridays are used by the staff for inservice training, staffings, conferring with the sending school teachers and other personnel, conferring with parents, assessing the week's progress of each pupil, and deciding on specific objectives, methods and materials for the following week.

All of the children who attend the Center have experienced failure and frustration in the academic setting although their measured ability is at least normal. Their achievement level, however, is below expectation. The major objective is to return the child to full-time regular classroom placement where the child is able to hold his own academically and socially.

One of the initial problems involved in understanding serious learning difficulty is that of determining those critical variables that influence the individual's behavior, positively and negatively. Early identification of these variables is extremely important in the diagnosis and treatment of a learning disability. It is assumed that most of these variables are subject to change. For example, if a negatively influential variable is not changed, it remains an impediment to instructional effectiveness. Similarly, a positively influential variable can be strengthened to contribute to the success of the treatment program. Of course, if a critical variable is never identified, its influence cannot be modified except by accident.

The Trail Analysis

There are several ways of identifying these critical variables. One can simply make a list of possibilities for random exploration; however, this approach is very inefficient. Another approach is through team diagnosis in which each discipline represented on the team explores the area in which it purports to be expert. A major drawback to this approach is that it results in considerable overlapping of the areas to be studied by the various team members. Both of these approaches were tried early in the Center program, but their disadvantages led to the development of a more systematic approach—that of the "trail analysis."

The trail analysis concept is quite simple and perhaps is not unique at all. In efforts to diagnose a child's learning difficulty it was noted that the critical variables were found most often along the actual path, or trail, on which the child moves in his daily activities. The trail is examined completely from the time the child wakes up in the morning to the time he goes to bed at night. The study follows him from his bedroom, to the bathroom, to the breakfast table, to the route he takes to school, to his classroom, to the playground, to the route he takes home after school, to his out-of-school play and hobby activities, to the dinner table, to the bathroom, and back to his bedroom at night. The trail also extends into the diagnostic and remedial phases of the Center program. For most youngsters the trail is quite consistent. The child's personal contacts, activities, and behaviors are examined all along this trail for signs that might lead to an explanation of his difficulty in school. For example, on the trail between home and school the child frequently may be threatened by a bully or feel threatened by a vicious-sounding dog. Within the home itself there may be several variables that contribute to the child's difficulty, such as physical violence, an absent parent, an unhealthy sibling relationship, or a relative who exerts a negative influence. Seldom is the child's problem traced to a single variable, although a particular one is often predominant.

Variables Outside the Remedial Setting

The trail begins when the principal contacts the parents to obtain authorization for diagnostic testing and bus transportation to the Center. The parental authorization form contains a letter to the parent indicating the purpose of the diagnostic testing and that the testing may lead to remedial instruction. Parental orientation regarding the diagnostic procedures is the first step in improving motivation toward subsequent remedial instruction for the child. If the parent does not understand, anxiety may develop and spill onto the child. Or a fearful attitude may develop through misunderstanding which negatively influences the child's learning.

Preliminary to diagnostic test administration, the test consultant establishes rapport with the child. Rapport is accomplished by explaining informally what is to happen and by chatting about the child's interests. Also, the child is shown around the Center so he can become familiar with the environment.

The first tests are the visual and auditory acuity screening checks. The visual screening exam is administered by the nurse after which the child is given a few M & M candies. The pleasant surprise that most children experience upon receiving the candy is a motivating influence in itself. Upon beginning the auditory exam the audiologist tells the younger children that they are pilots as the earphones are put on. This approach helps the children to relax and experience the exam with a pleasant feeling.

Data are gathered about the child's medical history and social development through home visits by the nurse and the social worker. The interaction between these staff members and the parents in a comfortable and safe setting of the home improves communication between home and Center. When the parents understand more precisely the child's problem, and when they feel that his needs will be met, parental cooperation is enhanced.

The trail continues at the sending school following the diagnostic workup at the Center. The sending school prepares the child for returning to the Center if there is to be remedial instruction. If a youngster feels he has sufficient reasons to give his peers for being gone part of the school day, then he will not worry so much about how the other children think of him. Most of all, he must not believe he is attending a class for "dumbbells." In many programs this aspect of counseling is neglected and a child must develop his own reason to give to other children for his attendance for special instruction. Sometimes his reasoning is based on erroneous assumptions and serves only to stimulate his peers to reject or antagonize him.

Counseling is provided by the Center social worker to explain the benefits of Center instruction and to help develop a positive attitude toward Center attendance. This enables the child to verbalize more adequately to his peers the reasons for his absence from class.

Another matter considered is the regular daily classroom schedule. It is important to note the activities from which the child will be absent. For example, it has been found that boys who miss their physical education are usually unhappy about it. Secondary school boys must be assured that they will not miss football or basketball practice. Usually the elementary youngster is rescheduled to participate in physical education activities with another class.

If the Center attendance schedule would interfere with participation in a special class activity such as a field trip, the child is excused from attending the Center for that day. Another matter given consideration in the sending school is whether or not materials are available in the classroom with which he can be successful. For example, if his basal reader is beyond his capabilities, then it is recommended that other materials be tried. Center teachers recommend materials and methods for this purpose.

Some children return to their school too late to eat lunch with their classmates. In this instance, a hot lunch is put aside for him, and he is permitted to have seconds if he so desires. This matter is quite important to some of the youngsters.

The bus ride itself to and from the Center can create problems. In previous years, both elementary and secondary students rode the bus together. The secondary students frequently teased the younger children making the latter more anxious and less receptive to instruction at the Center. In the current year, elementary and secondary children are separated, resulting in fewer bus problems. In addition, the skill of the bus driver in dealing with children can make a difference. The Center has been fortunate in having a particularly understanding driver who is able to interact favorably with the children.

Only elementary children attend the Center in the mornings. They are given a half pint of milk and two graham crackers daily. The purpose of this milk break is to alleviate possible disturbing hunger pangs. It also permits them to relax from the bus ride and to enjoy something pleasurable. During the milk break the children hear an interesting story which not only helps to improve listening skills, but serves also to develop a mental readiness for subsequent Center activities.

Variables Within the Remedial Setting

The environment in which remedial activities take place is an important factor in motivation. The Center was deliberately designed not to look like a school in order to reduce the number of cues capable of arousing anxiety (Teevan and Birney, 1964; Sarason et al., 1960). Most rooms are carpeted. Numerous paintings and sculptures are provided by the local Arts and Humanities Educational Program. The colors and interesting shapes make the setting attractive. The Center classrooms are much smaller than a regular classroom. A

18

teacher and three to five students fill these rooms. The children seem more settled in a smaller space. Larger spaces appear to stimulate hyperactivity in children with learning disabilities.

Somewhere along the trail a physical problem may be indicated. If so, the nurse arranges with the parents for help. For example, if teeth need attention, arrangements are made for dental care. If a child seems to have a visual acuity problem, local funds are obtained for an eye exam and for buying corrective glasses. It seems logical to think that a child whose eyes or body is easily fatigued will be less motivated to learn. Or, if the child's teeth hurt, he will not be motivated to give sustained attention to learning activities.

One of the functions of the social worker is to clarify parents' questions about the nature of the Center and its objectives. Parents are encouraged to visit the Center to see what it looks like. Anxieties and fears are usually alleviated after a tour of the Center. If there is a need for parental counseling beyond the usual orientation, the social worker does it. If intensive or extensive help is needed in the way of counseling or therapy, the family is referred to a local counseling service or mental health center.

It becomes clear that there are a number of blocks to motivation that need to be overcome or circumvented along the trail. The above blocks were discovered by teacher observation and from the children's remarks. These blocks can be moved or manipulated by personnel other than the child.

Variables Within the Pupil

A third general dimension of motivation might be labeled internal motivation variables. Several variables are considered by Atkinson (1964) who suggests that individuals have a tendency to succeed and a tendency to fail. These two tendencies are present in people who are being or will be evaluated. The degree or amount of this variable differs among individuals.

A second variable according to Atkinson is the probability of success in performing an activity. An individual is most highly motivated to work at a task when he feels there is a 50-50 chance of success. If he feels his chances are less, then success is considered less likely. If he feels his chances are better than 50-50, then he may feel success is so likely that there is no sense in trying.

A third variable suggested by Atkinson is the value associated with completion of a task. The accomplishment of a task must have correlated with it or in association with it, some sort of incentive that is prized or valued by the learner.

Certain assumptions are inherent in Atkinson's theory. First, the individual must consider himself responsible for the outcome. He must feel that he, rather than others, is in control of the results. In addition, he must know when he has succeeded by receiving explicit knowledge of success or failure. Third, success must not be a sure thing; there must be some degree of risk involved in the pursuit of achievement.

Center teachers attempt to motivate pupils in terms of Atkinson's theory. The small number of children with whom the Center teacher works permits her to interact closely with each child in the learning situation. It permits her to assess the level of task difficulty for each child; it permits her to correct, when necessary, the child's estimate of success or failure on a task; it permits her to assist the child in estimating his probability of success on a task; and it permits her to reinforce the successfully completed task. All these matters are relevant according to Atkinson.

The disabled learner's level of aspiration is typically low for learning in school. It is paramount that a teacher consider the child's own feeling about what his chances are for success in a given activity and, secondly, the incentives that are attached to the accomplishment of a task. However, there are complications. If the child has fantasies about being able to do well when actually he cannot, the task of the teacher becomes more difficult. She must interact closely with the child to assist him to feel successful on the tasks which will improve him academically.

There is information available to assist the teacher in the matter of task success. The teacher has access not only to the report of the test consultant, but also to the report of the sending school teachers. In addition, the Center teacher may work with a child for a time in order to clarify some areas of doubt. She may want to probe the child's readiness level to a greater degree. For example, the child may not know how to coordinate himself in order to skip, hop, jump rope, use scissors in cutting, use a pencil and paper, and so forth. Almost automatically, if not automatically, the Center teacher reacts to the child's performance of failure by saying, "That was quite hard," or, "That was difficult, wasn't it?" This technique permits the child to correct his thinking on his probability of success at the task. The need for starting with a task that can be accomplished on a 50-50 probability is important. He must feel both some confidence and some doubt in his ability to do the task.

Several ways are used in making the completion of activities seem valued or important. One general method can be called the extrinsic method. Center teachers frequently reward the attainment of a goal or the completion of an activity with M & M candies. Most of the youngsters are elementary boys who enjoy eating the candy or trading the candies for something more valuable to them. Candy has less appeal to secondary school boys—frequently their motivation derives from wanting to do better in school work and, consequently, to become more prestigious in their peer group. Giving verbal praise and also verbalizing how the activity will help them in attaining their goal, seems to help. Verbal praise, incidentally, is effective with a number of children, but not all. A few children have such a negative self-concept that praise does not fit their scheme. Changing their self-concept becomes a real goal for the teacher.

Another method of dealing with the assignment of value to task completion might be called the intrinsic method. This aspect of motivation seems crucial. Changes within the child that give pleasure to him probably will improve his motivation more than the extrinsic method. There seems to be more transfer of learning with intrinsic motivation than extrinsic. Oppenheimer (1968) mentions the pleasures occurring with new insights or from new awareness. He mentions that he has attained a "thousand horizons," each of which has given him pleasure and the persistence to look for even more horizons. It would seem that when some form of information has been integrated, there is a feeling of satisfaction or happiness on the part of the individual child.

Program Results

Efforts are being made to evaluate the Diagnostic and Special Learning Center program in several ways. Because the program is relatively new and subject to occasional modifications, the evaluative criteria and procedures have also been subject to change. This has made it difficult to provide a consistent assessment on a longitudinal basis.

One general criterion is the percentage of children who are able to resume fully their regular classroom program following therapy at the Center. Of the fifty-seven cases treated in 1967-68, thirty (52%) were successfully remediated, seven moved from the district, and twelve were continued into the 1968-69 program. In 1968-69 a total of forty-four cases were treated; twenty-five (56.8%) were successfully remediated, six moved from the district, and thirteen were carried over into 1969-70.

Other criteria include classroom teacher ratings, parent question-naires, and the STANFORD ACHIEVEMENT TEST.

For the two previous years (1967-68 and 1968-69) referring class-room teachers rated each pupil on a pre-and-post basis in four general attitudinal/behavioral areas: hostility, introversion, security, and work-study skills. The rating scale consists of twenty-seven items. Ratings were obtained upon initial referral and again at the end of the year. A t-test for correlated means was used to analyze the data.

Analysis of 1967-68 data (N=21) showed a slight but insignificant increase in hostility, a significant decrease in introversion ($p < .05$), and positive but insignificant growth in the remaining areas. Data for 1968-69 (N=22) showed positive but insignificant growth in all areas.

A parent questionnaire was used for the first time in 1968-69. It asks four general questions concerning improvement in the child's overall success in school, interest in reading, participation in school activities, and attitude toward school as evidenced by comments the child makes at home. Parents are asked simply to indicate "No," "Yes," or "No Change" for each question and, in addition, they are invited to make amplifying comments. Responses were highly posi-tive, and a consistent response pattern appeared for each question. Total responses in each category for all four questions were as fol-lows: "No" = 12, "Yes" = 47, and "No Change" = 4.

In both 1967-68 and 1968-69 the STANFORD ACHIEVEMENT TEST was given on a pre-and-post basis with a 7- month interval between tests. Scores of subtests for Word Meaning, Paragraph Meaning, Spelling, and Work-Study Skills were used for comparisons. Data were analyzed by obtaining the difference between the expected and actual gains for the 7-month period and applying the t-test for correlated means. Expected gain is determined on the basis of the previous rate of learning for each child. This is calculated by subtracting the pre-test achievement score from the grade placement norm and dividing by the years of school attended.

The twenty-one pupils for whom complete data were available in 1967-68 were of low-average mental ability and had an average learning rate of 4.1 months per year. Their expected gain for the 7 months between pre-test and post-test was 2.87 months; their actual overall gain was 4.79 months. Analysis of subtest data yielded significant gains in Work-Study Skills and Total Achievement ($p = <.05$). Positive but insignificant gains were made on the remaining three subtests, and in no case did the group achieve less than expectancy.

The 1968-69 group (N=22) were of average mental ability and had an average learning rate of 5.11 months per year. Their expected gain for the 7-month interval between tests was 3.58 months; their actual overall gain was 4.8 months. Analysis of subtest data yielded no significant gains, although the results were positive on all four subtests. Again, the actual gains equalled or surpassed the expectancy level.

Discussion of Results

It has been difficult to obtain an objective assessment of the program's effectiveness. Because the children treated at the Center differ greatly in the nature of their disability, their accomplishments cannot be measured on the basis of a single standardized instrument. Achievement tests are basically designed for normal learners, and the children undergoing educational therapy at the Center cannot be classified as normal learners. The cause of their learning problem must be identified and overcome before normal learning progress can be realized. Furthermore, the children referred to the Center have a poor self-concept because of past failures. The Center staff believes strongly that improvement in attitude and self-image must occur before significant improvement in scholastic achievement can be expected.

In 1968-69 the TEST ANXIETY SCALE FOR CHILDREN was administered to twenty-six Center pupils in conjunction with the Lie Scale to help determine how much reliance can be placed on achievement test scores for these children. The Lie Scale was used to identify those children who had developed such strong defense mechanisms that they could not answer the Test Anxiety Scale questions objectively. Nine of the twenty-six were found to be test anxious. On the basis of Lie Scale results, an additional ten children proved to be so defensive that they too could be classified as inordinately test anxious. On the basis of these results, it was felt that achievement test results could not be considered a valid evaluative measure for a majority of the group.

It is also evident that data obtained by means of the teacher rating scale is not valid. For example, teachers are asked to select among the choices "Always," "Usually," "Sometimes," or "Never" for each of the twenty-seven brief attitude/behavior descriptions on the instrument. Each choice is assigned a numerical value for each separate item. The choice that would most clearly indicate behavior typical of a well-adjusted, normal, healthy child carries the highest value. The Center staff and the evaluator agreed upon these values beforehand; however, the teachers doing the rating were not aware of the specific values and obviously placed different values on the available choices. For instance, the item "is able to accept authority," where the choice "Usually" carried a higher value than "Always," and the item "Is fearful in new situations," where "Sometimes" was keyed higher than "Never," were often rated by teachers at the absolute extreme of "Always" and "Never," respectively. Because the teachers' comments that accompanied these items suggested a great deal of improvement, it appears that teachers felt they were giving students the highest rating possible when, in terms of the key, they were not. This limitation of the questionnaire casts doubt on the validity of the data obtained. The nature of the teachers' comments suggests that in some areas students improved to a greater extent than the data indicate.

Evaluation criteria and procedures have been modified for the current year's program (1969-70) in an effort to produce more meaningful data on the program's effectiveness. The "Pupil Rating Scale" of the GRADY ADJUSTMENT BATTERY will be used in place of the locally developed teacher rating instrument to measure attitude/behavior change. The "Pupil Rating Scale" contains fewer items and describes more fully the behavioral characteristics that are appropriate for specific response choices. This should eliminate most of the ambiguities noted in the instrument used previously.

A more significant modification is the change in the focus of the overall evaluation effort. Heretofore, the focus has been on the degree of change in the students' level of academic achievement on the assumption that removal of the disability or a reduction of its severity should be reflected in improved performance on the STANFORD ACHIEVEMENT TEST. While this remains a valid assumption, the procedure does not produce the information needed about the effectiveness of the various techniques employed to help overcome specific disabilities. The criteria being used in the current year consist of the various instruments for diagnostic purposes. These include the following: DEVELOPMENTAL TEST OF VISUAL-MOTOR INTEGRATION (Beery), BENDER-GESTALT TEST FOR YOUNG CHILDREN, FROSTIG DEVELOPMENTAL TEST OF VISUAL PERCEPTION, HARRIS TEST OF LATERALITY, ILLINOIS TEST OF PSYCHOLINGUISTIC ABILITIES, PERCEPTUAL-MOTOR SURVEY (Purdue), DIAGNOSTIC READING SCALES (Spache), and the WECHSLER INTELLIGENCE SCALE FOR CHILDREN. Data from these instruments are being collected on a pre-and-post basis and will be analyzed at the end of the current year.

The assessment problems experienced thus far are not surprising. The area of learning disabilities is a relatively new one for most public school systems; and in 1965, when the Diagnostic and Special Learning Center idea was conceived, there were few programs in existence from which to draw useful information. Likewise, the district lacked the necessary expertise, and our staff had to feel its way and learn from experience. In this regard staff members have made intensive efforts to increase their knowledge about learning disabilities and to develop more effective diagnostic and therapeutic procedures. Much has been accomplished to this end through extensive reading, visiting other programs, attending workshops, and using the services of outside consultants.

Despite the lack of concrete, objective assessment data to date, other indicators suggest that the Center program is making steady progress toward the effective diagnosis and treatment of learning disabilities. Definite improvement in attitude, self-image, and learning skills among most of the children in the Center program has been noted by the staff, classroom teachers, principals, and parents. It is, no doubt, fortunate that no undue pressure was brought to bear in demanding instant success. One of the primary objectives has been, and will continue to be, the acquisition of useful knowledge about the nature of learning disabilities and the development and testing of promising remedial techniques. The staff has the freedom to try out a variety of techniques and the freedom to fail. As much has been learned from failure as from success.

Summary

As suggested in this discussion, there are many variables which may affect a child's motivation positively or negatively. A trail analysis assists in identifying some of these variables and helps in determining approaches which enhance motivation.

Dealing successfully with learning disabilities requires diverse expertise—educational, medical, and social—all cooperating to isolate problem areas and recommend solutions. Effective strategies for intervention require close interaction between teacher and pupil. A very low pupil-teacher ratio permits greater consideration of the complex motivational variables within each child.

27

Evaluation procedures heretofore employed have not provided a satisfactory assessment of program effectiveness. Because of the diversity and complexity of learning disabilities and their damaging effect on attitude and self-concept, conventional measures of achievement such as the standardized test have failed to reflect, for the most part, the subtle kinds of progress that a child may be making in overcoming his disability. Currently, a series of diagnostic tests appraising performance in specific areas (motor, perceptual, psycholinguistic, and others) is being administered on a pre-and-post basis. Analysis of these data should yield an improved assessment of pupil progress and a more definitive evaluation of the various techniques employed.

References

Atkinson, J. W. **AN INTRODUCTION TO MOTIVATION.** New York: D. Van Nostrand Company, Inc., 1964.

Oppenheimer, J. "Strictly for Parents," **JOURNAL OF LEARNING DISABILITIES**, 1968, **1**, 68-81.

Sarason, S. B., Davidson, K. S., Write, R. R., and Ruebush, B. K. **ANXIETY IN ELEMENTARY SCHOOL CHILDREN.** New York: John Wiley and Sons, Inc., 1960.

Teevan, R. C. and Birney, R. C. **THEORIES OF MOTIVATION IN LEARNING.** New York: D. Van Nostrand Company, Inc., 1964.

BEHAVIOR THERAPY WITH LEARNING DISABLED CHILDREN

Roger A. Severson, Ph.D.
Associate Professor, Department of Educational Psychology
and
Co-Chairman, School Psychology Training Program
University of Wisconsin
Madison, Wisconsin

In this article, Dr. Severson describes a program of behavior therapy for children which is implemented at the Psycho-Educational Clinic at the University of Wisconsin in Madison. The children for whom the program is designed range from third to fifth grade level and usually demonstrate both serious learning disabilities and attitudes of passive dependency. The behavior modification model is designed to move toward four goals simultaneously: academic remediation, desensitization of negative emotional reactions, restoration of appropriately assertive behavior, and development of a sense of pleasure in academic activities. Dr. Severson discusses the diagnostic process by which initial target behaviors are selected and describes the construction of a hierarchy of tasks aimed at reaching those behaviors. An important part of the program model involves the determination of the scheduling of secondary reinforcers. One of the significant features of the program is the verbal sharing with the child of the contingencies involved and the emphasis on the child's freedom of choice. The program activities are seen as a way to facilitate the child's ability to make choices which will help him achieve goals that are important to him. Dr. Severson outlines the phases of the behavior therapy, which, when completed, transfer the process of maintenance and restoration from the clinic to the home and classroom. Involvement of parents and teachers is a crucial part of the process described. The article concludes with a recognition of the limitations of the approach and of the resources of the center to deal with the needs of all the persons who may be involved in the problems of an individual child.

M.B.R.

BEHAVIOR THERAPY WITH
LEARNING DISABLED CHILDREN

Children who are referred to a clinic primarily because of severe learning disabilities often reveal two equally impressive impairments. Not only have these children failed to make adequate progress in learning to read, according to a standard of general intelligence, but a similarly impairing behavior pattern is also noted in most of the children. This nonacademic pattern is one of a general lack of adequate assertiveness (Dudek & Lester, 1968). The marked compliance is often accompanied by a suppression of underlying aversive reactions to academic materials. These children usually seem quite cooperative and appropriately concerned over their school failure. Because of this surface picture, parents, teachers and remedial reading specialists are inclined to focus solely upon the missing academic skills, assuming that the achievement of school success will concomitantly erase any feelings of guilt, poor self-esteem or depression, and result in an increasingly positive approach to school. Such reasoning seems to make sense, but close inspection of behavior in these children often reveals a different pattern.

For the past 4 years we have been attempting to develop behavior modification procedures which are effective with the deficient academic and nonacademic behaviors in children referred to our clinic due to severe learning disability. During the early cases, operant procedures for improving reading were reasonably successful, but a number of the children failed to reflect anticipated improvements in self-concept, as shown by a sense of pleasure over reading improvement, more positive comments about school, and increased efforts in school tasks. Furthermore, in these particular children the clinicians observed a continuing degree of overcompliance, occasional patterns suggesting depression, and frequent signs of tension which built up during the sessions.

The Behavior Modification Model

When it became apparent that many of these children were retaining underlying aversive reactions to learning tasks, it seemed that a desensitization procedure prior to reading remediation might not only remove the aversive reactions, but might also result in more rapid improvement during the attempts to modify academic behaviors. In addition, the lack of appropriate assertive behavior, together with the lowered ability to actively seek enjoyable experiences, became increasingly viewed as deficiencies in themselves. We have begun to refer to this problem as an "underground school phobia."

Putting these children through a complete desensitization schedule, using imagined aversive academic experiences paired with relaxation (Franks, 1969), seemed like an overly extensive procedure, and *in vivo* procedures were sought which might be applicable to the remedial situation where aversion to academic material was involved. A format was conceived allowing the behavior modifier to approach four goals simultaneously, that of academic remediation, desensitization of negative emotional reactions, restoration of appropriately assertive behavior and the development of a sense of pleasure in academic activities. This paper describes the general aspects of the paradigm developed for dealing with children with learning disabilities in the third to fifth grades who present serious learning disabilities and a general picture of passive dependency. Figure 1 presents a typical session, and the various features will be described one by one.

There are three essentially different levels within the hierarchy itself, all of which are related along an approach-avoidance dimension. At the top is a task which is presumably least intrinsically attractive for the child, but which is an important academic deficiency. This may be virtually any target behavior which is highly school-related, such as learning letters, words, phonic rules, accuracy of oral reading, speed plus effective comprehension, arithmetic operations, sustained attentional behaviors, or others. Prior to describing the remaining features of the hierarchy, it would seem important to clarify the process of selecting the initial target behaviors.

FIGURE 1
Sample Behavior Hierarchy

Name_____

5. Memory drill with vocabulary.   10 per 5 minutes   1 for each word read correctly at end of session.

4. Memory practice with numbers.   7 per minute   5 for each extra number beyond 3.10 for 2 correct trials in a row.

3. Chess or dominoes.

2. Talk to me, or do anything else in the room you want to.   Zero

1. Leave the room.   Zero

---

40 tokens = 25¢
60 tokens = 35¢
100 tokens = 50¢

500 bonus tokens = Trip Downtown and Special Surprise Present!

Bonus: A) 9 out of 10 words correct of those taken home during week: 10 tokens
        B) Known multiplication of 6's, 1 through 9: 10 tokens

Diagnosing the Academic and Behavior Impairments

Since every child will usually have more than one important academic deficiency, the initial task is to choose one of the most important academic deficiencies for placement at the top of the first hierarchy. A current trend in operant management of behavior is to dismiss the value of standardized test assessment on the grounds that report of deficiencies by the teacher and parent is sufficient for selection of target behaviors. The issue is not a simple one, but we have moved sharply in the direction of abandoning detailed behavior sampling in the form of IQ testing, perceptual assessment, language assessment, and similar skill assessment prior to the beginning of behavior modification. Since one of the real values of standardized testing lies in the opportunity to observe the child under standard conditions, there is no reason to expect testing to exceed this model of behavior modification in this respect. Since the format is presented in a relatively standardized way, except for variations from child to child in the content, the diagnostic power in reference to important school-related behaviors is usually comparable. Of course, in this format we are looking for consistent patterns of responding, rather than right or wrong responses.

Two kinds of standardized tests, however, have won a place in our approach. We do administer a standardized test of curriculum (the Gates-McKillop Reading Diagnostic Test and the Wide Range Achievement Test are currently being used), together with an informal sampling of curriculum items drawn from the child's current books used in school. If the findings are generally compatible with a school report of deficiencies within the actual classroom, we are satisfied that we have sufficient background information from important areas for starting remediation. Where there are multiple deficiencies of apparently equal importance where we begin is often arbitrary; but we aim for starting with that skill which if strengthened would have the most immediate beneficial effect in classroom functioning.

We have made impressive strides in developing a new approach to the initial diagnosis of learning difficulties through the use of diagnostic teaching. The approach involves careful observation of the child *as he actually learns new academic material.* These approaches will be described more fully in a forthcoming book. In the majority of cases we find that effective progress can be made without ever resorting to extensive testing, but when such test information is available from a prior school or clinic assessment, though interesting, we usually find it to be of negligible value in formulating a behavior therapy program. It is worth noting that picture projectives and the Rorschach are still found to be quite useful when there is a need to probe more deeply into interpersonal areas. These are forms of behavior sampling which are not readily obtained in other ways, and they often reveal important interpersonal and emotional target behaviors not otherwise observed, reported or suspected. This soft and impressionistic information, however, must be followed by more precise kinds of behavior sampling.

Construction of the Hierarchies

Once the target behavior for a session is chosen, the next step in composing the hierarchy is to choose the intermediate level of tasks. These tasks should involve decreasing amounts of specifically academic operations and show an increase in capacity to attract the involvement of the child. The content of these tasks should also be conceptually related to the target task. The general strategy is to break down the top target task into simpler and less demanding tasks for one or two levels. For example, if connected reading in a book is the top target behavior, the next level of the hierarchy might include a task where the child reviewed individual vocabulary cards and then read sentences composed of these cards. The next lower level might involve learning new words on the Language Master or similar machine.

The intermediate tasks should increasingly involve either a game format or some activity known to be highly enjoyable to the child but still involving certain academic operations. Here we draw from the wide variety of academic games marketed by such firms as Milton Bradley, Kenworthy, Charles E. Merrill and many others, or we make up our own. Such easily constructed activities as a bingo game involving words, or a hopscotch game on the floor using words, can be easily made to fit the need for an emphasis on fun while learning. The number of these intermediate tasks can vary considerably. The general rule is to include sufficient numbers to allow the child a real choice in getting away from the academic emphasis, and have sufficient variety to be genuinely attractive to the child. Usually we try to include three such tasks, but occasionally, where variety is observed to be an important variable for maintaining involvement of a child, early hierarchies will include several games.

The third level of the hierarchy involves tasks which require no formal academic activities, and which are included as safety valves for dealing with the arousal of strong aversive reactions within the child. These are tasks which allow the child to escape completely from academic tasks, yet stay in the session. Usually two levels are included, one permitting interaction with the therapist and one permitting complete withdrawal from contact. The two illustrated in Figure 1 are "Talk to me about anything" and "Play with toys in the room." The setting is a playroom where there are a large number of toys available to the child. The last item included is "Leave the room," which is included as a safety valve for the intensely phobic child or for the moderately fearful child to use in early sessions when things build up to the point where complete withdrawal is desired.

Setting the Contingencies of Reinforcement

The next significant aspect of the model involves the determination of the scheduling of secondary reinforcers. These can be anything

36

of neutral or minimal initial value, such as marks on a page, tokens, chips, and so on. Occasionally we employ actual money with children who cannot grasp the connection at a conceptual level between acquiring these tokens and their exchange value with the back-up reinforcers employed. In this case the money (usually pennies) is simply used as a secondary reinforcer with value determined by us, rather than having the actual value of the money as secondary reinforcers in our society. In general, the tokens are the leverage which we use to guide the children toward the increasingly frequent selection of academic target behaviors. This is done by offering lesser numbers of tokens for lower levels of the hierarchy, with the greatest amount being offered for the target behavior. The number of tokens available at each level is frequently modified between sessions in order to increase the probability of choosing behaviors toward the top of the hierarchy.

Three different contingencies determine the dispensing of tokens. The first contingency is simply the presence of the child at the clinic. On a variable interval schedule (random time intervals) the child is given a token "just for being here." These tokens are designed to communicate genuine feeling of acceptance to the child without regard to how he performs during the session. They account for about 10 percent of the total number of tokens dispensed. The second contingency refers to the task difficulty chosen during a 5-minute session. The higher on the hierarchy the task is, generally the greater is the number of tokens given at the completion of the 5-minute session. Occasionally this contingency is divided into two contingencies; first, the *choosing* of a task and second, the *completion* of a task. This is done when a child shows such markedly nonassertive behaviors that he is almost unable to make a decision on a task, or when he shows reluctance to complete 5-minute segments with a given task. On occasion it has been worthwhile to include a bonus if a child chooses the next task within a 10-second time limit. These modifications are incorporated when particular deficits fail to disappear with the initial options presented.

Five-minute segments are purposely arranged, rather than permit indefinite involvement for any activity, in order to provide opportunities for choosing. Since sessions typically run 45 minutes in length, this requires the child to make nine activity choices within a session. The third contingency consistently employed is that of success, based on the child meeting certain contingencies of *amount* or *quality* of performance. These are generally not introduced in the first sessions until some general base line of performance is observed in various activities. It is only introduced for an activity when an observed skill level seems to be below what a child can be achieving, and when it seems likely that performance will vary as a function of reinforcing outcome.

Some real skill is involved in the determination of token values for each level of the hierarchy and each success contingency, as well as the establishment of the value of tokens in earning back-up reinforcers. Not only is it necessary to vary the token value of each level of involvement in order to increase probability of the child choosing a higher level, but it is important that the range of probable token earnings be such that the child neither fails to earn a minimal level of tangible reinforcement nor achieves a level of reinforcement which is unrealistically high. Failure to achieve any back-up reinforcement merely confirms the failure pattern experienced in the schools, and an unrealistically high level of reinforcement in early sessions takes away leverage for later improvement. The tokens are spread out in such a way that effective leverage can be generated between levels of the hierarchy, and sufficient increments are offered for successful achievement to make these worth working for. After arranging for differences of presumed effectiveness at each level, the highest and lowest amount of tokens possible to be obtained in a session are determined. To do this add the lowest figure to the number of noncontingent tokens planned to be dispensed and set a figure somewhat above this for the first session as a minimal amount needed to earn a back-up reinforcer. A higher level is set for earning an additional amount. Generally, there are three different levels established, each providing for an increased amount of back-up reinforcer, and the ratios are set in such a way that after earning a minimum amount (which is quite easy), greater amounts can only be earned by moving up well into the hierarchy. Only after observing the child in actual response to a hierarchy can we be sure we are bringing his behavior under effective control. By circling each level of hierarchy chosen during the session (see Figure 2 for a sample recording sheet), we can note the pattern and see if the child is responding effectively to the arrangement, or if a modified spread of token values would be better during the next session.

FIGURE 2

Sample Recording Sheet for Each Session

1	2	3	4	5	6	7	8	9	10
5	5	5	5	5	5	5	5	5	5
4	4	4	4	4	4	4	4	4	4
3	3	3	3	3	3	3	3	3	3
2	2	2	2	2	2	2	2	2	2
1	1	1	1	1	1	1	1	1	1

Since the emphasis in this report is on bringing the behavior under stimulus control, some minimal discussion of control seems required. Since we communicate to the child before each session just what outcomes are associated with each activity (except for the social reinforcement, which is administered operantly), we are not presenting a medium where involuntary control is involved. We could arrange for more extensive operant control, simply by bringing the child into a situation where a variety of activities exists and then differentially reinforcing him when he chooses varying activities. However, we see the establishment of choices by the child as a part of the hoped-for outcome, and we see no reasons not to verbalize the contingencies to him. Since the goal is to provide a vehicle for the child to achieve goals of importance to him, the differential arrangement of contingencies is simply to make it easier for him to achieve these goals under conditions where aversive reactions are kept to a minimum. The child is constantly reminded that the choice of what to do is up to him, including ending the session at any time. Since it is possible to set up an apparently "free" situation when in truth it is otherwise, we carefully discuss the emphasis on choosing with the parents so they are not forcing a reluctant child to come to the clinic. The success of this emphasis can be found in the increasing anticipation of most of the children to visit the clinic after the procedure has captured their interest and involvement.

The use of tangible reinforcement is a second area where great care is required not only in the choosing and application of effective reinforcers, but in the understanding of their purpose by all concerned. We carefully explain the purpose of using tangibles to the parents, including particularly their purely "pump priming" value in getting the child started toward successful attempts at learning. We also carefully review how the parent can avoid using tangible and social reinforcement in an ineffective or inappropriate way in the home. We also help them to see that only when the natural and acceptable reinforcers of the home and school are maintaining behavior up to a desired level, will the reconstructive process be finished. This eases concern over dependence on tangibles, or reactions against their inappropriate use. (O'Leary, Paulos, Devine, in press).

The Determination of Effective Reinforcers

The selection of effective reinforcers is an empirical operation for which there are currently inadequate guidelines. In some situations we get long-term mileage out of a soft drink, and in others it is necessary to advance to moderate levels of monetary reinforcement in order to maintain effective high levels of continued involvement.

Generally, there is a dependable feature of oral deprivation in this population (where things such as candy seem to have powerful reinforcing value), and we therefore start by offering either candy or a soft drink as an outcome reinforcer. Social reinforcement in the forms of praise, smiles and personal attention is usually effective with these children, and is frequently used to enhance effort. Parent report plus empirical discovery quickly turn up other effective choices, but we continue to evaluate a child's list of reinforcers. If candy is used, place about ten different kinds of inexpensive candy in front of a child at the end of the first sessions and ask him to rank them according to his preferences; then permit him to choose three or four pieces to eat. It is always interesting to note that early choices vary from session to session, and that actual choosing varies from the rank ordering. Eventually it is possible to narrow down the selection to a few preferred kinds of candy. Usually a tangible food reinforcer is retained, often as something that can be earned and obtained during the session itself. In order to acquire the most effective leverage for later stages of involvement, however, a more expensive tangible reinforcer is used: money. We set a dollar a week as an arbitrary maximum, on the grounds that many of our families cannot afford to sustain higher levels of tangible reinforcement. Beyond this the child is allowed to collect bonus tokens, which allow for long-term buildup of large amounts. These may accrue up to a thousand tokens and are backed by some special outcome, such as a surprise present (known to be highly reinforcing to the child), or a trip to a museum, store or other activity.

The Four Phases of Behavior Therapy

The contacts with the clinic proceed systematically through four distinct phases. In the beginning sessions the children typically avoid the highest task, preferring the levels saturated with game-like qualities. As the contingencies are readjusted, they move increasingly toward choosing the top task, although the individual patterns remain over time. Some children avoid the academic

41

target behavior until the last part of the session, or at a point when they must get down to work if they are to earn the tangible reinforcement. Others select the top task early and use lower levels as a "breather." These selection patterns are always diagnostic in themselves and help in acquiring larger insight into the character patterns of the child which affect relationships at home and school. Once we have worked out effective selections of tasks in the hierarchy, and rearranged the token values in such a way that the child is choosing the top task at least once each session, a bonus arrangement may be introduced. Not long after this, most children enter what is referred to as Phase Two, or the choosing of top levels of the hierarchy a majority of the time. At this point most of the children are set on earning as large a number of tokens as possible and they enter into competition with their own past performance. We may enhance this emphasis on accelerating the rate of purposeful learning by charting the number of tokens earned in each session.

During these phases we are observing the child carefully to see if certain behaviors are present or absent, for example a child who moves too early for the top levels of the hierarchy and stays there out of grim determination to learn. When this happens we can invariably observe motor features of distress, and the child can usually verbalize how terribly important it is for him to learn these skills. In these cases, either vary the choices available or the value of the task, so that the child is more likely to engage in activities of enjoyment to him. After involving him in enjoyable activities with these manipulations, try to return him to a situation where stress builds up to an undesired level. Occasionally a child is so inhibited behaviorally and emotionally that we put in activities which try to elicit behaviors incompatible with constriction. Very effective techniques have been those which require large motor activity, such as putting material on squares on the floor and presenting a game requiring the child to hop from one word to the next.

Extremely deviant response patterns in reference to positive reinforcement are also found. With one girl who would invariably respond to social reinforcement by saying, "No, it's not good," we
replaced positive social reinforcement by a neutral response whenever she responded correctly. First we used a card suspended by
pins and spun it following a correct answer. Then the child was
involved in spinning the card. Next a bell was introduced as
having somewhat more powerful reinforcing qualities. When these
procedures were tolerated without chaining into a negative comment, neutral words such as *correct*, *OK*, and *yes* were gradually
paired with the bell. If she responded, "No, it's not correct,"
we dropped that word from the session, but gradually, by pairing
increasingly more positive verbal responses with more neutral responses, it was possible to reintroduce the word *good* into the
session and eventually to put back high levels of enthusiastic reaction. What appeared to be markedly deviant behavior with
masochistic qualities was effectively modified, at least superficially,
by this change of procedure.

Although the individual patterns are too numerous to report here,
all children eventually enter Phase Two and work hard to acquire
tokens. After several sessions of Phase Two, when we feel the
child is working well at mastering academic tasks, Phase Three is
introduced. This involves the opportunity to earn additional tokens
through mastery of tasks within the home. These between session
tasks generally involve such activities as reading paragraphs in books,
drill on such activities as vocabulary learning, learning phonics rules,
or memorizing the multiplication tables. The problems involve being
able to bring the behavior under effective management in the home
so the child has a place and time to attempt the tasks and some way
of getting correct answers. We have developed several procedures
which involve ways of getting correct feedback, but wherever possible
we involve the parent. Often the parent is not an acceptable resource
in working with the child because of underlying resistance on the
part of the child toward him. We test this out by putting the parent

on the hierarchy at some point, with the child having the option of doing some academic task with him. If the child fails to choose this option during the session, we help the parent to understand the undesirability of working directly with the child at this time. Other procedures are then worked out such as sending the material home on a cassette tape, introducing an acceptable sibling as "tutor," or giving the child material where his answers can be checked against a list of correct responses such as a programmed instruction format.

The task is purely elective, and at the start of the next session the child is given an opportunity to earn bonus tokens through demonstration of mastery of the task taken home. He may elect not to do so. Where there are obvious difficulties because of avoidance or ineffective involvement, the procedures are modified at the stimulus and reinforcement level until the child begins to extend his active academic mastery into the home. One particularly effective task has been the building up of sight vocabulary words through the construction of an expanding dictionary. The child takes from five to ten words home for drill, either by himself or with the aid of the parent, and each week the new words are added to a pack at the clinic. Mastery of the new words plus a successful recollection of any ten words drawn at random from this pack are both bonus tasks and help to consolidate the long-term mastery of these words. Because so few of these children know how to employ drill procedures in an effective and nonaversive way, we give them careful instructions as to how to go through the words and make a game of mastering the set. Tokens are often given initially based on the number of trials engaged in at home, as well as for actual mastery.

Along with the focal attention to the academic problems found in the child, invariably there are problems in many other aspects of the family life. Although only rarely are we involved in marriage counseling (preferring to refer the family elsewhere) the existence of certain character patterns in the child is usually related to parental patterns of handling the child. Although we are careful not to imply that the parents have caused any current problems, we offer to work with them on modifying behaviors in the home. We also let them know that it will be necessary for them to become involved in the academic program of behavior modification so that the contact with the clinic may be phased out. Since it takes about two months (one clinic visit per week) to effectively develop the behavior modification program with the child and clinician, another clinician spends this time examining the home and the school.

The order of attention to these two natural settings depends on where the primary problems seem to be and on availability of clinician time. If as many as three clinicians are available for a single case, then attention can be given immediately to both home and school behaviors. The initial effort regarding the home is to interview the parents and clarify the problem behaviors they wish to see modified. Since rarely is it possible to visit the home, we ask for careful descriptions by each parent independently, always supplemented by observation of the family interacting in the clinic. One of the most useful measures involves having the child read to one or both parents on one of the same passages previously read to a clinician. Significant deterioration of performance is often observed, and the reactions of the parents are valuable clues to impairments in the parental pattern of reinforcing the child. When a parent spontaneously shows the ability not only to cover up critical reactions to errors, but also to praise the child for effort or good performance, we know that the prognosis is excellent for speedy improvement.

If initial interviews do not reflect parental agreement to the most important problem behaviors, we first ask the mother and father to keep a list of problem behaviors as they occur during the week. Usually within about two weeks there is a fairly useful list of missing or excessive behaviors in the home, and we ask the mother (usually) to shift into a more exact documentation of daily frequency of certain behaviors. If the behaviors are of the high intensity, low frequency type, we ask for a careful description of events leading up to it, and reactions which follow.

45

After about 2 weeks of gathering a baseline of daily frequencies, during which time the parents are reading a manual on how to handle problem behaviors (Patterson and Gullian, 1968), a carefully discussed procedure is instituted. In a case, where procrastination was the primary home problem, we asked the mother to record every time it was necessary to remind the child to complete a task. The mother was told to put a check beside each behavior when one reminder was made, and two additional checks if a second reminder was needed after an interval of 15 minutes. The boy had a baseline of sixty-three checks weekly, based on an average of fifty-four weekly tasks (almost eight per day!). Bonus tokens were made contingent on the boy being able to improve to the extent of forty or less checks. As he successfully met this initial contingency in the first week, in subsequent weeks the threshold of forty checks was made a necessary condition in order to visit the clinic, whereas improvement below this number was reinforced with tokens and praise. As behavior improved, the schedule was modified and within only a few weeks the child was able to get through the week with only two reminders. From that point on, the clinic visit itself was contingent on keeping below five reminders, and a sharply increasing schedule of tokens was given for improvement within this range. He maintained an average of two reminders for the remaining several weeks of contact. Although improvement in this boy was unusually fast, the families are usually amazed at the speed of improvement in their children when effective modifications are made in their patterns of child management.

Whenever we establish conditions for the child to continue visiting the clinic it is always accompanied by praise of accomplishment and a statement not only of our confidence in the child being able to meet the expectations, but also how much we look forward to seeing him the next week. The apparently unwise withdrawal of ourselves from an accepting and noncontingent position with regard to clinic visits is rendered more acceptable by our genuine expressions to the child, plus a clear expression as to why we are doing what we do. We make it clear that above all else we are committed to seeing that things improve for the child and family.

It is not uncommon, when focus is on only one natural setting such as the home, to find behavior deteriorating in another setting. We are not entirely sure what causes this phenomenon, but it seems possible that it could reflect the child's conscious or unconscious awareness that performance in one setting is receiving positive attention, but in the other setting persons are not responding similarly. That is, it may be a commentary on the sudden awareness of the child that deficiencies exist in these settings from the standpoint of the adequacy of reinforcers available. Furthermore, it may be the child's way of coercing those who dispense reinforcers (in the words of Patterson and Reid, 1969) to provide the same improved ways of responding. For whatever reasons, it is best, when time allows, to give simultaneous attention to both the home and school. We view an actual visit to the school as more logical than a visit to the home since a simulated school situation with the actual persons involved cannot be created as easily in the clinic. Also, a classroom visit is more convenient since it occurs during daytime hours.

After one visit to discuss the objectives of the program and briefly observe the classroom interaction, the clinician returns to gather baseline information on the functional analysis of the child's behavior. This means an examination not only of what is typical behavior over time, but what expectancies and reactions on the part of the teacher and other children are responsible for maintaining this typical behavior. Several rating scales have been adopted or created to allow examination of the child's responses in several areas, the teacher's characteristic responses, and the interaction of the two over situations. Figure 3 shows a typical rating scale useful for examining both individual student-teacher interaction and whole classroom interactions. We have profited from the work of Becker, Madsen, Arnold and Thomas, 1967; Bijou, Peterson and Ault, 1968; and Patterson (in Benson, 1969), in constructing and using these rating scales.

FIGURE 3

Rating Form: Whole Class-Teacher Interaction

Alternate one full class sweep with 4 minutes of rating teacher response. Rate both class and teacher only during homogeneous activity periods. Avoid split session and non-study activity. *Whole Class.* Observe each student, beginning with first pupil in first row from left, for 10 seconds, recording at the end of the 10-second interval. Record marks from left to right for each row so that each child can be identified.

		Row 1	Row 2	Row 3	Row 4	Row 5	Row 6
First Sweep	Task						
	Non-task						
Second Sweep	Study						
	Non-study						
Third Sweep	Study						
	Non-study						

Teacher Responses

Observe and record continuously by 30-second intervals. Rate each category + or − (or O for category #6).

	30″	1′	1′30″	2′	2′30″	3′	3′30″	4′	30″	1′	1′30″	2′	2′30″	3′	3′30″	4′
1. Physical contact																
2. Verbal attention task																
3. Verbal attention non-task																
4. Helps S at desk																
5. Punishes S																
6. To whole class																

Date _____   Number of students present _____

Time rating started _____   Terminated _____   Class activity _____

Name of teacher _____   Rater _____

After about four visits of 30 minutes each, or when an apparently stable baseline is obtained while observing the child under similar task conditions, the clinician discusses with the teacher methods of modifying expectancies or reactions in order to increase or decrease various patterns of behaving in the target child. The clinician then keeps returning to the classroom once or twice a week for about a month or until some initial improvement is observed in the target child. Following this phase, or where classroom visits are not feasible, teachers are asked to chart certain behaviors for a short period each day.

Although exact frequency counts of behavior during the important instructional periods are obviously more precise, too few teachers can both teach and take frequency counts on their own for even a short portion of the day. We therefore employ a fairly gross reporting form (see Figure 4) and provide the teacher with general guidelines for using it. Then some guidelines are developed for what constitutes *little improvement*, *some improvement*, and *much improvement*. These same guidelines are given to the child so that each may be aware of the general expectancies. Generally, a maximum of four target behaviors are charted, two of which are deficient behaviors directly related to classwork and two of which are nonacademic problem behaviors.

There is a considerable amount of stereotyped classroom behavior in this population, particularly with the boys, and the most frequent kinds of academic deficiencies reported are failure to complete assignments, messy work, failure to engage in effective seat work, misunderstanding instructions, and similar behaviors. So-called nonacademic problem behaviors most frequently reported are time off task, talking to others, clowning, being "lazy," being either hyperactive or quite withdrawn, unpopular, tendency to cry easily, playing with girls (in the case of boys), and similar behaviors. The general male performance syndrome is one of avoidance when confronted with difficult material, plus general inability to develop effective masculine

49

relationships. The girls are more often reported as overcompliant, quiet and withdrawn.

FIGURE 4

Example of Recording Card for Teacher Report

	Target Behavior		
1	2	3	4
MUCH IMPROVEMENT	MUCH IMPROVEMENT	MUCH IMPROVEMENT	MUCH IMPROVEMENT
Some improvement	Some improvement	Some improvement	Some improvement
No improvement	No improvement	No improvement	No improvement

Instructions: circle one level at end of day
            for each target behavior

Date _____

Tokens are given at the beginning of the session for improvement according to schedules discussed in advance. These add to the bonus tokens, rather than to those earned during the session itself. Generally, contingencies are set low initially, such as requiring *little improvement* in an average of two target behaviors each day of the week. Just as with home behaviors, these are gradually tightened up until, for example, we may ask that *much improvement* be achieved in two or three out of the four target behaviors for 4 of the 5 days of the week in order to get a bonus. We also set a minimum standard of classroom performance for visiting the clinic after impressive improvement. The standard for determining improvement is the initial baseline, rather than the performance of the previous week. A graph is kept so the child can see the week by week improvement.

After considerable involvement with classroom teachers, we have concluded that effective modifications of classroom management are not nearly as simple as one might believe from reading previously published reports. Much seems to depend on the desire of the child to improve in order to gain approval from the clinician, the initial cooperation of the teacher, the power base of the clinician in entering the school, and the amount of time one can spend in establishing an effective relationship with the teacher. It is fair to say that most teachers want to help but charting procedures which demand time, and suggestions based on reinforcement principles which often run counter to ways of viewing behavior learned earlier, are not easy for teachers to adopt. Despite these problems, if the teacher can continue to report behaviors from the classroom and learn to modify certain expectancies and reactions, then social reinforcement plus bonus tokens are usually sufficient to obtain improvement of effort, achievement and nonacademic problem behaviors.

When impressive improvement can be observed in the clinic, home and school, and when the child is extending his academic efforts effectively into the home, and when the parents have mastered the basic principles of behavior modification (Patterson and Gullian, 1968), Phase Four is initiated. This involves the transfer of the process of restoration and maintenance completely to the home and school. If the parents were involved in the academic program during Phase Three, they are changed from simple givers of correct feedback to persons who learn how to use simplified hierarchies themselves, typically with only three items: target behavior, game, and nonacademic activity. They are given hierarchies to be used for two weeks during a standard time. Initial sessions start at 15 minutes and build up. Whichever parent elects to spend the time with the child first does so at the clinic while being observed. This may take place in three or four clinic sessions for about 15 minutes each time. As with the clinic visits, the child may elect not to engage in the home session, and if he does not it results in a postponement of the visit to the clinic. At this point the clinic visits are usually shifted completely into being rewards contingent upon involvement, as well as successful mastery of various behaviors in the home and school. Generally, a visit every other week is still available to the child, which is faded out to one visit during the next month if things have been proceeding smoothly. If the child's behavior deteriorates at this point, we do not increase the clinic visits, but reduce the expectancies the following week in order for the child to earn a clinic visit. The time spent at the clinic is then reduced to half the usual time. These procedures not only provide leverage for continuing improvement, but allow the gradual undoing of the frequently strong attachment to the clinic personnel by the child. It also accomplishes the reversal of the implied contingency that the child is coming to the clinic because of things he does wrong. The bonus trip and surprise present are earned sometime toward the end of this phase, and at the same time that the clinician takes the child for a visit and presents him with a present, he is given a diploma of graduation.

After the last clinic visit, contact with the parents is maintained on an interim basis by telephone for a brief period of time. In most cases it has been possible to fade out the record keeping in the home but to instruct the parents that if behavior drops below a certain level, they should immediately start charting for a week. If behavior does not improve, currently noncontingent rewards such as allowance or privileges (TV or movies) are put back on a contingent basis. This is generally sufficient to maintain a certain level of threshold behavior, and in most cases the family is now equipped for dealing with any new problems.

In families where there are several children, it is not at all uncommon for a sibling who has otherwise been doing fairly well to begin to deteriorate somewhat, or hint that he would very much like to get into that room, or to express direct jealousy to the referred child. Usually it is possible to spot these children early and to alert the parents to the situation. It is preferable to build in a whole-family contingency for the successful completion of the clinic contact by the referred child, such as a weekend vacation for everybody. If siblings do drop off in performance, they may be put on some similar procedures themselves. Improvement seems to be in direct relationship to the degree of initial impairment, so it almost never represents a serious problem.

In conclusion, comments can be offered regarding certain limitations of this approach. For one thing, we have never worked with a seriously acting-out child. Although conceptually these children might be viewed as differing only in the open expression of their rebellion, it is possible that this format, so oriented toward reinstituting assertive behaviors, might not be the most appropriate one. For example, in one child who seemed not to be particularly deficient in assertive behavior, the 5-minute segments ran counter to what was finally chosen as the most important target behavior, that of keeping at a task for extended periods of time. In this case the choosing sessions were extended from 5 to a choice of 10 or 15 minutes, and he was given more tokens for choosing 15-minute tasks.

We have tried on occasion to work with children only, independent of the involvement of the parents or the classroom teacher. Almost invariably this has sharply limited the speed or ultimate success of the efforts. Parents who drop off their children at the clinic but who remain uninvolved are too readily inclined to dismiss what we do as "fun and games," particularly when initial school improvement is not rapidly forthcoming. When classroom performance improves spontaneously, it is usually because the teacher is already dispensing reinforcers in some effective balance, recognizes improved behavior, and immediately reinforces it.

We have learned that we must approach the total environment of the child and in any individual case be prepared to deal with the fragile lives of a whole family, or of a classroom teacher. The needs of one child may easily lead to the needs of others. We try not to let our focus on the child obliterate our awareness of the needs of others, yet we cannot assume that we are the healers of all mankind. As in any form of therapy, we strive to keep ourselves aware of the time, place and extent of our best involvement as helping agents. The sharpened tools of behavior therapy do not obliterate the problems of personal choice and human values, nor do the increased attempts at direct control lead us to abandon caring, acceptance of feelings, and other ingredients assumed to be important for the humanization of a client-therapist contact.

The author wishes to express appreciation for contributions made by the following students in the practice and development of this model of behavior therapy: Linda Goodsell, Barbara Marwell, Kristin Guest and William Dickerman.

References

Becker, W. C., Madsen, C. H., Arnold, C. R., and Thomas, D. R. The contingent use of teacher attention and praise in reducing classroom behavior problems. JOURNAL OF SPECIAL EDUCATION, 1967, 1, 287-307.

Benson, F. A. M. (Ed.) MODIFYING DEVIANT SOCIAL BEHAVIORS IN VARIOUS CLASSROOM SETTINGS. Eugene, Oregon: University of Oregon, 1969, No. 1.

Bijou, S. W., Peterson, R. F. and Ault, M. H. A method to integrate descriptive and experimental field studies at the level of data and empirical concepts. JOURNAL OF APPLIED BEHAVIOR ANALYSIS, 1968, 1, 175-191.

Dudek, S. Z. and Lester, E. P. The good child facade in chronic underachievers. AMERICAN JOURNAL OF ORTHOPSYCHIATRY, 1968, **38**, 153-160.

Franks, C. (Ed.) BEHAVIOR THERAPY: APPRAISAL AND STATUS, New York: McGraw-Hill, 1969.

O'Leary, K. D., Paulos, R. W., and Devine, V. T. Tangible reinforcers: Bonuses or bribes? JOURNAL OF CONSULTING AND CLINICAL PSYCHOLOGY, in press.

Patterson, G. R., and Gullian, E. LIVING WITH CHILDREN: NEW METHODS FOR PARENTS AND TEACHERS. Champaign, Illinois: Research Press, 1968.

Patterson, G. R. and Reid, J. Reciprocity and coercion: Two facets of social systems. In C. Neuringer and J. Michael (Eds.) BEHAVIOR MODIFICATION IN CLINICAL PSYCHOLOGY. New York: Appleton-Century-Crofts, 1969.

REMEDIALDIAGNOSIS AND PROJECT TEACH

Keith E. Beery, Ph.D.
Faculty, University of California,
   San Francisco Medical Center and Dominican College
Director, Institute for Independent Educational Research
San Rafael, California
      and
Consultant, U.S. Office of Education

Dr. Keith Beery describes here his proposal for bringing the skills and approaches gleaned from special education to regular education programs. He hopes that the thorough diagnostic attention that is given to handicapped students could be extended to all students to provide them with a more appropriate education. At the same time, he is well aware of special education's biases and shortcomings and would want to eliminate them where possible.

(Ed. Many diagnostic forms have been eliminated from Dr. Beery's original manuscript. If you are interested in them, they may be obtained from Dr. Beery.)

M. B. R.

REMEDIALDIAGNOSIS AND PROJECT TEACH[1]

Introduction

Special education has been flirting with education in general for a number of years. It is past time for the two fields to combine their strengths for the benefit of all learners.

On the negative side of the coin, special education has labeled, categorized, and stigmatized children to the point where our good intentions have paved the road to hell for thousands. On the positive side of the coin, we have learned a tremendous amount from disadvantaged children which, if introduced to the mainstream of education, will assist *all* children. These gifts from "handicapped" children must be shared with others.

What follows is a capsule summary of the thinking and experience of a multidisciplinary team which began a series of explorations in 1966 in an effort to discover and share how "specialists" and "generalists" can help one another. Our earliest fumbling efforts have been reported elsewhere (Beery, 1967). In this chapter, which is extracted from an application for funds from the U.S. Office of Education, our past 2 years and our plans for next year are summarized.

In closing this introduction, an invitation: Please correspond with us. Please share your experiences and thoughts with us. We, like children, are *thirsty* for growth!

Objectives of Project TEACH

The overall objective of the project is to demonstrate the effectiveness of models whereby local communities, in particular public

[1]TEACH: Teacher Education Approaches for Handicapped Children

schools, can provide pre-service and in-service education programs which will facilitate the development of handicapped children. Within this broad objective are eight more specific objectives:

1. To better educate handicapped children. (Although some children in the proposed project would come under the headings of mentally retarded, hard of hearing, speech impaired, visually handicapped, crippled, etc., the majority would come under the heading of "other health impaired"—emotionally disturbed and learning disabilities.)

2. To teach special education teachers to provide continuous in-service education regarding handicapped children to classroom teachers.

3. To teach special education teachers to assist handicapped children in regular classrooms.

4. To teach special education personnel (school psychologists, nurses, speech therapists, etc.) to provide in-service education to classroom teachers and special education teachers.

5. To teach special education personnel to assist handicapped children in regular classrooms.

6. To teach pre-service teachers basic concepts and practices in assisting handicapped children in and out of regular classrooms and to encourage such teachers to enter the field of special education.

7. To teach parents to assist handicapped children in the schools and in the home.

8. To teach preschool teachers, pre-service teachers, and parents how to assist handicapped preschool children in situations where preschool special education personnel are not employed (i.e., to create preschool special education personnel).

Problems Addressed by Project TEACH

Great Numbers of Handicapped Children. Throughout the country, special education and regular classroom teachers have become increasingly frustrated by lack of understanding of ways to teach handicapped pupils more effectively. For example, the program for Educationally Handicapped children fostered by the State of California has led to an increased awareness by teachers of the critical importance of individual differences in learning. This awareness has been accompanied by increased sophistication in the diagnosis of individual differences among pupils to the degree that many educators now estimate the percentage of pupils with significant learning difficulties to be closer to 20 percent than to the 2 percent defined by the Educationally Handicapped legislation. Approximately 10 to 30 percent more of the school population is from lower socio-economic populations. Many more children within the schools are working well below their potential because of inadequate instruction. Thus, teachers are all too keenly aware of the large numbers of handicapped children and their needs are staggering. Unfortunately, teachers frequently lack adequate knowledge of ways to render assistance.

Lack of Special Teachers. All of these children cannot be placed in special education classes. Even if the funding for sufficient classes were available, administrators would be unable to find adequately trained teachers. According to Lucito (1968):

> It is obvious from even a casual examination of the present status of the manpower needs and the availability of personnel that a crisis exists. One often quoted estimate indicates only forty per cent of the handicapped are receiving

the educational services to which they are entitled. Admin-
istrators of local school programs, state departments of
education, and university departments of special education
can testify to the difficulty of hiring quality personnel.
(p. 531)

At current rates of preparing teaching personnel, sixteen
years would be needed to close the gap between supply
and need. (Heller, 1968, p. 539)

Inadequate Pre-service Preparation. Even if we had sufficient special
education personnel, as presently prepared, special education teachers
are usually not equipped to deal with the problems they encounter.
Kass (1968) suggests that:

All too often educators are trained in a "how to" approach
rather than in a problem-solving approach, and further training
can only add some rationalizations for habitual patterns of
teaching. (p. 545)

The present nature of pre-service preparation, with emphasis upon
books and lectures, with little practicum experience, does not adequately prepare personnel for meeting the needs of children in
actual teaching situations. New models for the transmission of
instructional technology to special education teachers are urgently
needed.

The preparation of teachers cannot be left entirely to colleges and
universities. The critical needs cannot be met in this way in the
foreseeable future.

The responsibility for continuing education is shared by
institutions of higher education, professional organizations,
state and local agencies, federal agencies, and by the individual
teacher. (Kass, p. 545)

61

Need for Continuous In-service Training. Conclusions by John I. Goodlad, Dean of the Graduate School of Education, UCLA, suggest a major direction which needs to be explored to help handicapped as well as other children:

> *Public schooling probably is the only large-scale enterprise in this country that does not provide for systematic updating of the skills and abilities of its employees and for payment of the costs involved . . . general failure to do so for large numbers of people constitutes the greatest failure of our educational system.*

We need pre-service programs which have a stronger practicum base but, probably even more importantly, we need strong in-service education programs in the schools themselves so that school personnel are continuously motivated, informed, and actively extending the frontiers of ways to help children. Basic systemic changes (e.g. interfaculty communication) in a school are often needed to accomplish these goals.

Need for Improved In-service Models. In-service programs in schools typically occur at the end of the day, do not involve pupils directly, consist of one-way communication from "experts," and in other ways contradict basic learning principles. Models should include characteristics such as:

> Teachers are given prime time for participation.
> *Time for study and re-training should be built into the daily school schedule. This does not mean simply more free time or in-service courses tacked on the end of a draining day of teaching. Time should be scheduled during the school day for teachers to come together and learn.* (Ryan, 1969, p. 83)

Teachers are provided with adequate personnel for in-service training.

Adequate materials for training are provided.

The alternative in-service models must also provide for continuing renewal of school systems. Data such as the following must be considered and incorporated:

Innovative classroom teacher roles must be considered.

The human relations aspect of the school must be considered (Gross, 1964).

Persons whose roles are modified must be involved in pre-planning (Blanke, 1965).

Relationships between new and old programs must be delineated (Olson, 1965).

Potential and existing role conflicts must be identified and dealt with (Gross, Mason & McEachern, 1958).

Teachers must participate with administrators in planning in-service (Kinnick, 1957).

In-service education must provide for individual teacher self-analysis (Childress, 1965).

Group factors (Stogdill, 1959; Festinger, 1942; Kidd & Campbell, 1955; McKeatchie, 1954), leadership variables (Hemphill & Coons, 1950; Halpin, 1956; Getzels & Guba, 1955), administrative roles (Ohles, 1964; Lipham, 1964), communications variables (Charters, 1964; Guest, 1962; Charters, 1957; Mott & Neff, 1962), diffusion variables

(Katz, Levin & Hamilton, 1963; Rogers, 1962) provide necessary background for planning.

In-service education should further

Use pupil behavioral changes as criterion

Provide for continuing assimilation and education of new personnel

Incorporate both laboratory approach and classroom experience model of in-service (Bessent et al., 1967)

Provide for systematic feedback from pupils (Gage, Runkel & Chatterlee, 1960)

Utilize background data on conditions which influence the introduction of new technology (Miller, 1967; Ryan, 1969)

Embody most or all of the following characteristics:
1. Relate to what is going on in individual schools and communities
2. Involve teachers and administrators in planning
3. Choose as initial participants personnel who express interest in change.
4. Differentiate various kinds of programs appropriate for various groups and individuals
5. Assess individual teacher readiness for various kinds of programs
6. Specify cognitive, affective, and skill objectives in performance terms
7. Emphasize process as well as content (teacher as catalyst in learning process rather than information dispenser)
8. Utilize appropriate patterns (intensive group experience, task team, interaction analysis, microteaching, etc.)

9. Choose appropriate media (open or closed circuit television, video tape, programmed instruction, etc.)
10. Use staff appropriately (staff teams, principal, supervisor, consultant, etc.)
11. Provide prime time and adequate support money
12. Provide for evaluation and develop evaluation instruments that emphasize feedback based on classroom situations (self-evaluation, peer evaluation, pupil feedback, etc.)
13. Cooperate where appropriate with colleges and universities, R and D Centers, regional laboratories
14. Enlist a high level of community understanding and support

Need for Desegregation and Reorganization. Although it is clear that we need many additional, well-prepared special education personnel, it seems increasingly apparent that many of these personnel need to be functioning differently on the job than they have in the past. Many leaders in the educational professions believe that we have gone too far in the direction of segregating exceptional children, both in terms of labeling and, particularly, in terms of removing them from the mainstream of their school and peer societies. In removing handicapped pupils to special classes, we frequently stigmatize them, create loss of self-esteem, overly reduce expectancies, and create self-fulfilling prophecies that they are "unable." Many of these children can profit most if they remain as much in the regular classroom as is possible, particularly if the classroom teacher is taught to more adequately meet their individual needs and is helped to do so. Better education for *all* children is achieved in such circumstances. In order for this to be accomplished, however, we need to reconceive the roles of special education teachers and other special education personnel, such as school psychologists and language specialists. Instead of simply *removing* handicapped children from the regular classroom for special education services, special education services need also, as much as possible, to come *to* the regular classroom, to work there with handicapped pupils and, most importantly, to provide in-service education for the classroom teacher in the process.

Need for Early Assistance. Research and experience increasingly indicate that the earlier we can assist handicapped children, the more they can be helped to meet their full potentials. Special assistance programs should concentrate at least upon the elementary school years and should be extended to the preschool years (Westman, Rice & Bermann, 1967; Kirk, 1966).

Need for Inexpensive, Practical, Productive Models. Too often, productive knowledge and programs are not implemented:

> *Until very recently, we have depended upon a very simpli-fied transmission of "knowledge into action" model. . . It has proven to be a magnificent failure.* (Gallagher, p. 485)

Frequently, transmission fails because it is not practicum based. Failure also often occurs because school districts and other agencies cannot afford to institute the procedure, or its application is impractical for other reasons. We need accentuation of effort to translate productive discoveries into applied models which can be readily adopted on a broad scale.

Developmental Background of Project TEACH

In the course of the past two years, an experienced and sophisticated multidisciplinary team in Marin County, California, has developed a model for the in-service education of school systems, special education personnel, classroom teachers and parents who deal with handicapped children. This model, called Remedialdiagnosis (Beery, 1967), has proved to be highly effective. During the intensive 4-week in-service education programs which were held in a variety of elementary schools, children with learning difficulties gained, on the average, over 6 *months* in reading and nearly as much in spelling and arithmetic. Shifts in social status, self-concept, classroom and out-of-classroom behavior have been equally dramatic. Trainee enthusiasm has been very high, and significant school system changes have been evidenced.

The Remedialdiagnostic Process, in brief, consists of defining the individual differences of a child, and most importantly what actually helps him to learn, through experimental *teaching*. In essence, it is application of scientific method to teaching. The teacher is taught to:

Survey the child's development as a learner and a personality

Select an instructional area in which to focus

Define a behavioral objective and a criterion measure

Analyze the teaching task

Identify strengths and weaknesses on the task ladder

Design two or more methods for teaching to the objective

Test these methods and refine them through experimental teaching

Evaluate and interpret results

In addition, the teacher is taught a number of basic principles, such as behavior modification techniques, and is introduced to new materials.

Heavy emphasis is placed upon the process of "Sharing":

Identifying and exchanging available resources in one's environment including one's self

Establishing fuller and more active communication within the system, including parents and other members of the professional and lay community

Reorganizing or otherwise making better use of resources

In particular, the teacher is taught to respond more fully to children, to see each child as her "teacher" of what needs to be taught and how to teach

In developing the curriculum and models for implementing it, the following basic format was used:

A large trailer was brought to elementary schools for a period of 4 weeks at each school.

The trailer contained space for teaching individuals or small groups of pupils, instructional materials, a secretary, two master teachers with experience in both special education and regular classrooms, two release teachers, and—one day per week— a neurologist, pediatrician, psychiatrist, psychologist and speech and language therapist.

Eight classroom teachers in the school volunteered to participate.

Each classroom teacher selected, with help, at least one handicapped pupil from her classroom to serve as her "teacher." Pupils were told honestly that their teacher would be taking a course to help her to become a better teacher and that she would need them to help her learn.

Special education teachers and other special personnel from the building and district were involved as resource teachers to the classroom teachers. Pre-service personnel, interns, and others (such as the children's personal physicians) were also frequent participants.

Each master teacher worked with four classroom teachers per day, 5 days per week, for 4 weeks. Each teacher was released for 1 hour per day for this purpose. In most cases, at least during the initial week or two, the classroom teacher and her focal pupil came to the trailer to work with the master teacher and ancillary personnel for 30 minutes. The pupil would then leave while participating adults discussed the session and made plans during the second 30 minutes.

As the ultimate goal was to assist handicapped children in the regular classroom as much as possible, teachers were increasingly encouraged to transfer their work to the classroom. Some teachers chose to begin and to stay in the classroom throughout the 4 weeks. Most started in the trailer with one pupil and gradually worked back into the classroom, often through a transition stage of working with a small group.

In addition to the practicum time, group seminars involving all participants and—usually—other faculty, etc., were held frequently during the noon hours and after school. On the average, three noon sessions and two after-school seminars were held each week, so that the 4-week course was quite intensive.

Increasingly, parents and administrators were involved as members of teaching teams, both in the trailer and in the classrooms.

Increasingly, handicapped pupils and other pupils in the classrooms were actively engaged as team members and had teaching responsibilities for both adults and classmates.

Further explication of the curriculum will be gained through examination of the materials which follow. First is an example of a daily schedule for a 4-week program. Each school's schedule differed somewhat depending upon time commitments and the particular needs and interests of the participants. Next is an objectives checklist which the teacher completes in consultation with the master teacher and principal.

The program was highly individualized for both teachers and pupils. Participating teachers had a great deal of choice and concomitant *responsibility* in the program. The master teachers and other consultants structured and directed whenever the individual or situation seemed to require direction, but the emphasis in the instructional process was upon the creativity and accountability of the teacher taking the course. By constantly working for increased competency, confidence and creativity on the part of the participating teacher, we were able to leave a building and its personnel with a high level of motivation, determination, confidence, and competence to be *responsible* for continuing self-improvement and system-improvement. Discovery and reinforcement of *strengths* within individuals and systems was a keynote of the program which was complemented by direct, "hard-nosed" examination of areas of weakness and how to improve upon them.

We have found that it mattered little which handicapped pupil a teacher chose to focus upon; nor did it matter what instructional area was chosen for focus—the same basic gains were realized in almost all cases:

> Pupils accelerated growth markedly, both academically and in social-emotional behavior spheres. Again, reading gains have been, on the average, 6 *months* in the 1-month period of work. Similar gains were realized in spelling and arithmetic. These gains, upon follow-up months later, have not only held, but been built upon further. Sociometric and

other behavioral data reveal similar marked gains in social-emotional behaviors.

Spread of effect to all children in the classroom occurs as the results of improved attitudes, concepts and techniques gained by the teacher. Teachers are very enthusiastic about the value of the program to them, their classrooms and their school system.

Significant systemic changes resulted. For example, participating teachers in one school, as a result of the project, have:
1. Led the district in which they work in totally revising the reading program so that it is sequentialized, individualized, and systematized.
2. Shifted the role of the remedial reading teacher from ineffective "patchwork" remediation outside the classroom to working in the classroom in in-service and preventive capacities as well as remediation.
3. Increased interfaculty communication, sharing and responsibility.
4. Encouraged special education personnel to work more in the classroom in a collaborative fashion.

One of the most common system changes which has been effected has been recognition of the need for and ways to increase interfaculty communication and in-service growth. Scheduling to allow teachers to observe one anothers' classrooms, team teaching, and release time for in-service have been among the means developed to meet these needs.

In summary, a very powerful curriculum for in-service education of teachers and others dealing with handicapped children in the schools has been developed. However, the *most critical* juncture of development has been reached: transmission of the curriculum and processes

REMEDIALDIAGNOSIS WEEK #1

D A T E With Pupil	Noon Seminars Voluntary and Open To all Faculty and Community - 12:05—12:35	Consultation	Afternoon Seminars 3:10-4:40	Recommended Reading
M Classroom teacher introduces Child Center teacher (and others) to the pupil. A time to share one another as people— *no work!*	REMEDIALDIAGNOSIS: The Marin County Implementation Study, Keith E. Beery Patrick A. O'Donnell	(a) Discussion of each others strengths, weaknesses, and goals. (b) Plan means for evaluating pupils' development as a person and as a pupil.	(a) Review of goals and expectancies in project. (b) Needed modifications? (c) Speculation vs. action as means for discovery and progress. (d) What *can* the school change?	*Remedialdiagnosis* Beery (especially pages 18-23, 34-39, & 44)
T Classroom teacher evaluation of pupil development (a) Wide Range Achievement, (b) Other informal means as desired.	*EVALUATION OF PERSONAL AND EDUCATIONAL GROWTH. Diane G. Wilkinson	(a) Discussion of pupil as a student. (b) Introduction to various academic evaluation materials and techniques.	NONE	*(1) *Temporal Learning,* Bateman, p. 29-30
W (a) Introduce other consultants to pupil. (b) Continue evaluation survey.	PSYCHIATRIC FACTORS IN LEARNING, Gerald G. Jampolsky, M.D.	(a) Discussion of pupil as a person. (b) Introduction to various personality evaluation materials and techniques.	(a) Jerry Jampolsky People *discussion* (45 minutes) (b) Gayl Westerman: Reinforcement discussion (45 min.)	(1) "Psychiatric Consideration," Jampolsky, p. 61-72, (2) Diagnostic Teaching, Rosenberg, pp. on learning styles.

Continued on next page

REMEDIALDIAGNOSIS WEEK #1 – continued

D A T E	With Pupil	Noon Seminars Voluntary and Open To all Faculty and Community - 12:05—12:35	Consultation	Afternoon Seminars 3:10—4:40	Recommended Reading
Th	Continue evaluation survey.	BEHAVIORAL DESCRIP-TION AND OBJECTIVES, Gayl Westerman	(a) Discuss survey. (b) Select area in which to focus, e.g. reading, spelling, arithmetic, independence, (c) Plan evaluation in area of focus.	NONE	*(1) *Preparing Instructional Objectives,* Mager (the entire book takes less than an hour to read, humorous very important.)
F	Begin more detailed evaluation in area selected for focus. (Testing is permissible, but teaching is preferable now.)	*TASK ANALYSIS Diane G. Wilkinson	(a) Discuss behavioral objectives and task analysis (b) More planning re specific ways to evaluate subskills.	NONE (first 1-page progress report due— EVALUATION SUMMARY SHEET)	*(1) *Temporal Learning,* Bateman, p. 54-57

73

REMEDIALDIAGNOSIS WEEK #2

DATE	With Pupil	Noon Seminars	Consultation	Afternoon Seminars	Recommended Reading
M	Continue subskill evaluation in area of focus.	METHODS DESIGN AND COMPARISON, Keith E. Beery	(a) Complete task analysis, (b) Final subskill evaluation plans.	(a) Constructive gripe session (15 min.) (b) Diane Wilkinson, Behavioral Description, objectives, criterion, tasks, task analysis discussion.	(1) "Remedialdiagnosis: Experimental Teaching," Beery, (ditto, 4 pages)
T	Complete subskill evaluation (should be definitely discovering through teaching by now!)	SPEECH AND LANGUAGE FACTORS IN LEARNING, Jean M. Hartley	(a) Begin designing Method #1	NONE	(1) *Auditory Learning,* Zigmond & Cicci, p. 55-75 (2) Verbal Learning.
W	Begin to try out instructional ideas which might be included in Method #1	NEUROLOGICAL FACTORS IN LEARNING, Wm. E. Drake, M.D.	(a) Evaluate pupils' responses to initial instruction. (b) Continue to design Method #1	(a) J. Hartley: Speech and Language Factors discussion (45 min.) (b) Bill Drake: Neurological factors discussion (45 min.)	(1) "Clinical and Pathological Findings in a Child with a Developmental Learning Disability"
Th	Continue to try out instructional ideas for Method #1	*ATTENDING RESPONDING & REINFORCEMENT, Gayl Westerman	(a) Evaluate response (b) Continue to design Method #1	NONE	(1) *Conceptual Learning,* Engelmann, Chap. VII (this is a classic) (2) *Attending and Responding,* Haring, p. 32-43.
F	Try out ideas	STRUCTURE AND PROGRAMMING, Diane G. Wilkinson	(a) Evaluate response (b) Finalize Method #1	(Second 1-page report due: TASK ANALYSIS AND SUBSKILL EVALUATION)	*The Engineered Classroom,* Hewett.

REMEDIAL DIAGNOSIS WEEK #3

DATE	With Pupil	Noon Seminars	Consultation	Afternoon Seminars	Recommended Reading
M	Experiment with alternate methods	*INDIVIDUALIZING INSTRUCTION, Pat A. O'Donnell	(a) Evaluate responses (b) Design alternate method	Progress reports and discussion of Group (15 pupils - 15 min. each—focus on methods development)	1. *Reading,* Strang 2. *Arithmetic,* Berieter 3. *Writing,* Westerman
T	Begin systematic application of methods (in classroom if feasible)	MOTOR LEARNING, Barbara A. Wander	(a) Evaluate (b) Modify methods as indicated.	NONE	(1) *Haptic & Motor Learning,* O'Donnell
W	Application of methods	HEALTH FACTORS IN LEARNING, E. Muriel Bennett, M.D.	(a) Evaluate	(a) Progress reports & discussion on Group B. (2 pupils - 15 min. ea.) (b) Muriel Bennett: Discussion of health factors (30 min.) (c) Jerry Jampolsky: Discussion of parental involvement (30 min.)	(1) "The Pediatrician's Role. . ." Bennett
Th	Application of methods	SOME OF THE LATEST & BEST TEACHING PROGRAMS, Pat A. O'Donnell	(a) Evaluate	NONE	
F	Application of methods	SOME OF THE LATEST & BEST SUPPLEMENTARY MATERIALS & EQUIPMENT, Pat A. O'Donnell	(a) Evaluate (b) Plan for parent conference	NONE (Third 1-page progress report due: DESCRIPTION OF TWO OR MORE METHODS.)	

REMEDIALDIAGNOSIS: WEEK #4

DATE	With Pupil	Noon Seminars	Consultation	Afternoon Seminars	Recommended Reading
M	Application of Methods (Extend to classroom groups if feasible.)	*CLASSROOM APPLICATIONS OF REMEDIAL DIAGNOSIS, Gayl S. Westerman	(a) Evaluation (b) Plans for total classroom application if feasible.	Individualizing in the classroom discussion, P. A. O'Donnell	
T	Application	*PARENT-SCHOOL TEAMWORK, School Staff	(a) Evaluation	NONE	(1) "Strictly for Parents" (2) Parent Section in all Dimensions in Early Learning volumes (3) Ipsilanti: *Parent Education Handbooks*
W	Application	NONE	(a) Evaluation (b) Plan parent conference	(a) Summary reports 10 min. ea. (b) one "indepth" report, 30 min. (Last 1-page report due: TEACHING FACTORS SUMMARY)	
Th	People time: No work discussion of project and fun together.	(a) Pupil ceremony awards for teaching.	PARENT CONFERENCES	PARENT CONFERENCES	*(1) *Citizenship*, Gibson, p. 31-32 & chapter V. (2) *Humanity*, Lavaroni
F	NONE	NONE	NONE	NONE	

Teacher's Name _____   Pre-Date _____
   (or code if preferred)

School _____   4-Week Date _____

Grade _____   8-Week Date _____

                                       6-Month Date _____

OBJECTIVES CHECKSHEET

General: Some of the major objectives of the project are listed below.
Since the focus of the project is upon in-service education for classroom
teachers, the objectives are stated in reference to classroom teachers.
However, it is important to recognize that the responsibility for teacher
growth is *mutually shared* by teachers, principal, parents, and others.
The checksheet, then, is a measure of how we have worked together
to help the classroom teacher in his or her efforts to help children.

    5 = major strength

    4 = a strength

    3 = OK

    2 = somewhat weak

    1 = weak spot

	Pre-	4 Wks	8 Wks	6 Mo
I. SHARING (Two-way exchange of information, responsibility and support)				
1. Faculty meetings				
2. With teachers individually				
3. With teachers in your classroom				
4. With principal				
5. With principal in your classroom				
6. With resource teachers				
7. With resource teachers in your classroom				
8. With guidance personnel				
9. With guidance personnel in your classroom				
10. With health personnel				
11. With health personnel in your classroom				
12. With speech & language personnel				
13. With speech & language personnel in your classroom				
14. With parents				
15. With parents in your classroom				
16. Classroom interaction				
17. With pupils individually				

	Pre-	4 Wks	8 Wks	6 Mo
II. INDIVIDUALIZATION SKILLS				
1. Evaluation of pupil growth				
2. Selection of focal behavior				
3. Analysis of subskills				
4. Evaluation of subskills				
5. Statement of behavioral objective				
6. Define criterion measure				
7. Obtain baseline measure				
8. Sequence steps to reach objective				
9. Design & describe methods				
10. Teach methods				
11. Record results				
12. Interpret results				
13. Communicate results				
14. Translate to classroom practice				

III. SELF-CONFIDENCE

1. In general, as a person				
2. In general, as a professional				
3. With class				
4. With individual pupils				
5. With fellow teachers				
6. With principal				
7. With parents				
8. With other professionals				

which were developed into models which are practical and economically feasible for schools and communities to finance and conduct themselves.

We recognize that there are few school districts which could afford the format within which the curriculum and processes were developed. Sophisticated multidisciplinary teams simply are not available in most areas of the country and, even if they were, most districts could not afford to employ them. However, we are convinced that most school districts can and will adopt one or both of two inexpensive models of the program once these models have been demonstrated to be effective. These models will be explained in detail in the pages that follow.

It is clear that the heart of our process development model was the master teacher-to-teacher consultation which was built around the curriculum and the practicum experience. These master teachers can teach other teachers to be master teachers and thereby set in motion an expansion effect which would result in continuous in-service education in schools. "Master teachers" are available to every school district, either from their own ranks or from local colleges and clinics. A master teacher, according to our experience, can come into a school building and, in a relatively short time, effect highly important changes in the school to the benefit of handicapped children. Special education teachers employed by the district make the most logical candidates for this instruction and role, as they are usually more highly trained than classroom teachers in the education of handicapped children and usually have greater flexibility in role definition and in scheduling. Ideally, each building would eventually have a special education teacher whose role is to provide continuous in-service education for the faculty in the process of performing direct pupil service. Once taught to so function, all that would be required to implement the role are clarity and acceptance of the role by the faculty and administration, and administrative facilitation of scheduling to permit the special education teacher to work in regular classrooms to a greater extent than is usually the case.

It should not be necessary for a master teacher to come to every school in a district in order to activate the model in all of the schools. After one or two or three buildings have reoriented and are functioning successfully, the special education teachers from these schools can then teach teachers from other buildings to function in the model. Furthermore, pre-service and intern teachers can train with this new breed of teacher and thereby increase the roster and competencies of special education personnel. This new "Multi-Purpose Teacher" would therefore function for the following purposes:

In-service education for teachers and special personnel

Classroom assistance to teachers, especially for marginally handicapped pupils in the classroom

Direct assistance for moderately to severely handicapped children

Pre-service and intern education

Mention was made above to *two* inexpensive models which schools would adopt to their advantage if the models had demonstrated effectiveness. The second model has at its core the Multi-Purpose Teacher model just discussed. However, the preparation of the Multi-Purpose Teacher is an outgrowth of a reorganization of the special services of a district, rather than the result of direct instruction by a master teacher. In this second model, a district, using its *own* special education personnel (special education teacher, school psychologist, school speech therapist, school nurse, and so on) simply replicates the format used by the multidisciplinary staff which worked out of a trailer in developing the curriculum and processes of our program. That is, for negligible additional expense, the district leases a trailer and reallocates existing special education staff time and role definitions to permit this staff to tour the schools in the district and implement the program that has not been developed.

Districts adopting this model could go one of two basic ways after initiation: 1) simply continue the trailer tour indefinitely, thereby having intermittent services of Multi-Purpose Teachers and Special Education teams or 2) the trailer staff could develop a Multi-Purpose Teacher in each building, much after the fashion of Model I, so that a Multi-Purpose Teacher is left in each building for continuous service. The objective of having a Multi-Purpose Teacher in each building would seem to be the preferred direction, but simple continuance of the traveling special education team would certainly go far to meet the needs addressed by this proposal.

Only brief mention will be made here of the need for assistance to handicapped children during the preschool years. The need is quite clear, and our third proposed model will address this subject.

It is possible to derive many models for implementing the program which has been developed with the expensive multidisciplinary team. It would be worthwhile to test several more of the models which show promise of adoption by schools and communities. For example, the concept of the "Outside Change Agent" deserves further empirical investigation in this context. We think, on the basis of our experiences, that many changes in attitudes and systems require the stimulus of people who are not employed by the system itself. We also think that for such changes to last and be extended, "outside" and "inside" change agents must work closely together.

Clarification of the Three Models

Model I: The Multi-Purpose Teacher Model. In this model, the major focus is upon teaching special education teachers, hereafter called "Multi-Purpose Teachers," already employed by the public elementary schools to work with and to teach regular classroom personnel in the system. (These Multi-Purpose Teachers, in most instances, will be currently functioning as Remedial Reading Teachers or as Learning Disability Teachers.) The major purpose of this focus

82

is to achieve a multiplier effect in the upgrading of teacher skills to assist marginally handicapped pupils in regular classrooms.

As described below, pre-service teachers, other special education personnel, administrators, parents and the school system are also foci of the program. However, the heart of the model is the teaching of the school's Multi-Purpose Teacher to do this job. The teaching of the Multi-Purpose Teacher is done, primarily, by a master teacher who has both special education and regular classroom experience and expertise.

The master teacher spends a total of 7 weeks at an elementary school. During the first 5 weeks, she and the school's Multi-Purpose Teacher work with three of the most able and child-oriented classroom teachers in the building. All of these teachers are enrolled for college credit and spend a minimum of 10 hours per week working on the project.

Each classroom teacher is helped to select at least one handicapped pupil from her classroom with whom to work each day *in* the classroom, with the guidance and assistance of the Multi-Purpose Teacher, supervised by the master teacher.

Conferences are held daily between the classroom teacher, Multi-Purpose Teacher, and the master teacher.

Joint classroom work and conferencing are facilitated by the classroom aides. These aides will usually be parents who will be introduced to this role by the project. In addition, frequent noon-time and after-school seminars are held with the three classroom teachers, the Multi-Purpose Teacher, and the master teacher, plus ancillary personnel in attendance.

The program will duplicate in all its essentials, the program which was described earlier and which has been successfully tested.

Ancillary personnel at each school include at least one pre-service teacher from the local teacher colleges (or special education intern), the three classroom aides, the principal of the school, and the school's special education personnel. These ancillary personnel will be scheduled into the classroom work and daily conferences as frequently as their schedules permit. Others will be included from time to time, as one of the major processes taught is that of identifying and using available resources more fully.

A mental-health consultant will consult 2 hours per week with principals and guidance personnel. A speech and language specialist will consult with the principals and with the school nurses. This consultation is not considered critical to the success of the model, but we believe that the basic model will be enhanced significantly by it, particularly because the consultation is systems-oriented (e.g. how the principal uses his resources). One expected outcome of such consultation will be a recognition by the systems involved of the value of consultation, so that this finding can be communicated to other systems. However, we feel that it is important to have this consultative interaction primarily to help the project, in a research sense, better identify system problems and their solutions so that these can be communicated to the field.

Three master teachers will be conducting in-service programs in three different elementary schools within the same or adjacent districts at any one time.

Five school districts will participate in the project. Each district will provide three schools for participation. The three schools in the district will participate simultaneously (each serviced by a different master teacher). At least once per week, the three schools will hold a conjoint seminar to facilitate cross-fertilization and maximum impact upon the district.

Each of the five districts will send at least two of their best teachers to an 8-week summer workshop for intensive *follow-up* work with the master teachers. This workshop will provide not only follow-up, but will provide interdistrict cross-fertilization, and—most importantly— will provide districts with personnel who can continue the work of the master teachers after they leave.

At the conclusion of the year, each school in which the master teachers have worked will have at least one Multi-Purpose Teacher who will provide in-service education for the faculty of that school as well as assist classroom teachers to meet the needs of handicapped children within the classroom. (Participating schools must agree to have their Multi-Purpose Teacher continue to work with additional classroom teachers.) In addition, districts will have at least two teachers who can carry on the process of teaching other special education teachers in other district schools to perform these functions. In essence, an each-one-teach-one multiplier system will have been established. It is also anticipated that, by concentrating initially upon the most outstanding classroom teachers in a building that, should the building's special education teacher leave for any reason or if the district decides to expand their special education staff, that district personnel have been prepared for the Multi-Purpose Teacher role.

With each of the three master teachers working 7 weeks at a school (5 weeks to teach the processes and 2 weeks for follow-up and supervision of the Multi-Purpose Teachers' work with two to three additional classroom teachers), fifteen elementary schools can be educated during the school year. The equivalent of three more schools can be educated during the summer workshop, for a total of eighteen schools during the fiscal year. In addition to the eighteen principals, approximately forty-five special services personnel, fifteen pre-service or special education interns, at least seventy-five classroom teachers and at least seventy-five teacher aides will have been educated.

At least seventy-five handicapped[2] children will have benefited, but since the classroom and special education teachers will have learned so much of value to *all* of their pupils, it is not exaggerating to say that approximately 2,200 elementary school pupils will have benefited immediately. Many more pupils, as a result of the multiplier effect, will benefit in the very near future.

Most importantly, a model will have been demonstrated which can then be adopted by teachers colleges and school districts all over the country.

Model II: Trailer Team Model. Among the major findings of our work to date are observations concerning the relationships among the school's special education personnel and between special education personnel and the regular classroom programs.

Not only are special education teachers terribly isolated, but the rest of the special education personnel (school nurse, speech and language therapist, psychologist) usually function in isolation from one another and from the classrooms.

By and large, handicapped pupils are pulled out from regular or special classrooms to see an individual adult who functions in a very fractionated manner, not only with regard to the child, but with regard to the environment or system within which they operate. As a result, the pupil, the specialist, the classroom teacher, and the system itself not only fails to grow from interrelationships, but weakens due to fractionation.

---

[2]Although some children in the proposed project would come under the heading of mentally retarded, hard of hearing, speech impaired, visually handicapped, crippled, etc. the majority would come under the heading ot "other health impaired"— emotionally disturbed and learning disabilities.

We have found it tremendously productive to simply bring these elements together from time to time so that communication and in-service education from and to one another can occur.

If, in addition, special personnel are enabled and encouraged to work *in* the classrooms, they provide in-service education for themselves and the classroom teacher and are much more successful in helping handicapped children than they were in pursuing the isolated clinical model.

Because our own multidisciplinary team was so successful in working together for brief periods with special education and regular classroom personnel, we believe that most school district special education teams can achieve similar success.

To test this model, all that is required is space (in the form of a mobile unit), secretarial service, and reallocation of special education personnel time. The in-service process to be taught by these new teams (same as in Model I) can be quickly and easily communicated, so that extensive pretraining would not be required for these new teams to duplicate the work of the original multidisciplinary team which developed the process.

This model is a natural extension of the original and may have great potential for most school systems in the country. It is basically simple, inexpensive, and can be tremendously beneficial to the pupils, adults, and system.

Model III: Preschool Model. As noted above, it is increasingly clear that most handicapped children can be maximally helped if assistance begins in the preschool years.

Unfortunately, it is precisely during the preschool years that there is the smallest number of adults with any background in special education to assist the children. In addition, a relatively small proportion of handicapped children are enrolled in any kind of school prior to kindergarten, and their preschool education is almost totally in the hands of their parents. Most of these parents are uneducated in childrearing and teaching techniques; furthermore, they are usually interacting inappropriately with their children because they are concerned and confused as to the nature of the difficulty and what to do about it.

We recently conducted a pilot program for preschool handicapped children which consisted of 4-week sessions. Fifteen children between the ages of 3 and 6 years were enrolled in each session. These children were referred by Head Start, Welfare, preschools and pediatricians for a wide range of reasons, but most of them were "bottom-of-the-barrel" referrals.

The children attended a 3-hour morning session 5 days a week, conducted by an experienced classroom and special education teacher and three staff teachers. These teachers devoted the other half of their time to working with the children's parents and teachers (if they had teachers), comparing perceptions, exchanging teaching ideas, and so forth.

Positive changes in the children and in the parents' attitudes and behaviors were startling in this brief period of 4 weeks. We are, therefore, convinced that the processes we have developed have important applications to preschool which need to be taught to pre-service and in-service teachers as well as to parents.

Basically, we will apply Model I to the preschool program in modified form. Because many preschool children are not enrolled in a preschool, we will bring all of the children to a preschool center. If the children *have* teachers, they will come to work at the center at least one day per week for active, supervised teaching experience and seminars.

Similarly, *parents* of the children will be actively engaged in teaching sessions, afternoon seminars, and evening seminars.

Outstanding parent trainees will be taught to conduct home visit consultations and evening seminars (which will include fathers as well as mothers).

At least two pre-service or special education intern teachers will participate full-time for 6-week periods and will actively engage in supervised teaching of the children as well as in seminars.

It is anticipated that almost all of the children will be enrolled in local preschool programs by the time the 4-week special session is concluded. Their *new* teachers will be engaged as soon as possible in the session so that all children leave with someone at least initially trained to work with them who has the benefit of in-depth perceptions of the children and a recommended initial teaching program to meet their needs.

Three months following this initial 4-week session, the children, their parents, and their preschool teachers (as well as pre-service trainees and interns) will have a second 4-week program to follow up on their initial training.

At this time, however, focus will shift from our own preschool center to the child's preschool and home. Our teachers will go to the child's own environments to assist their parents and teachers to further understand and implement individualized teaching programs for the children.

A total of ten 4-week sessions will be held during the year.

A multiplier effect will be set in motion in the parent population, with parents being taught to teach other parents in the community. A number of these parents will undoubtedly be stimulated to enter the field of special education through these experiences, thus enlarging our special education teaching roles. At the very least, these parents will become knowledgeable of special education needs and many will become active supporters at the classroom, building, and school-board levels for needed special educational programs.

Plan for Forthcoming Evaluation

An external evaluation team will be engaged to 1) refine the evaluation plan described below, 2) collect data, 3) analyze data, and 4) report the results of data. This team will be directed by Dr. Glenn A. Ohlson, Associate Professor of Special Education, San Francisco State College, with Dr. Patrick A. O'Donnell, Assistant Professor of Special Education, San Francisco State College, as Associate Director. Pending further refinement by the evaluation team, the following is planned:

Overall Objective: To Demonstrate the Effectiveness of the Models. Achievement, sociometric, behavioral, and self-report data gathered during the 1969-70 school year by the multidisciplinary program development project will be statistically (analysis of variance and other appropriate techniques) compared to data on the same variables obtained during the 1970-71 year. With 1969-70 data as a baseline, a cost-benefit analysis of the implementation models will be possible. That is, we can compare the relative benefits of the expensive and inexpensive models and relate them directly to costs. We will expect to show that 90 percent or more of the academic and other gains obtained by the 1969-70 (expensive) model will be gained by the inexpensive models. This finding will have not only scientific value, but will demonstrate that school districts can conduct effective programs with their own resources.

Objective 1: To better educate handicapped children
A. The Wide Range Achievement Tests will be administered as pre- and post-test for each 7-week project. All pupils in the project will

also be tested at the end of the academic year. Mean gain scores will be computed for pupil participants by individual schools and as a total group.

B. The Stanford Achievement Test will be administered at the end of the academic year and compared to results from the previous year.

C. Each teacher participating in the project will be guided in the development of behavioral objectives for the individualized practicum teaching. Assessment of the degree to which each pupil attains the criterion measure for the stated objective will be made. Individual pupil graphs and/or other records will be maintained.

D. A sociometric test will be administered as a pre- and post-test to each participating class to measure change in pupil-peer relationships.

E. A checklist of pupil behaviors will be rated pre- and post-project by his parents to assess changes in behaviors.

F. This same checklist of pupil behaviors will be rated pre- and post-project by the classroom teacher.

G. The same checklist will be rated pre- and post-project by the Master Teacher and Multi-Purpose Teacher.

H. The same checklist will be rated pre- and post-project by the principal.

Objective 2: To teach special education teachers to provide continuous in-service education regarding handicapped children to classroom teachers

A. The ultimate measure of teacher learning is pupil performance, as outlined above.

    1. Measures on pupils during the project

    2. Measures on pupils served after the project

B. Pre- and post-project tests of teachers' basic concepts related to the education of handicapped children in and out of the classroom. (Seigel, E., SPECIAL EDUCATION IN THE REGULAR CLASSROOM as basic text.)

C. Pre-project and end of school year checklist of teaching practices to reflect use of ancillary personnel in the classroom, special materials, etc.

D. Pre- and post-project Objectives Checklist (changes in degree of understanding and utilization of the basic processes of Remedial-diagnosis and of Sharing).

E. Pre- and post-project Teacher Attitudes Inventory

F. Pre- and post-project Interaction Analysis data

G. Log of number of teachers taught and hours devoted to in-service education post-project.

Objective 3: To teach special education teachers to assist handicapped children in regular classrooms

A. Pre- and post-project counts of
1. Number of Special Education Teacher times in classroom per week
2. Duration of Special Education Teacher time in classroom per week
3. Number of Classroom Teacher consultations outside classroom per week
4. Duration of Classroom Teacher consultations outside classroom per week
5. Number of pupils actually instructed by Special Education Teacher *besides* those pupils on her roster

Objective 4: To teach special education personnel (school psychologists, nurses, speech therapists, etc.) to provide in-service education to classroom teachers and special education teachers.

A. Objective 2 (A) data

B. Objective 2 (B) data

C. Objective 2 (C) data, modified to fit the job (psychologist, nurse, etc.)

Objective 5: To teach special education personnel to assist handicapped children in regular classrooms

A. Parallel data to Objective 3 (A)

Objective 6: To teach pre-service teachers basic concepts and practices in assisting handicapped children in and out of regular classrooms and to encourage such teachers to enter the field of special education
A. Same as Objective 2 (B) data (wherever possible)

Objective 7: To teach parents to assist handicapped children in the schools and in the home
A. Duplicate and parallel Objective 2 data as much as possible

Objective 8: To teach preschool teachers, pre-service teachers and parents how to assist handicapped preschool children in situations where preschool special education personnel are not employed (i.e., to create preschool special education personnel)
A. Duplicate and/or parallel data for other models as much as possible

Concerted efforts will be made to provide continuous periodic feedback of results to project staff so that as high a level of performance as possible is maintained and program adjustments can be made as indicated. Technically, this feedback loop should be considered a program as well as an evaluation input and will be communicated as such in dissemination reports. In most cases, evaluation feedback loops do effect program outcomes positively.

References

Beery, K. E. **REMEDIALDIAGNOSIS.** San Rafael: Dimensions Publishing Co., 1967.

Bessent, E. W. (Ed.) DESIGNS FOR IN-SERVICE EDUCATION. Austin, Texas: The University of Texas, Research and Development Center for Teacher Education, 1967.

Blanke, V. Lesson in Change, THEORY INTO PRACTICE. 1965, 4, 131-132.

Blanke, V. The Issue: Planning for Educational Change, THEORY INTO PRACTICE. 1966, 5, 1-4.

Charters, W. W., Jr. "The Communication Structure of School Staffs." Paper presented at American Sociological Association. Washington, D. C., August, 1957.

Charters, W. W., Jr. An Approach to the Formal Organization of the School. In Daniel E. Griffiths (Ed.) BEHAVIORAL SCIENCE AND EDUCATIONAL ADMINISTRATION. Sixty-third Yearbook, Part II. Chicago: National Soc. for the Study of Education, pp. 243-261, 1964.

Childress, J. R. In-Service or Continuing Education for Teachers, JOURNAL OF EDUCATION. 1965, 147, 36-45.

Corey, S. M. ACTION RESEARCH TO IMPROVE SCHOOL PRACTICES. New York: Teachers College, Columbia University, 1953.

Cruickshank, W. M., Junkala, J. B., Paul, J. L. THE PREPARATION OF TEACHERS OF BRAIN-INJURED CHILDREN. Syracuse University Press, p. 169, 1968.

Cunningham, R., and Assoc. GROUP BEHAVIOR OF BOYS AND GIRLS. New York: Bureau of Publications, Teachers College, Columbia University, 1951.

Festinger, L. Wish, Expectation and Group Standards as Factors Influencing Level of Aspiration, **JOURNAL OF ABNORMAL AND SOCIAL PSYCHOLOGY.** 1942, **37**, 184-200.

Gage, N. L., Runkel, P. J. and Chatterlee, B. B. **EQUILIBRIUM THEORY AND BEHAVIOR CHANGE: AN EXPERIMENT IN FEEDBACK FROM PUPILS TO TEACHERS.** Urbana, Illinois: Bureau of Educational Research, University of Illinois, 1960.

Gallagher, J. J. Organization and Special Education, **EXCEPTIONAL CHILDREN.** 1968, **34**, 7.

Getzels, J. W. and Guba, E. G. The Structure of Roles and Role Conflict in the Teaching Situation, **JOURNAL OF EDUCATIONAL SOCIOLOGY.** 1955, **29**, 30-40.

Goodlad, J. I. Schooling and Education, **THE GREAT IDEAS TODAY.** Chicago: Great Books Division, Encyclopaedia Britannica, Inc., 1969.

Gross, N. Some Research Findings of the National Principalship Study and Their Implications for Educational Change. In Harry V. Anderson (Ed.) **CONFERENCE ON TRAINING PROGRAMS FOR PERSONNEL WHO WORK WITH EDUCATIONALLY DISADVANTAGED STUDENTS.** Coop. Res. Project No. F-030. Boston: Boston University Human Relations Center, 1964.

Gross, N., Mason, W. S. and McEachern, A. W. **EXPLORATIONS IN ROLE ANALYSIS.** New York: John Wiley & Sons, Inc., 1958.

Guest, R. H. **ORGANIZATIONAL CHANGE: THE EFFECT OF SUCCESSFUL LEADERSHIP.** Homewood, Illinois: The Dorsey Press, Inc., and Richard D. Irwin, Inc., 1962.

Halpin, A. W. "The Leadership Behavior of School Superintendents," School-Community Development Study Monogram, Series No. 4, Columbus, Ohio: Ohio State University, 1956.

Heller, H. W. Training of Professional Personnel, EXCEPTIONAL CHILDREN. 1968, 34, 7.

Kass, C. E. Continuing Education for Teachers, EXCEPTIONAL CHILDREN. 1968, 34, 7.

Katz, E., Levin, M. L. and Hamilton H. Traditions of Research on the Diffusion of Innovations, AMERICAN SOCIOLOGICAL REVIEW. 28: 237-252, 1963.

Kidd, J. S. and Campbell, D. T. Conformity to Groups as a Function of Group Success, JOURNAL OF ABNORMAL PSYCHOLOGY. 1955, 51, 390-393.

Kinnick, B. J. The Teachers and the Inservice Education Program. In Nelson B. Henry (Ed.) INSERVICE EDUCATION. FIFTY-SIXTH YEARBOOK, PART I. Chicago: National Society for the Study of Education. 1957, pp. 131-152.

Kirk, S. A. The Diagnosis & Remediation of Psycholinguistic Disabilities. URBANA, INSTITUTE FOR RESEARCH ON EXCEPTIONAL CHILDREN. University of Illinois, 1966.

Lipham, J. M. Leadership and Administration. In Daniel Griffiths (Ed.) BEHAVIORAL SCIENCE AND EDUCATIONAL ADMINISTRATION SIXTY-THIRD YEARBOOK, PART II. Chicago: National Society for the Study of Education, pp. 119-141, 1964.

Lucito, L. J. Division of Training Programs—Its Mission, EXCEPTIONAL CHILDREN. 1968, 34, 7.

McKeatchie, W. J. Individual Conformity to Attitudes of Classroom Groups, JOURNAL OF ABNORMAL AND SOCIAL PSYCHOLOGY. 1954, **49**, 282-289.

Miller, R. I. "Educational Technology and Professional Practice." Address to the John Dewey Society Annual William Heard Kilpatrick Memorial Meeting. Dallas, Texas, March 11, 1967.

Mott, P. E. and Neff, F. W. "Some Criteria for the Effective Acceptance of Organizational Change." Paper presented at American Sociological Assoc. Meeting, 1962.

Ohles, J. F. How of Educational Reform, CLEARING HOUSE. 1964, **39**, 214-216.

Olson, C. O., Jr. New Programs Race, EDUCATION. 1965, **86**, 221-225.

Rogers, C. R. A Plan for Self-Directed Change in an Educational System, EDUCATIONAL LEADERSHIP. 1967, **24**, 717-731.

Ryan, K. A. Where Are We Going and How Can We Get There? THE TEACHER AND HIS STAFF: DIFFERENTIATING TEACHER ROLES, Washington, D.C.: National Education Assoc., National Commission on Teacher Education, Professional Standards, p. 83, 1969.

Siegel, E. SPECIAL EDUCATION IN THE REGULAR CLASSROOM. New York: John Day, 1969.

Stogdill, R. INDIVIDUAL BEHAVIOR AND GROUP ACHIEVEMENT. A THEORY. THE EXPERIMENTAL EVIDENCE. New York: Oxford University, 1959.

Taba, H. Techniques of Inservice Training, SOCIAL EDUCATION. 1965, **29**, 464-476.

Westman, J. C., Rice, D. L. and Bermann, E. Nursery School Behavior and Later School Adjustment, AMERICAN JOURNAL OF ORTHOPSYCHIATRY. 1967, **37**, 725-731.

THE PROGRAM FOR RESPONSIBLE BEHAVIOR

Fred A. Rowe, Ph.D.
Counselor, Provo City School District
Provo, Utah
        and
Staff Consultant, National Council of Juvenile Court Judges
University of Nevada
Reno, Nevada

The following article by Fred Rowe outlines the Program for Responsible Behavior conceived in Provo, Utah. The program was designed for use with students who are involved both in legal problems and school discipline and motivation problems. The basic assumptions made in formulating the program are as follows:

Children must learn to be responsible for their actions.

Anti-social behavior is peer group sanctioned.

The student must adjust to his own world, not a structured replacement, if significant permanent change is to occur.

Only changes in behavior are acceptable—no excuses or alibis.

Within the group context the student should be honest, responsible for his actions, and helpful to others.

After setting out the theoretical framework for the program, the author describes the functional operations, which include emphasis on group therapy and on development of work skills. The last section of the chapter describes evaluation procedures which have been used to determine the effectiveness of the program.

M. B. R.

THE PROGRAM FOR RESPONSIBLE BEHAVIOR[1]

Definition of the Problem

One of the problems confronting education today is that of finding effective ways to respond to the student who exhibits anti-social behavior. Our society is geared to sequential steps in learning for the process of maturing to adulthood; most young people find this process to be congruent and are able to meet the daily challenge without undue frustration. However, some young people find at times that behavior not acceptable in our society is more suitable to them for fulfilling their needs.

As this student progresses through school his cumulative record and confidential file become increasingly large. Anecdotal records, teacher summaries, counselor conference memos, psychological diagrams, and social work evaluations of his home all become a part of his image which each new teacher uses in order to "save time," and to "know the student."

Throughout the nation new programs have emerged to meet the challenge of changing the behavior of extreme discipline problems. These programs have ranged through remedial, custodial, and therapeutic. The children have become participants in these programs during their regular classes, in place of their regular classes, or in addition to their regular classes.

To implement the programs additional staff has been added to our schools. On the scene we see administrative assistants in charge of discipline, more counselors, tutors, community volunteers, teams of school staff combined with central office staff, and added probation committees.

[1]A description and evaluation of a project in education aimed at combining the efforts of various civic agencies for the rehabilitation of the child with severe social problems.

To add to the complexity, a variety of therapeutic methods have been oriented to the educational setting. In an effort to become agents of change, personnel often see themselves as the effector of conformity within the school. Rules are established, a violation of which results in a program where constant surveillance is required. Another approach has been to effect change through building self-concept. Nondirective methods of interaction are instigated in hopes that the child will become "free to learn." Yet another, resulting perhaps from the frustration of the first two, holds the child totally responsible for his own predicament and for removal from his predicament. Here the change agent sees himself as a record keeper, analyzer, diagnostician, and disperser of information to staff members related to the case.

Still another approach depends on identification. If a teacher, administrator, or counselor can become the proper model, the student will respond by changing to match the model. A final approach to be mentioned here views the child as capable of change, if he has help. The central mechanism used is reality. Frank, open discussions are held which develop into plans for betterment on the part of the student.

Fritz Redl (1955) explains that there is a difference between delinquency and juvenile crime. This is an important concept that is applicable to the school setting. There is a difference between capers that sometimes backfire and chronic misbehavior. Education should be cautious in extending the scope of special programs to all children whose behavior is not in perfect harmony with the desires of the educational staff.

Voluminous research points to a high correlation between boys who drop out of school, those who have extreme discipline problems in school, and those who are juvenile delinquents. Delinquency is official when it is entered into the court record. In a preliminary study, Utah County, of which Provo is a part, showed a high correlation existing between students who had records in the juvenile courts and those who had extreme difficulty in school, school drop-outs, and students from low income families. Many of the characteristics of juvenile delinquents are therefore the same for dropouts and discipline problems. Therapy, in a school setting, could theoretically approximate the same procedure for delinquents with both preventive and compensatory goals being attained.

As a result of this information, a program to help students experiencing difficulty in school, and involved with the juvenile courts, was established. The Program for Responsible Behavior (PRB), was developed to help all such students. The objectives of the Program were: 1) to help the student assume responsibility for his own behavior, 2) to assist the student in establishing functional relationships in school, the world of work, and the community in general, and 3) to end delinquent and harmful school behavior.

Theoretical Framework

To insure maximum benefits in implementation, the current literature was surveyed and a theoretical model developed for the program. Dr. William Glasser's concepts, as outlined in **REALITY THERAPY** (1965), were of specific value. Neither work with juvenile delinquents, dropouts, and discipline problem students nor therapy is new. However, working with this type of adolescent boy and girl, using this particular approach resulted in methods different from the traditional techniques used in an educational setting.

Five assumptions basic to the research and practice of the PRB will be discussed in the following paragraphs.

First, we assume that the basic problem of the children in trouble with the school and the court is that they consider themselves unaccountable for their actions. Through experiences in life, the child has come to avoid and even to deny reality. As anxiety mounted, from not being able to fulfill his needs in a conventional manner, flight from existence, fighting, and the development of a self-fulfilling prophecy grew. In other words, he became skilled in avoidance, in denial, and in saying to himself, "Everyone treats me in this manner, therefore I have the excuse to act this way."

Second, we assume that a large part of anti-social behavior is not secretive but is largely a group phenomenon. The goals of the child, what he is after to enhance his own position, are group oriented. He is a social being. He looks at success and failure, to a large extent, in light of his relationship with others. Treatment, therefore, cannot ignore group membership nor the impact of the group on the behavior of the child. Instead, the vehicle for change may be the group itself. Group life, the building of relationships, testing and feedback can become the tool in helping the student learn how to become more involved with other people.

Third, in-context therapy, where a student learns to fulfill his needs in his natural environment, is quicker and more permanent than being placed in a unique community. It is impractical to place a child in an abnormal situation and then expect him to become normal. In essence, we want the child to say to himself, "In spite of my parents, my economic situation, my past failure in school, and everything else, I must now learn to cope with these factors and be responsible for my own decisions and behavior." This is not easy. To help, it may be advantageous to have as many of his actual peer group in the therapy situation as possible. Often a child may see the inadequacy of his own behavior and make a commitment to others in a group therapy situation to quit the behavior. As he gets on the outside, still with honest intentions, the old group slowly breaks him down. However, if several of the group members are in the therapy situation, it becomes observable that the norms of his peer group are changed. In this situation, on the outside, he can receive positive reinforcement.

Fourth, only behavioral changes can be accepted as "change." Excuses, good intentions, promises, alibis, can be by-passed! As the student begins to recognize reality, he should learn to live successfully with it, to use it. He must plan new ways of behaving to replace the old inadequate ones, then commit himself to action. Self-respect, necessary for a success orientation to life, grows as he becomes more productive.

Fifth, the student must see himself and others in the group as possessing three important characteristics: a) complete honesty, b) responsibility for his actions inside and outside the group, and c) helpfulness to himself and other members whether it is comfortable or not. By complete honesty, the student must learn that his opinions and feelings are important. Part of reality is being able to identify what his feelings are and to verbalize them. At no time can the student or other members of the group let irresponsible behavior go unnoticed. There need not be a certain punishment affixed, but awareness of the correct behavior is imperative. To be helpful one must discuss the differences between ratting, nagging, attacking, teaching, suggesting, and the many other actions that can make the difference between encouragement and discouragement.

Functional Operations

Based on the above assumptions, the students in the PRB were helped to perceive their involvement in the program as having extremely high priority in their activities. Any attempt by students to dilute the program's effectiveness, such as flight from the program by absenteeism or by refusal to honestly cooperate, was met with immediate challenge. This kept the students from manipulating the therapist, school administrators, parents, or other group members. The member was forced to meet his problems squarely. This, of course, created anxiety—which is necessary for change—in the student.

Since anti-social behavior is viewed largely as a group process, the group setting became the major vehicle of change. The core of the program was group meetings in which the student's behavior, as it related to authority figures, school and community personnel, and other members of the group was discussed and analyzed. This was enriched by a work program in which the boys learned job expectations from other people and limited occupational skills.

The selection of the group took into account the following factors: age, sex, seriousness of the school problems, and involvement with the court. Involvement with the court was the first factor considered. No student was allowed in the program unless he or she was on probation with the Juvenile Court. Judge Monroe J. Paxman of the local Juvenile Court, in reviewing the case and upon recommendation from the school, entered the students' participation in the Program as part of their probation. This was necessary for legal support when sanctions were issued. Originally, the program was set up for boys only. However, we discovered that more girls than boys were on probation so girls were also included. The meetings were held separately for the different sexes. Age range for the participants extended from 14 to 16 years.

The meetings lasted for 2 hours daily during the school year. The first 1-1½ hours was focused on group discussion. The remainder of the time was spent in nonstructured interaction. During the summer months the meeting time was shortened to 1½ hours because the participants worked all day. The week was divided into 3 days for the boys and 2 for the girls during the school months. This was modified with both groups meeting, at different times, 3 days per week during the summer. The meetings were held after school hours and after work hours.

Meetings were held in the Dixon Junior High School in the Provo City School District. A large vacant room was remodeled into two smaller rooms and one larger room. Any apprehension felt about including this program in the school was mitigated by the emphasis that this was not part of the regular school day program. The facility was set up with microphones and tape recorder installations enabling a person to record or monitor any activity going on in any room. Precautions were strictly followed in using only that part of the building assigned to the program. In addition to this, maintenance and housecleaning in the program's complex was carried out by the students.

Work Projects

The Program was very fortunate to have an ideal work program for the participants. During the winter months, the boys worked in the Employment Youth Program which was functioning in Provo. Every Saturday was a workday. This extended to full-time responsibilities in the summer. The boys earned 75 cents per hour and had duties of maintaining city property. The girls had no jobs in the program during the winter but worked with the city recreation department for 6 weeks of the summer vacation. One girl worked as an assistant in Project Head Start in an elementary school.

Initially, not much effort was made to have the parents involved in the program. This was due partly to the concern that the parents' participation would lessen the cohesiveness of the group. However, it was decided that they were good reinforcement agents and could be helpful, not in a strict family therapy situation, but to help the student keep his commitments. There was no meeting held with the parent without involving the child. This proved to be very profitable to the child and improved the communication between the child and the family.

The success of this program was enhanced greatly by the support offered by the Juvenile Court, school administration, teachers, and public officials. The communication channels were always open and staff meetings were held periodically to insure a coordinated effort for the students.

Because group therapy is demanding and concentrated, it was decided from the outset that a lone therapist could not handle the details of the meetings by himself. This decision proved to be most wise. Two counselors from the Dixon Junior High School acted as group leaders and largely handled the program under the policies of the school administrator. Actual time in the group meetings was not the only time involved. The counselors spent additional time working with various agencies, in parent conferences and staff meetings, tape editing, evaluating processes, and preparing for group meetings.

Characteristics of the Group

The Program began officially in February or close to the beginning of the third term of school. Being an open group, new members were added as they were assigned by the court. We evaluated the program based on the seven boys and nine girls who were involved most of the school year. Most statistical information in the evaluation will be about these sixteen students.

Some identifying characteristics showed the range in IQ to be from the seventh percentile to the ninety-third percentile, the average being at the thirty-fifth percentile. In the eighth grade Iowa Basic Skills tests, participants scored an average of .8 grades underachievement in their composite scores. This average was at the thirty-ninth percentile. Thus we can conclude that, as a group, these students are nearly one grade behind their peers in achievement but they are working near their potential using IQ percentiles as the criteria.

The program was open-ended. This allowed the groups to exist on a continuous basis. While the data presented here is specific to those listed above, further study indicated that this was typical for all groups conducted.

Evaluation

One measure of the effectiveness of the program was the rate of change in absenteeism from school. Information about this is presented in Table I. Sixteen students were in the program during the school months from February until the present time. The range of absences from school varied for individuals. The most extreme change was shown by one girl who dropped from 43 absences the first term of school to 6 during the last term. The minimal change occurred with a boy who had 5 absences his second term and 4 his last term. Only one student, a girl, exhibited an increase. She increased from a low of 0 during the first term to 10 the last term. Part of this term, however, was spent in the Youth Home under the direction of the PRB. There were four students who had perfect attendance the last term of school. As can be seen from Table I, the boys had a greater rate of decrease than the girls. The percent decrease in absenteeism, overall, was 21 percent from the first half of school as compared to the last half in which the students were in the program. The greatest change occurred with 51 percent decrease in absenteeism of the last term compared to the first term. It is also interesting to note that there was no trend indicating better or worse attendance in school before the program started.

Another way in which the program has been evaluated has been through progress reports by the teachers involved. Progress was identified in two areas. In the first area, classroom management, teachers recorded improvement by all participants. Behavior indicating cooperation, self-discipline, and concern for others was noted to have increased while the student was in the program. This improvement was sustained over long periods of time. Only two boys and one girl had frequent recessions in their improvement.

The second area, centering around academic growth, was not perceived by the teachers to have been a field of growth as much as the first. In both achievement and assignment preparation all

109

participants displayed improvement but frequently, among the boys, no assignments were handed in. No boy at any time became completely caught up with his classwork. They averaged 50 percent preparation in assignments. The girls averaged 72 percent preparation with two girls being completely prepared at frequent intervals.

TABLE I

Rate of Change in Absenteeism of Students in PRB School Year 1965-66

	Number Absences First Term	Number Absences Second Term	Number Absences Third Term	Number Absences Fourth Term	% Decrease Last Sem. Compared to 1st Semester	% Decrease Last Term Compared to First Term
Boys (7)	34	33	31	9	40	74
Girls (9)	67	51	70	36	13	49
Total (16)	101	84	101	45	21	54

Grade reporting was given separate consideration from the teachers' progress reports. Table II shows that the students made some progress in raising their grade point average after they were in the PRB. From the outset, while not indicated on a table, it should be mentioned that there were no trends in either a decrease or increase of individual GPA before admittance into the program.

Table II indicates that the girls, as a group, showed slightly greater increase in GPA the semester following involvement in PRB. Nearly one-half grade point raise was shown. The boys increased .3 grade points as a group. Individually the range was from a decrease of .5 grade points for one girl to an increase of 1.9 grade points for a boy. Four students experienced slight drops while the other twelve raised their grades.

TABLE II

Comparison of Group Grade Point Averages the Semester Before Admittance to PRB as Compared to the Semester After Admittance to PRB School Year 1965-66

	First Semester Average GPA	Second Semester Average GPA	Average Change for First and Second Semester
Boys	.9	1.2	+.3
Girls	.8	1.2	+.4
Total	.8	1.2	+.4

At the conclusion of 5 months, parents were asked to assist in the evaluation by responding to a questionnaire on which they were to indicate any changes they had observed in their child. The eight general areas are summarized in Table III. According to the parents, no child showed an overall negative change in behavior. All trends that were observable were positive. This, however, does not indicate frequent problems in family living nor does it claim that problems no longer existed. Rather, it simply indicates a trend. The areas of least change were "duties around the home" and "talking things over with members of the family other than parents." The greatest change came in the communication between parents and the child. All of the girls' parents indicated a change for good in this area.

There has been contention for many years over the value of Juvenile Court records being used as the sole criterion for determining juvenile delinquency. However, it was not within the scope of this project to go beyond this source. Evaluation was therefore determined by comparing the number of referrals to the Court before and after each individual began the program. These data are presented in Table IV.

TABLE III
Parent Appraisal of Change in Behavior of Children in PRB (February 1966 through July 1966)

	No Change			Slight Change For Better			Great Change For Better		
	% Boys	% Girls	% Total	% Boys	% Girls	% Total	% Boys	% Girls	% Total
1. Duties around the home	25	—	9	50	41	45	25	59	46
2. Appreciation to members of the family	25	—	9	25	29	27	50	71	64
3. Personal cleanliness	50	—	18	—	29	18	50	71	64
4. Cooperation with parents	50	—	18	25	14	18	25	86	64
5. Honesty	25	—	0	50	14	27	25	86	64
6. Talking things over with parents	25	—	9	50	—	18	25	100	73
7. Talking things over with other members of family	25	—	9	50	41	45	25	59	46
8. Effort to improve problems	—	—	—	25	29	27	75	71	73

More girls' referrals entered the court prior to entrance into the program than referrals for boys. The girls, as a group, showed the greatest change after entrance into the PRB. They averaged 43 percent decrease in referrals for 6 months after getting into the program as compared to 27 percent decrease for the boys. The overall referrals to the court decreased 38 percent during this same time.

This decrease would have appeared greater except for the fact that many referrals to the court came as a result of PRB sanctions rather than violations of the law. These sanctions consisted of detention to the Youth Home for therapeutic reasons. While at the Youth Home a full school schedule was provided by a teacher employed by the District.

The actual number of students who were referred to the Court became another factor influencing the data. Table V shows that all of the students came before the Court during the 6 months prior to involvement in the Program. Throughout the first 3-month period after entrance, 63 percent of the group were sent to the Court by various agencies. This decreased to 25 percent during the second 3-month term. It is interesting to note that all the referrals to the Juvenile Court during the second 3-month period involved only four students. Thus twelve participants in the program did not come before the court at all during this time.

Although not of an empirical nature, observations by contributing agencies proved to be of utmost value. The principal of Dixon Junior High School was a great help in the PRB Project and his encouragement and honest appraisal greatly assisted its effectiveness. Principal Ronald Last made the following observations:

> *Generally the feeling of the administration toward the Dixon PRB Program is most positive. Without empirical data, the reasons for this support are:*

TABLE IV

A comparison of Referrals Made to the Juvenile Court about Participants in the Program for Responsible Behavior (August 1965 through July 1966)

	# Referrals 6 Months Before PRB	# Referrals First Month After PRB	# Referrals Second Month After PRB	# Referrals Third Month After PRB	# Referrals 4-6 Months After PRB	Total Ref. 6 Months After PRB	% Decrease Before and After PRB
Boys	11	3	2	1	2	8	27%
Girls	21	6	2	1	3	12	43%
Total	32	9	4	2	5	20	38%

TABLE V

A Comparison of the Number of Participants in PRB Referred to Juvenile Court (August 1965 through July 1966)

	# Participants Referred 6 Months Before PRB	# Participants Referred First 3 Months After PRB	# Participants Referred Second 3 Months After PRB
Boys	7	5	2
Girls	9	6	2
Total	16	10	4
% of Total Participants	100%	63%	25%

1. For the first time someone is coordinating the work of several agencies in working with our school children who have serious problems. The relationship between court and school has been excellent.

2. Students whose actions create problems for others are forced to take responsibility for the things they do. They are showing more concern when they are in trouble. They are unable to remain aloof as they are involved in PRB.

3. Teachers report an improved attitude in the classroom. In some instances students have changed their achievement pattern to a marked degree. In every instance referrals to the principal's office have decreased.

4. Attendance at school has improved for some members of the group. One boy has missed only 2 days of school since entering the program. Before entrance he attended school less than one-third of the time, even though the school made numerous contacts with home and court to improve attendance. This pattern, to a less marked degree, is noted with the group generally.

5. This program is perceived as giving legitimate group action to those who are isolated from the larger core of society in the school and community generally. The group has greater sanctions to force conformity than the informal structure. At the same time, the power of the organization is so derived as to encourage decisions within the laws of society.

6. The program enables students to remain in a more normal situation than complete incarceration would afford. It has the advantage of keeping very close attention focused on the action of those assigned and at the same time enables them to remain in the school and other normal social organizations.

A vital part of the program was felt to be the development of work skills of the participants accompanied by an association with community officials and civic organizations. This phase was supplied by the Youth Program of Provo City Corporation. Brent Birtcher, director, writes:

. . . One of the most welcome aspects of this program (overall community youth program) has been the opportunity to participate in your Program for Responsible Behavior. This program has been not only helpful to us, but absolutely necessary in channeling the behavior of these youth into socially acceptable behavior patterns.

116

I feel the Program for Responsible Behavior and the youth work program of Provo City Corporation can be coordinated more effectively and can complement each other further by:

> *(1) Instituting more frequent meetings between the staff of the city employment program and the group counselors of PRB.*
> *(2) Drafting a set of rules for on-the-job behavior pertaining to misconduct, dress, etc.*
> *(3) Having, when possible, the boys and girls work directly with, and be supervised by, regular city employees.*

Finally, our evaluation included reports from the Juvenile Court. It was imperative that efforts between the program and the Juvenile Court be coordinated. Judge Monroe J. Paxman was largely responsible for the implementation of this program in the community of Provo. His follow-through and support has been a necessary force in its effectiveness. Mrs. Edna Hill, probation officer, was chosen to work with the PRB. After 5 months of activity she reports the results of a Juvenile Court staff meeting about the value of the program as seen by the court:

> *The PRB has replaced the necessity to commit students to State Industrial School which I see as a real threat to parents and a blight to the family in the eyes of some of the citizens.*

Mrs. Hill named eleven participants in the program who would have been committed. Foster care, ranch type and SIS cost many times more than a probation program like that of PRB.

> *Parents are helped by having the child remain in his own home in a program such as the PRB, whereas an institution often has difficulty providing help for parents.*

117

The PRB is more closely correlated with the court structure and programming than most institutions.

The staff working in the PRB program seems to be more oriented to the needs, the philosophy of limitation, and the requirements of the court than do outside agencies. The involvement of school counselors is less threatening to many parents and children than is that of probation officers.

We feel there has been a closer working relationship obtained with the school, the community, and the court in helping the child assume total responsibility.

There is better utilization of existing agencies in the community. This means that we can obtain professional people, like the counselors involved without having to look beyond our area.

Conclusions and Discussion

Students involved in the PRB increased in their effectiveness in school. This was illustrated in two ways: 1) greater ability to manipulate the situation they were in and 2) an intrinsic effort to do better in their school work. While no empirical evidence is available, it is thought that while both factors were operating, the most influential was the honest effort.

Students involved in the PRB increased their ability to become involved with people. This was indicated in parents' perceptions of increased communication at home, teacher's evaluation of more cooperation with them and fellow classmates, and work supervisors' reports of assignments.

Students involved in PRB increased in their problem-solving abilities. Greater insight into problem identification, alternative solutions, and

consequences were visualized both in the evaluation of tape recordings of group discussions and in reports of personal problem-solving
situations by students while they were on the job.

Delinquent acts among the students involved in PRB became less
in number and in seriousness. This was reported as being noticeable
both in the Juvenile Court and in the school. In court the number
of referrals increased for some students. This can be accounted for,
in part, by the fact that many referrals were made by PRB and were
not infractions of the law but were for motivation of the apathetic
delinquent child.

The Program acted as a coordinating tool, for the child's welfare, of
several agencies including the school, court system, child welfare
office, and various community agencies.

The PRB is unusually effective when evaluated with respect to 1)
comparative costs for rehabilitative efforts, 2) coordinating effects,
3) in-service training of local public agencies and school personnel,
4) family participation, 5) effect on delinquent acts of the child,
and 6) socialization and problem-solving skills of the child.

References

Redl, F. Who is Delinquent? **THE PTA MAGAZINE** (National Parent-
Teacher), December, 1955.

Glasser, W. **REALITY THERAPY**. New York, Harper & Row, 1965.

EXPERIMENTAL EDUCATION:
BASIS FOR STRATEGIES OF SERVICE,
RESEARCH AND TRAINING

Norris G. Haring, Ed.D.
Director, Experimental Education Unit of the
    Child Development and Mental Retardation Center
Professor, College of Education
Lecturer, Department of Pediatrics
School of Medicine
University of Washington

Thomas C. Lovitt, Ed.D.
Associate Professor, Experimental Education Unit of the
    Child Development and Retardation Center
University of Washington
Seattle, Washington

This paper describes an effort to apply scientific principles to education, on the assumption that the science which has produced our rapidly changing environment can help man to learn how to successfully adjust his behavior to that environment. Drs. Haring and Lovitt describe the program of the Experimental Education Unit at the University of Washington in Seattle, where they have attempted to incorporate the scientific principles of direct observation, repeated measurement, and systematic manipulation of variables into three basic strategies of experimental education—service, research, and training. The authors define service as "the designing of procedures for the current population of school children and the extension of these procedures to field settings. Research is characterized by the exploration of future teaching techniques and methods. Training attempts to extend the scientific elements of diagnosis and remediation throughout a wide community of therapists and to discover those variables relevant to the process of instruction."

I think that the present approach is a significant effort to bring logic and clarity to the educational process and to translate theory into practical action in the classroom. However, I always find myself troubled theoretically with behavior modification. What bothers me about behavior modification is the underlying assumption that the school context is humane and only the students' behavior needs to be altered. From the classrooms I have observed around the country I see this as a doubtful assumption.

M. B. R.

122

EXPERIMENTAL EDUCATION: BASIS FOR STRATEGIES OF SERVICE, RESEARCH, AND TRAINING

While the American educational system of 100 years ago seems to have fulfilled societal needs, education today is subject to criticism from a variety of social segments. This increasing disenchantment is largely the function of the rapid technological advances during the past century which have drastically altered the American way of life. While requisite skills for the rural and relatively nontechnical environment of several generations ago were few and basically simple, today's environment requires a variety of complex social and technological skills. As science has provoked technological change at a rapid rate and created an environment of constant flux, education has not provided man with the behavioral process necessary to adjust at a corresponding pace.

The critics of contemporary education, noting with alarm that many individuals are unable to function adequately in the current society, are, in effect, demanding an educational renaissance. From these critics—the military, the industry, the political community, and the citizenry at large—educators have received a barrage of suggestions concerned with administrative, curricular, and instructional revisions to increase educational excellence.

Throughout the country educators have sought to answer these criticisms by revising certain aspects of their programs. Such administrative plans as team teaching and nongraded classrooms have been attempted by a number of schools. Curricular innovation, in the form of different courses and materials, is widespread. Instructional and methodological revision is noted by the exploration of such procedures as the discovery or inquiry method.

These reformation attempts by educators have been, for the most part, random and unsystematic. One curricular text is changed, and then another; one grouping plan is attempted, then revised; one instructional method is advocated, then followed by others. However, these changes in method, procedures, or materials are rarely evaluated to gain objective information concerning their effect on pupil performance.

A further proliferation, then, of advocates for new educational plans or theories is not needed. Sorely required, however, are sound experimental methods for evaluating teaching and learning and educators who support educational growth based on scientific principles. Each educator, in order to fulfill his prime mission of assisting pupils to acquire certain academic and social behaviors, must base his curricular, procedural, and instructional decisions on experimental objectivity. If education is to progress efficiently and systematically, the principles of experimental inquiry and evaluation must permeate the entire educational structure, from the classroom teacher to the U.S. Commissioner of Education.

These scientific principles—direct observation, repeated measurement, and systematic manipulation of variables—are neither revolutionary nor new; they are, rather, the basis by which every scientific discipline has been able to advance from speculation to demonstrated knowledge of complex phenomena.

The first of these principles, direct observation, requires precise specification of what is to be evaluated. Just as the physiological scientist might observe the synaptic mechanisms; the psychologist, visual perception; or the physical scientist, atmospheric conditions, the educator would directly observe performance in reading, writing, or mathematics. Secondly, the educator, like other scientists, would make repeated observations of the specified behavior in order to make reliable statements as to its extent or probability of occurrence. Finally, the educational scientist would systematically manipulate variables, alternately introducing and removing some environmental element to determine its effects on the specified behavior.

Before these scientific principles of direct observation, continuous measurement, and systematic manipulation can be achieved, however, several steps must be taken to arrange a scientific atmosphere which will allow educational evaluations. First, as in any other scientific endeavor, the independent variables must be precisely described. Just as in a laboratory where such variables as size of room, intensity of stimulus, or type of reinforcement are defined, the classroom variables—class size, materials, or teacher interaction—must be described.

The second step toward establishing a scientific atmosphere is to define the unit of measurement being employed. Academic variables might be measured by rates of reading, of computing math problems, or of completing language exercises, while social behaviors might be measured by time spent sitting, standing, studying, or talking.

The third requisite for a scientific environment is that some situational stability must be imposed so that behavior may be systematically recorded. All the independent variables except the one being manipulated must be kept constant; otherwise, if constant alteration is taking place, one is uncertain which variable was associated with change in pupil behavior.

Finally, the classroom must utilize materials and procedures that lend themselves to recording; a dependent measure is only possible to the extent that it can be noted. Many classroom responses are easily recorded, for example, arithmetic computations, words read, or sentences written. Other activities, however, do not readily lend themselves to measurement—for example, group listening activities, show and tell sequences, silent reading exercises, or field trips. Such activities must, nevertheless, be followed by some method of evaluation if their effect on pupil behavior is to be determined.

After these steps have been accomplished, the classroom is arranged for scientific inquiry. Now, after existing conditions have been measured, a new independent variable may be added or the prevailing independent variables modified to determine effects on student performance. A replication might also be performed—returning to the original condition, then reintroducing the manipulation phase—to demonstrate conclusively the effects of the manipulated variable.

Such a scientific situation has been established at the Experimental Education Unit (EEU) of the University of Washington. The independent variables—curricular materials, teacher instructions, seating arrangements, contingency systems—have been defined. Further, the materials and procedures used facilitate recording. Programmed materials are employed extensively, instructions and procedures individualized, and pupil performance on academic and social behaviors continuously measured. Finally, after a stable environment is established, an environmental alteration is encouraged *only* as a rational attempt to modify or rehabilitate some behavior, not as an impulsive effort to effect sheer novelty or innovation. Thus, seating arrangements, instructions, or contingencies are not altered unless their effects have been observed over a period of time and the data indicate that a change is warranted.

At the EEU the scientific principles of direct observation, repeated measurement, and systematic manipulation of variables have been incorporated within three strategies essential to the total learning process: service, research, and training. Service fulfills the needs of current pupils enrolled in the experimental school and teachers in the field. Research seeks to explore and investigate procedures that may in the future add precision and efficiency to the learning process. Training is designed to discover and arrange the relevant skills of teaching so that the programmers of the future may accommodate the intellectual needs of children in a scientific manner.

Strategy for Service

The primary concern of any educational unit is to accommodate the current intellectual needs of the children in that setting. Thus, at the EEU, although activities and projects of a research and training nature are constantly underway, the major interest is serving the pupils.

When a child first enters the EEU for possible placement he is seen by members of the Behavioral Analysis staff, who determine the child's functioning level in a number of academic areas such as reading, writing, mathematics, and spelling, and in a variety of social situations as well. A number of observations are obtained relevant to each skill to increase the probability of obtaining a reliable index of performance, since often, if but one measure of a behavior is obtained, the variability of subject performance is entirely undetected. The data yielded by these observations are reported as rates of response per minute, thus incorporating both a measure of frequency of responding and the temporal period encompassing such efforts.

This evaluation not only determines which skills the pupil possesses, but also reports the environmental circumstances that were in effect during the assessment period, such as a description of the materials used, the instructions given by the evaluator, and the events that occurred subsequent to the pupil's responding. It is important not only to report how well the pupil performed on a certain task, but to detail the events that prevailed during such an evaluation; for both performance rates and environmental contingencies must be included in a functional analysis. The probability of providing meaningful evaluation data that will extend into the classroom setting is increased when both product and process are considered; then the teacher who will instruct the child not only knows the level of the pupil's skill development, but has some information as to which procedures and materials to use for preliminary programming.

In the second step of the instructional process, educational objectives are established for each child. This is the joint responsibility of the Behavioral Analysis staff and the assigned classroom teacher at the EEU. The objectives are generally reported and specified in terms of direction, that is, to increase or decrease the behavior. The objectives might be to increase the children's skills in a number of areas— more reading or mathematics skills or more involvement with peers. Or these objectives could be to decrease the occurrence of such behaviors as hitting or talking out of turn. In addition, the extent of improvement expected is also specified.

Following detailed assessment and specification of objectives, the pupil is assigned to one of the classes at the EEU. The teacher's task now is to incorporate the data pertaining to the child's initial evaluation into the ongoing management system of the class. She first selects academic materials which correspond to the child's current level of performance and which enable her to provide immediate feedback regarding the pupil's efforts. For this reason, programmed materials are used whenever possible, whereby the child himself, once he makes a response, can receive immediate confirmation regarding his efforts. If programmed materials are not available, every effort is made to use curricular materials that may be subdivided into small teaching units that allow some continuity to the performance-evaluation cycle.

The child is then placed on a contingency system which states, in effect, that when a child successfully completes so much work, he is granted so many points that may later be redeemed for leisure time pursuits. Thus, initial contingencies might be that for every two math responses the child is given one point or minute of free time. The management design of the classrooms at the EEU, based on the research of Premack (1965) and Homme (1966), has been detailed by Haring and Kunzelmann (1967). Essentially, the premise of this management design states that any high probability behavior (such as coloring, listening to music, or building models) will reinforce any preceding low probability behavior (such as reading, mathematics or spelling).

When the contingency system has been placed in operation, daily performance records are obtained. Each day performance data are recorded regarding the pupil's rate of correct and incorrect responding on a number of academic areas, and pertaining to other behaviors originally designated as target behaviors, such as behaving inappropriately in some social circumstances. Data are also maintained relevant to the number of times the teacher interacted or assisted the child, how many points he earned, when he redeemed the points for free time, and how he used these minutes of earned free time.

During this beginning period of classroom observation, where daily performance records are obtained, the environmental conditions must remain stable. The student's seat is not changed, the material and instructions remain constant, and the number of points granted for each activity does not fluctuate. The teacher thus is able to assess the effectiveness of her procedures and to what extent, if any, the child is progressing toward the desired goals. If, as revealed by the data, the student is not increasing his rate of sight word recognition or is not decreasing his rate of talking out of turn, the teacher can make a procedural revision based on this evidence. She might choose, for example, to increase the number of contacts with the child. By again observing the pupil's performance rate, the teacher will be able to determine whether the increased interactions have been effective. Similarly, the teacher might choose to alter the pupil's program to increase his rate of academic responding. Or the teacher might choose to manipulate the point-per-response contingency rather than the program content or the teacher involvement. She might raise or lower the number of points granted for academic responding or reschedule the dispensing of points or free time by allowing the student to take his free time only after so many minutes, or after so many correct responses have been made, or both.

The effects of manipulating either the contingencies or the frames of the program itself is being studied by Nolen (1968). In past efforts to evaluate programmed materials as a function of pupil performance, she has found that some pupils' error rates have decreased by a simple rearrangement of environmental contingencies, where the point-per-answer ratio was in some way altered. If, however, high rates of error or low rates of correct responding continue, the programmer must in some way alter the program itself, either by rearrangement of steps or by the addition of supplemental sequences.

Therefore, several alternative remediation tactics are available to the teacher in her attempts to direct her pupils toward certain educational objectives. However, only by manipulating one of these variables at a time and by maintaining daily response rate data will the teacher be in a position to evaluate the effectiveness of any of these remediation attempts. Because of high teacher-pupil ratios or lack of auxiliary personnel such as teacher aides, certain modifications in these management procedures are necessary when they are applied in the public school. A secondary service obligation of the EEU, therefore, is to adapt and extend scientific procedures to public school settings. To accommodate this aspect of service the EEU has developed a Field Service staff, whose personnel assist teachers in the field to use some of the procedures of evaluation, recording, and remediation that have proved functional at the EEU.

One such service project that began at the EEU and is now being extended to a field setting is a reading investigation conducted by Haring and Hauck (1968). Four severely disabled readers from the intermediate grades of a suburban school were brought to the EEU for daily 75-minute reading sessions. Prior to any remediation attempts, each pupil's skill level and range of competencies were determined. This examination revealed that all of the boys were functioning at the primer level in Sullivan programmed materials. Throughout the training program at the EEU, the boys were presented Sullivan materials and permitted to progress individually from one

book to another. During this investigation as many of the environmental variables were stabilized as possible—same seating arrangement, material, and teacher instructions. Performance response
rates were maintained and graphed daily. Only the type and scheduling of reinforcement was manipulated to determine their effects
on individual rates of performance. During some portions of the
study the pupils received nothing for correct answers except the
opportunity to make another academic response; at other times
they were provided counters indicating their number of correct
answers; finally, contingent upon correct responses they received
marbles that could be redeemed for some toy item. The results
of this 5-month program revealed that progress, as measured by
change in basal reading level, ranged from 1½ years to 4 years.

Following the 5-month period of instruction at the EEU, procedures
were designed to transfer the reading program to the regular classroom. Before the classroom teachers assumed the responsibility for
administering this program, three training steps were scheduled. The
three phases of this training included: 1) demonstrating to classroom teachers how to use the materials and procedures that had
been in effect at the EEU; 2) assisting the classroom teachers to
obtain daily performance measures from each child; and 3) aiding
the teachers to present the materials in a uniform and stable manner. Currently, the children, back in their respective schools, are
continuing to function adequately.

A second example of a service activity being extended into the public schools (Hauck and Haring, 1968) is being conducted in the
Bellewood Elementary School, Bellevue, Washington. The purpose
of this project is to establish a contingency management system
during reading for a total classroom and to use the pupils as monitors and data recorders. In this class, where reading levels range
from grade two to five, each child is assigned a pupil-teacher who
monitors his pupil's answers and records relevant data. Each day
the children are given an opportunity to read silently as many three-
page-sets as possible in a period of 30 minutes. When the silent

reading is completed, the pupil is required to answer comprehension questions corresponding to the reading sets. They are also given a list of words that had been incorrectly pronounced the previous day. When each child completes these lessons, he goes to his assigned proctor, who records the words pronounced correctly and checks the comprehension answers from a master sheet. The proctor also keeps time on the pupil's reading by requiring him to read orally for a short session, and then records lines read per minute. Every pupil graphs his own data from his reading record sheet. The more advanced students in this class gather the recorded information from each proctor and subsequently graph these data. Following a period of baseline assessment, extra recess, physical education, and free choice reading activities were made contingent upon the pupil's performing at higher and more stable rates.

Preliminary data from this project are very encouraging. Discipline problems have been minimized during the reading portion of the day, the pupils are advancing through reading materials at a high rate, and they are developing the ability to instruct and communicate with others.

A third project designed to serve eventually the public schools has been organized under the cosponsorship of the Renton and Seattle school districts and the University of Washington (Alton, Kunzelmann, and Haring, 1968). To accommodate this project a room was established at the EEU to approximate as closely as possible the environment of a public school situation; children were selected from the cosponsoring school districts; materials currently recommended by the districts were used; and free-time activities and reinforcers from the regular school setting were incorporated.

A contingency management system was placed in effect for this total group. Each pupil's rate of responding was recorded for each academic activity; and on the basis of his performance he was granted points to be redeemed later for free-time activities. While this plan has been in operation the classroom teachers from the school districts have been receiving training from the project teacher at the EEU, so that when the children are later transferred back to their regular classrooms, the procedures of contingency management will generalize to that setting.

These few projects exemplify the ways in which more precise educational methods can be applied in the natural school situation. A service program, to be functional, is one which identifies procedural, instructional, or evaluation problems in the field and attempts to design developmental projects which will resolve these issues.

Strategy for Research

The primary function of an educational unit, whether in a laboratory or field setting, remains one of service. The central focus, as previously stated, must be one of assisting students to acquire the necessary skills to discriminate successfully from among a wide variety of complex academic and social cues.

A program of developmental research which explores ways of increasing the precision of the educational process is also an essential element for the advancement of any educational enterprise. Some of the research that is currently underway at the EEU is of such an exploratory nature. Although the results from many of these projects cannot be immediately recommended to settings in the field, functional innovations may be anticipated. It is the dual responsibility, then, of the research staff at the EEU to explore systematically the educational processes of the future and to assess the efficiency of such innovations before their extension to the field is recommended.

Kunzelmann (1968), in an ongoing project of an investigative nature, is attempting to devise an observation system that would encompass simultaneously some independent variables of a classroom, and then to relate these variables to the dependent variable, academic response rate. Currently, two independent variables, teacher interaction and point-per-answer requirements, are plotted for each pupil on the same chart. This chart illustrates how many times the teacher was involved with each child and how many points per correct answer were granted. Also plotted on this chart for each individual are two dependent variables: rate of correct and rate of incorrect responses. By simultaneously illustrating all of these data, the experimenter is provided, for the entire class on any given day, a total view of behavior relevant to each of the four described variables. By presenting data in such a manner, the investigator can observe the effect on the entire class when an independent variable is introduced either for a single pupil or for each class member. For example, if a teacher decreases her frequency of interactions with one pupil, the function of this change could be detected on the entire class as well as on the single individual. Or similarly, if the same variable, a substitute teacher, was presented to the entire class, the effects on each individual and on total class performance could be measured.

Another exploratory project being undertaken at the EEU seeks to increase the precision of pupil evaluation. This project arose from the fact that often, when varying academic skill levels are employed, a performance rate discrepancy is noted. If a pupil performs complex mathematics problems at a rate lower than that for a simpler problem, the viewer of such records would be uncertain whether the difference in the two rates was a function of the type of stimulus material or of some other independent variable. Therefore, Kunzelmann (1968) has recommended counting responses by grapheme and phoneme units rather than using only the final answer to the problem as the response. For example, in a math problem such as 22 + 44 = _____, two responses would be counted in the newly recommended system since one computation is involved in the units column and one in the tens. Traditionally, the answer to the problem would have been considered a single response. In the language area, a phoneme rather than the complete word would be counted as a response. In this instance, if a child uttered ten words that contained forty-three phoneme units he would be credited with forty-three responses, as contrasted with the ten he would traditionally receive.

Preliminary investigations comparing grapheme-phoneme and traditional counting systems have indicated that this new method grants much more stability when varying complexities of problems are used. Thus, inter-educator communication may be facilitated when pupil performance is described as grapheme or phoneme units rather than the traditional unit as a dependent variable when information is desired relevant to the effects of some independent variable; for this system may allow more ready discernment of the effects of contingency alteration on performance rate.

Another research effort is planned to study the behaviors that constitute self-management. An initial investigation was designed in an attempt to specify those behavioral elements that comprise the total trait, self-management. During this investigation several self-management behaviors were required of a pupil. One variable was added, then another, until four self-management behaviors were scheduled; no effort was made to determine the effects of any one variable. The sequence of self-management steps was self-scheduling, where the pupil was allowed to arrange his own sequence of activities; self-correcting, where the pupil confirmed his own answers; self-recording, where the student kept his own performance records; and self-contingency specifications, where he detailed his own work-per-reinforcement ratio. The purpose was to evaluate continuously the pupil's academic performance as more complex management requirements were imposed to determine whether his rate of responding would in some way be affected. If a general decline in academic performance were observed it would, perhaps, indicate that either too few self-management steps had been detailed or that some of the frames were out of sequence. The data from this initial survey revealed that the pupil's academic rate did not suffer as self-management behaviors became increasingly more complex; in fact, as one variable was added to another, his rate of academic responding steadily increased.

Following this initial survey, a study was then designed to assess the effects on academic performance of a single aspect of self-management, self-contingency specification. This investigation (Lovitt and Curtiss, 1968) studied the effects of pupil response rate when the teacher imposed the contingencies versus when the child himself arranged his environment. In the first stage, the teacher set the contingencies, with so much work being granted so much reinforcement. The second stage of the experiment allowed the student himself to set the contingencies. In a final stage, the teacher once again set the requirements. The data from this study revealed that, for this student, higher response rates were associated with self-management of contingencies.

Further studies have been planned to assess experimentally the individual effects of other self-managing behaviors. One ongoing attempt seeks to observe the effects on response rate when the pupil records his performance versus when the teacher conducts the recording.

A fourth project is being conducted in an attempt to specify some of those behaviors believed essential for effective teaching. In this study, a child at the EEU is being instructed to teach another child. This young man was first told to teach one of his classmates a list of sight words, using the teaching procedures of his choice. At the end of each day's session the pupil-teacher and his pupil were granted points, on the basis of the pupil's performance, to be used for free-time activities. In the second stage the pupil-teacher was given certain procedural instructions, how to present the material and in what order, and what to say to his pupil when a correct or incorrect answer was given. The data from this investigation indicated that the specified criterion of learning was reached in twenty-three sessions in the first sequence, while only seven sessions were required when certain teaching procedures were followed.

This "teacher-training" project is continuing. Now, however, the pupil-teacher is required to record length of session and number of correct answers, and to plot these data on a graph. After acquiring these recording skills, he will be requested to teach his pupil a second set of words. Next, the instructor will be observed as he teaches a set of arithmetic problems to the same boy, to determine how many of the teaching techniques he continues to use while training his pupil on a different skill. After the teacher successfully demonstrates his skills as an instructor for one pupil, he will be assigned a different pupil and will again teach word recognition. This final investigation, then, will demonstrate how a set of training techniques and procedures, once they have been taught to an instructor, will generalize to others of his pupils.

The teaching skills so described would represent only the remediation phase of teaching. Certainly instructors are required to possess additional skills in diagnosing, offering a remediation program, discriminating materials and techniques to effect remediation, evaluating data, and basing programming decisions on these data. Perhaps the most efficient way to discover other necessary skills required for teaching may be to evaluate these steps with children. It is difficult to evaluate the function of formal training with undergraduates or graduates who have been exposed to teacher training programs; for many of them are, in all probability, using skills developed through courses and other techniques that are remnants of their own student days. With young students who have short pupil histories, the probability is increased that, because of his limited teaching repertoire, he will be restricted to using only those skills demonstrated to him. The evaluation of teacher training programs, then, would appear to be, at least initially, more direct and valid when tutorially naive pupils are used.

Strategy for Training

A third strategy of the educational process encompassed within the framework of the EEU is training. This training is necessitated by the demands and requirements of a number of sources: parent groups; local and area teachers; pediatricians and nurses; students from the departments of education, psychology, and sociology; and students and instructors from a number of universities.

Training in these instances ranges from a short visitation accompanied by an explanation of the EEU, its intended function, operation, and purpose, to a more detailed arrangement of activities sequenced for the pediatric residents of the University's medical school.

Two major programs which exemplify the experiences and training sequence at the Unit are discussed here: One is the training of Master's Degree students in the area of Learning Disabilities,[1] and the other is a demonstration project designed to prepare teachers to use behavior modification procedures.[2] In the former program some course offerings, research facilities, practicum, and seminar experiences are provided the fellowship students at the EEU.

The training of the teachers involved in the Demonstration Project is totally centered at the EEU. The purpose of this project has been to prepare four former teachers to return to elementary school settings as resource teachers. The project seeks to demonstrate that individuals trained in the scientific principles of learning can assist regular and special classroom teachers to: 1) specify behavioral

[1] Learning Disabilities Fellowships funded by the Bureau of Education for the Handicapped, U.S. Office of Education, Grant No. OEG-2-7-003380-3380.

[2] The Application of Functional Analysis of Behavior by Teachers in a Natural School Setting, Demonstration Grant funded by Bureau of Research, Division of Handicapped Children and Youth, U.S. Office of Education, Grant No. OEG-0-8-070376-1857 (032), Project No. 7-0376.

problems; 2) design remediation plans to alleviate these problems; 3) arrange situations whereby such procedures might be implemented; and 4) evaluate the efficiency of these attempts.

The training of the four project teachers was to be completed at the end of two academic quarters; at the end of this time they would be functioning as consultants in their Seattle area elementary schools. Because of the time limitation it was necessary to restrict the curricular design to those aspects of teaching considered most relevant. Therefore, these future consultants were presented a series of rather discrete exercises, rather than a set of courses whose content and objectives were not, perhaps, totally relevant. Although it was not initially known which steps were necessary to train such a teacher, or how much emphasis should be placed on any step, some preliminary framework had to be developed and presented before the total sequence could be evaluated.

Basically, the sequences that have so far been presented to the project teachers include orientation to behavioral modification, observation and specification of behaviors, evaluation of academic and social behaviors, construction of remediation programs to modify behaviors, and communication of evaluations and recommendations.

The primary purpose of the first training step was to acquaint the teachers with the literature relevant to behavioral modification procedures. In addition to assigned readings, meetings were conducted to discuss the importance of describing behavior in a precise manner and maintaining graphic information relevant to attempts to affect this behavior.

To attain the second training objective, observation and specification of behavior, several exercises were designed requesting the project teachers to define the dimensions of a variety of behaviors in such a way that they might be tabulated and graphed in a valid and reliable manner.

Following this observation phase, the project teachers conducted several academic and social evaluations of children, observing certain behaviors and then determining the performance level of the child in each of these areas. These evaluations not only described the product of the child's performance in terms of number of correct answers per unit of time, but detailed the process of the evaluation, for example, the instructions provided by the examiner, and the remarks or events that followed a pupil's answer.

The fourth phase of the teacher training sequence involved designing and implementing modification procedures. First, the project teachers worked directly with a child in attempts either to increase his behavior in an academic area or to decrease his rate of activity in some socially unacceptable behavior. Following this direct involvement with a child, the project teacher then assisted another teacher to conduct a modification procedure through specifying a problem behavior, designing procedures for remediation, and obtaining graphic evidence of the results.

The fifth aspect of the training sequence has been one of communication. Since these teachers, as consultants to other teachers, parents, and administrators, must communicate their evaluations and subsequent recommendations in a precise manner, exercises were designed to train these skills. Meetings were scheduled involving the project personnel, fellowship students, and other teachers, during which time each participant presented data concerning an observation or modification attempt. The project teachers were required, as they conducted these meetings, to insure that each participant explained precisely the behavior in question, detailed clearly the teaching or observation procedures, projected implications coincident with the observed data, and suggested feasible recommendations as to the future course of the project.

To obtain data pertaining to the time each teacher devotes to project-relevant assignments, each is required to make several entries each day in his log. Certain aspects of this log data pertain to total time devoted to the project, time spent on reading assignments, and time applied to modification efforts. At the termination of the project, these data will state, to some extent, that these teachers perform as they do as a function of so much time devoted to certain sequences. With more specificity and precision of future programs, it will be possible to analyze functionally and manipulate certain elements of the training curriculum.

Summary and Conclusions

This report sought to describe the three basic strategies of experimental education—service, research, and training—as exemplified by the Experimental Education Unit of the University of Washington. Although the dimensions of these strategies are not rigidly defined and in many instances overlap, certain administrative parameters are apparent. Service refers to the designing of procedures for the current population of school children and the extension of these procedures to field settings. Research is characterized by the exploration of future teaching techniques and methods. Training attempts to extend the scientific elements of diagnosis and remediation throughout a wide community of therapists and to discover those variables relevant to the process of instruction.

When the educational process is based on sound scientific principles, the existing gap between education and technology will be reduced. By employing the thoroughly documented aspects of empiricism— direct, continuous observation and precise description and manipulation of variables—educational techniques and procedures will emerge systematically. By blending the efforts of experimental education in service, research, and training, service will effectively accommodate the present; research will provide for the future; and training will generalize the products of both.

References

Alton, C., Kunzelmann, H., and Haring, N. "Applied Behavioral Analysis in an Instructional Setting." Unpublished manuscript, EEU, University of Washington, 1968.

Haring, N. and Hauck, M. A. "Improved Learning Conditions in the Establishment of Reading Skills with Disabled Readers." Unpublished manuscript, EEU, University of Washington, 1968.

Haring, N. and Kunzelmann, H. The Finer Focus of Therapeutic Behavioral Management. In Jerome Hellmuth (Ed.) **EDUCATIONAL THERAPY, 1.** Seattle: Special Child Publications, pp. 225-251, 1966.

Hauck, M. A. and Haring, N. "Group Contingency Management of Reading in a Regular Classroom." Unpublished manuscript, EEU, University of Washington, 1968.

Homme, L. Human Motivation and Environment. **UNIVERSITY OF KANSAS SYMPOSIUM, THE LEARNING ENVIRONMENT: RELATIONSHIP TO BEHAVIOR MODIFICATION AND IMPLICATIONS FOR SPECIAL EDUCATION.** Kansas Studies in Education. Lawrence, Kansas: University of Kansas Publications, **16,** 1966.

Kunzelmann, H. "Data Decisions." Paper read at the Association for Children with Learning Disabilities, Boston, Massachusetts, 1968.

Lovitt, T. and Curtiss, K. "Academic Response Rate as a Function of Teacher and Self-imposed Contingencies." Unpublished manuscript, EEU, University of Washington, 1968.

Nolen, P. "Data Programming." Paper read at the Association for Children with Learning Disabilities, Boston, Massachusetts, 1968.

Premack, D. "Reinforcement Theory." Paper read at Nebraska Motivation Symposium. Lincoln, Nebraska, 1965.

AN INNOVATIVE PROGRAM FOR
SCHOOL-ALIENATED ADOLESCENTS

William R. Page, B.S.
Director, Educational Programs and Resources Division
Education Corporation of America
Nashville, Tennessee
        and
Director, Project ENABLE
Peabody College
Nashville, Tennessee

William Page outlines here a program, Project ENABLE, about which I am excited. I am excited primarily because of the high value I see accorded to students. Bill Page has built into the program the possibility for autonomy and interdependence for both teachers and students. He has indicated how all involved in education—student, teacher, parent, and administrator—fit into the program and how they have reacted favorably to the feel of a new role in the educational exchange.

M. B. R.

AN INNOVATIVE PROGRAM FOR
SCHOOL-ALIENATED ADOLESCENTS

Preface

The advent of new approaches, with new resignation and determination, to the diagnosis and remediation of learning problems has caused a resounding flourish of activity in the past decade. These innovative techniques and theoretical developments have focused on early childhood development and upon early discovery and prevention procedures.

While prevention is the obvious place for such focus, those concerned with adolescents cannot wait until prevention techniques are perfected. Even if in some wild dream a miracle would occur which would prevent learning problems at school entrance level, it would still be many years before problems ceased at the secondary level.

Introduction (Overview)

Project ENABLE is a comprehensive remedial and developmental program making operational a completely individualized program which uses self-initiated, self-directed learning for school-alienated adolescents.

The project is based upon fundamental and significant changes in the basic student-teacher relationship.

These changes represent not only new techniques in education but more importantly some new directions with new objectives.

The essence of the project is a creative communication procedure which permits the teacher to communicate openly and honestly with warmth, acceptance, and understanding, and to respond to students in ways which enhance the students' self-concept, personal responsibility, self-discipline and decision-making ability.

The Problem

Tomorrow, (or perhaps on Monday,) several million adolescent school children will sit through some 6 hours of schooling. While most of them may be expected to learn or in various ways to profit from the experience, the rest, a significant number, will suffer through just one more day of failure, frustration, embarrassment, intimidation or negative learning.

These children are likely to be told, shown, and reminded repeatedly that they are stupid, incompetent, and unacceptable. They will hear it, see it, and feel it, from the school with its structures, curriculum, labels and evaluative methods, from their peers, teachers, and parents, from their own subconscious and conscious judgments. Whether said subtly or blatantly, the inhumane message they receive is that they are dumb.

The strategies which they develop in their efforts to cope with this affront to their very existence as worthwhile human beings are literally strategies for survival.

In attempting to deal with adolescent problem learners it is necessary to recognize a distinction between the plots and ploys which all students use to pass tests, deceive the teacher, and so on, and the techniques which a "failure" finds necessary to withstand sustained blows to his very dignity and worth. Recognizing this distinction is the first step toward understanding that the "failure's" techniques are strategies for survival.

Dr. William Glasser (1969) says that there is no qualitative difference between a straight "A" student and a straight "F" student. Each has learned to cope with school—the "A" student by ultimate conformity and submission; the "F" student by ultimate rejection and retaliation.

Most of the strategies involve some form of survival manifested by either active or passive rebelliousness, deviant behavior or some form of a "to hell with it" attitude.

The specific problem, then, is this: A small but significant number of junior high school students are unprepared for regular junior high school programs; the junior high schools, on the other hand, are unprepared to offer any program as an irregular alternative to the regular program.

Too often the school, in coping with these alienated students, chooses one of two minimally effective programs. The first is a basic remedial type program which offers a "more of the same" approach or a watered-down, slowed-down program. It may offer a vocational program which is designed as a terminal program and which so stigmatizes the students that most of the real value is lost to the students' feelings of inadequacy and the pervasive futility of a dead-end program.

A junior high school student may have already experienced anywhere from 7 to 10 years of failure and frustration. To offer him such programs as these is analogous to putting a band-aid on an amputated arm.

An added dimension of the problem is that of the increasing pressure of society to have schools "do something." Previously schools could use kick-out and force-out techniques to alleviate their own problems—now schools are being forced to deal with the problem student rather than ignore him so he will "drop out."

One who has experienced years of failure in a particular program is not likely to change his attitude or feeling about that program. Unless he perceives the new program as significantly different from the old one, he is not likely to accept it or change his approach to it.

Project ENABLE was designed to be a genuine alternative to regular school programs and to traditional remedial and vocational programs.

Program Description

The essence of this project is that students make decisions, set goals, make commitments, make their own materials and are held responsible and accountable for their own learning. To complement and encourage such growth in students we want a teacher who is a sincere, honest human being who responds to and respects students as human beings.

The procedure for such a relationship is based upon the perceptual or interactional theory articulated by such authors as Arthur Combs and Carl Rogers as taken from PERCEIVING, BEHAVING, BECOMING (1962):

> *The perceptual view of human behavior holds that the behavior of an individual is a function of his ways of perceiving. That is to say, how any person behaves at a given moment is a direct expression of the way things seem to him at that moment. People do not behave according to the "facts" as they seem to an outsider. How each of us behaves at any given moment is a result of how things seem to him. What a person does, what a person learns, is thus a product of what is going on in his unique and personal field of awareness. People behave in terms of the personal meanings (perceptions) existing for them at the moment of action.* (pp. 67-68)

Arthur W. Combs describes the perceptual theory in this way (1965):

148

The basic concept of perceptual psychology is that all behavior of a person is the direct result of his field of perceptions at the moment of his behaving. More specifically, his behavior at any instant is the result of 1) how he sees himself, 2) how he sees the situation in which he is involved, and 3) the interrelations of these two. When I see myself as a lecturer, standing in front of an audience, I behave like a lecturer. My audience, on the other hand, seeing themselves as an audience, behaves like an audience. Each of us behaves in terms of what seems to him to be appropriate for the kind of person he sees himself to be in the situation he is in at that moment. The immediate causes of behavior are to be found in the perceptions existing for the behaver at the moment of acting. This seems like a simple, acceptable notion that fits very closely with our own experience.

Perhaps it is precisely because it fits so closely and comfortably that it is often overlooked. One's own perceptions of events seem so "right" and so certain that one is quite likely to jump to the conclusion that the way one sees things is the way things are. Our own perceptions have such a feeling of reality that when others do not see things in a similar fashion we are likely to jump to either of two conclusions: They are frightfully stupid for not seeing correctly, or else they are perversely trying to annoy and confound us. It is probable that such failure to understand how things seem to other people is the most persistent source of difficulties in human relationships. To understand human behavior, the perceptual psychologist says, it is necessary to understand the behaver's perceptual world, how things seem from his point of view. (pp. 12-13)

Applied to Project ENABLE, the approach attempts to understand and acknowledge the student's point of view through an innovative communication process. This communication involves skills which permit the teacher to abandon the use of student anxiety, intimidation, coercion and cajoling to move to self-direction, reasoning and logical consequences; to become a democratic leader rather than an authoritarian; a qualified human resource rather than a task-master.

Empirical research and clinical evidence indicate that an atmosphere of trust and respect must be created if the student is to share his perceptions and thus enable the teacher to become a resource.

A communication model has been developed which can help teachers to develop the skills necessary to create such an atmosphere. Teachers in the project are introduced to the model which follows:

A. Owning one's own position—the skill of sharing one's feelings honestly and openly in relationships with students. The teacher must learn to share his position without demand, without blame, and without making absolute statements. To help him do this, the teacher learns to use " 'I' statements that talk about me."

B. Listening to the position of the other person. Respecting and understanding that position unconditionally without calculative or judgmental statements. Teachers are taught to paraphrase the statements made by the student because it does the following:
  1. Shows the speaker that he has been accurately heard.
  2. Leaves the speaker feeling respected.
  3. Allows the listener to check understanding.

C. Resolving conflicts by mutual and cooperative procedures rather than coercively. This is accomplished by steps A and B being fully met. Having heard and having been heard, each party can mutually suggest possible solutions; then together they agree upon one of those suggested solutions.

The interpersonal relations—teacher to teacher, teacher to child, and child to child—are based upon this model of mutual respect. It permits the teacher and student to become equal as human beings— equal in thoughts, feelings, desires, and ideas. It also permits them to live with being unequal in knowledge, experience, accountability and responsibility.

Procedure

Selection. At the end of the school year, sixth grade teachers from the feeder schools were asked to list in rank order the students who could not be expected to be successful in the regular seventh grade program and who should be offered a special program. Reasons for the anticipated failure were ignored—selected students represented the bottom 10%-20% of the incoming seventh graders regardless of whether they were emotionally disturbed, slow learners, lazy or whatever.

Parent Conferences. Parents of the children selected for the program were invited to individual conferences at which the program was described. Parents were not told they had a choice to participate or not participate in the program, but had any of them had serious objection, their child would have been excluded. A couple of parents had some reservations, but none objected and no children were excluded.

Because to us motivation is based on the intrinsic value of what is learned, grades become inadequate to describe the child's progress. Therefore parent conferences were used in lieu of report cards. Progress was reported to the parents by the child in terms of what the child had learned (not what he did or how he compared with what other seventh graders were learning). The teacher's job is to make sure the child gives an accurate and complete picture of his progress.

151

Complete Individualization. The teacher rarely deals with more than one child at a time. Her goal becomes to establish a tutorial relation with each child.

The basis for the complete individualization lies in the child's understanding of his goals. If he knows what he is to learn, what he needs to know, and can determine for himself when he has learned it, he needs the teacher only as a resource to help him reach his goal. He can also use fellow students, or books or parents to reach his goals.

Once the goal is to learn the material—because the material is important to him—the child no longer needs extrinsic motivation to work. He works to learn, not to get grades, privileges, or approval, or to avoid punishment.

The way to insure that the goal is meaningful to a child is to let him participate in its selection. The teacher's primary function then becomes to help the child determine a goal worthwhile to him and in conformity with the school's goals.

Role of the Teacher. The teacher changes his or her role from taskmaster to resource person, from lecturer to tutor, from controller of activity to setter of limits according to the needs and goals of individual children in relation to her own feelings of responsibility.

The teacher must understand the inconsistent behavior of adolescents; be sensitive to their needs in addition to academic requirements; and be tolerant of diverse activities taking place in a limited area. She must perceive her job as helping a child to set or reach his goal rather than setting goals for him.

The teacher must have a repertoire of techniques to permit total differentiation of assignments and personality considerations.

She must feel secure enough to be willing to try new techniques and material and likewise be willing to fail.

Children work together according to their own choice and help one another. Once the child accepts the philosophy that the purpose of school is to learn—not to impress the teacher, to get a grade, or approval or to avoid punishment—he will seek help from whatever source is most efficient and convenient. Many children prefer to ask another child for help. If the teacher has taught one child a concept, one of the best ways of reinforcing that teaching is to refer other students to that child so he can teach it. The responsibility of playing the teacher role plus the positive self-concept effects involved in being "teacher" make it an especially worthwhile activity. Children may serve as worksheet checkers, test givers, note makers, and activity explainers.

Facilities. A self-contained single classroom, or two adjoining or adjacent classrooms are designated and equipped for certain types of activities. There may be an area of the room designated as quiet area, game table area, reading corner, conversation area, materials and supplies area, etc., as mutually decided. Normally the children initially decide and the teacher modifies the plans according to problems that arise.

Within the concept that the learner must be active, there must be raw materials and tools for making learning devices and a place to work on projects of a crafts nature.

Moveable partitions and furniture arrangements permit division of areas. Areas are frequently changed.

Introducing the Program. Each teacher uses his own method and style of introducing the program. One method of introduction is simply to begin without introduction. On the first day the teacher waits until the students are in the room. When he enters, he approaches a single child and begins discussion along the lines of, "Why are you here? What do you want to learn or do in this class?" As a group begins to gather around him, he excuses himself and goes to another individual.

His objective is to begin getting the individuals working toward a mutually determined goal. The teacher's initial goal becomes one of getting three or four of the children "going" each day so that it is possible to have the whole class "going" in a matter of 9 or 10 days.

The room would normally be set up with signs or notices such as "Here is a test that can tell you what you need to learn." (The test is the arithmetic portion of the WRAT.) Or, "Can you do these problems?" (Worksheets or exercises indicate to the students the course content.)

Another method of introducing the program is to have a class discussion on, "What is dumb?" This method is useful where children complain about being in the dumb-dumb class. In one class the group concluded that if you are dumb, it means you don't know what is expected of you; if you are average, you know what is expected; and if you are smart, you know more than is expected of you. The teacher then said, "You are in here because you don't know what is expected of you. I don't know why you don't know those things. It may be because you didn't want to learn. It may have been because you had a lousy teacher in the third grade. It may have been because you moved around from school to school or because you didn't want to learn. It doesn't really matter to me. All I know is that if you would like to get smart, I'll be glad to help you. I can't make you learn or learn for you but I can help you or get things or people that can help you. The main rule in this class is that you may choose to work or not to work, but you may not prevent others from working."

Another method of introducing the class includes beginning with the study of learning how to learn. In this class children might build learning machines or visit schools and classes as observers of learning.

The key factor in introducing the class is that the students have to be *shown* that the teacher means for this class to be different from other classes and that they see him as genuine and honest.

Materials, Equipment and Supplies. No special equipment, materials or supplies are required by the program. By being resourceful, teachers were able to get many extra but typical materials. The students use their own initiative and ingenuity to get materials for the room and build such things as study carrels and room dividers.

In classes where a special or extra budget is available, the main items needed or desired are a duplicating machine so students can make their own worksheets or tutoring worksheets; raw materials for making counting frames, flash cards, learning machines, educational games and manipulative devices.

Some of the materials which are used in the program are:

Teaching Aids	Standard Material
Cuisenaire rods	SPA Kits
Flannel board	Texts
Abacus	Workbooks
Charts	Worksheets
Maps	Programs
Games	Activity books

Equipment	Supplies
Tape recorders	Ditto masters
Record players	Paper cutter
Ditto machine	Scissors
Variety of furniture	Craft type supplies
Individual storage	Paper
File cabinets	

The Child as a Tutor. Children in Project ENABLE classes become tutors for lower grade level children. The tutoring program was begun as a way to get children to work at lower levels—to get them to do first and second grade work "because you are going to teach it," not "because they need first and second grade work." As the program developed, other values were found. The following are some observations made by teachers involved in the tutoring program:

The tutoring experience builds the self-concept of the tutor.

The tutoring assignment can be used to develop academic proficiency in the tutor since assignment can be given in the area where the tutor needs development. Because the tutoring carries assignment prestige, students are willing to learn many skills otherwise labeled as "baby stuff."

The tutoring experience creates a need for learning social skills and provides an opportunity for learning responsibility.

The tutoring experience causes the tutor to analyze the learning process and to apply what he sees to his own learning style.

The tutoring program demands role reversal and thus facilitates attitude changes toward school.

156

The activities of tutors vary. Tutors also play various roles for the teachers; some are teacher's aides who do clerical and monitorial tasks; some supervise whole class activities or give assistance as individuals in the group raise their hands; some instruct small groups in basic skills or drill activities; some listen to reading groups; some teach complex skills on a one-to-one basis; some lead learning games; some diagnose deficiencies and then ask for teacher directions for remediation or planned remedial exercises.

Tutoring helps to show a child that learning is a process. By analyzing lower level tasks, a sort of task analysis, the tutor begins to see that learning is more than just a matter of luck. It is a matter of determining appropriate steps and then being willing to go through those steps and get help when needed.

Evaluation of the effect of tutoring on the children being tutored showed consistent growth in achievement, self-concept, attitudes and peer relations. Having a tutor proved to be a real prestige factor.

Techniques. The child is taught that the object of school is to learn. Some of the techniques and teaching methods are these:

Children helping each other—working together and in groups.

Children making their own worksheets and tests.

Children charting their own progress.

Children tutoring children in lower grades.

Children doing independent projects.

Children using and devising diagnostic tests.

Children chart their own progress and learn to do self-diagnosis and task analysis. For a child to be responsible for his own learning he must know: a) what he is to learn (goal), b) what he already knows and doesn't know (self-diagnosis), c) what components are necessary for his task (task analysis).

Children make their own worksheets and tests. A child can frequently learn more through determining what material should be on a worksheet than he can by actually "working" the worksheet. He can prepare materials more appropriate to his level, interests, and needs while gaining self-confidence and practicing self-diagnosis.

Through individualization it is possible to give children completely engrossing, elaborate, on-going projects that necessitate the use of most of the skills we normally attempt to teach.

Results

Summary. Project ENABLE is a process based upon a philosophy. The techniques change from day to day, teacher to teacher, school to school, child to child. These techniques depend upon a myriad of factors and vary accordingly—the philosophy remains constant—dealing with the child as an individual on a human-to-human basis.

Because the teacher is concerned with each child rather than with "the class" or "this group" or "these kids," his ability to deal with each child is limited only by specific school policy, his own repertoire of techniques, his own personality and his ability to relate to a particular student. With the child participating in the goal setting and planning, the teacher has the latitude to do whatever is necessary for each child rather than having to determine what all (or even most) children need.

It is no longer a case of "how much structure do children need;" it is a matter of how much structure do I need in relation to this child, at this time under these circumstances. Programmed materials are neither good nor bad in and of themselves. The question becomes whether or not they are *appropriate* for this child with these problems at this time. Other considerations might include how the teacher feels toward it; whether the child failed in it last year; whether his little brother takes home the same book; whether his peers think it is worthwhile, and so on.

Within a single classroom one child may be on a contract schedule every minute of every day (if that is what he and the teacher decide to do), another may have no commitment of any kind for weeks at a time. Visitors to the classes frequently ask: "How do you motivate them?" "What kind of materials do you use?" or "When do they do their arithmetic?" These questions are impossible for the teacher to answer except when applied to a given child.

"How do you motivate John Jones?" or "What materials is John Jones using today for learning social studies?" or "Does John Jones do arithmetic? If so, when? If not, why not?" are all questions readily answered by the teacher.

The Research. Because of its totally individual approach, the program tends to be "all things to all children." The difficulty of researching programs under such conditions is obvious. The teacher's view is, "I'm doing whatever I need to do; it's up to the researcher to figure out what that is."

One researcher noted: "I can't conceive of any program with more variables, and I can't conceive of any way we could have had less control over those variables, or access to observation of the interaction."

Another of the researchers on this project once said: "This is like trying to evaluate a running dog that's changing into a camel as he runs."

Thoreau once said something to the effect that it doesn't take a team of statisticians or an elaborate research design to determine that something other than chance is at play when you find a trout in the milk. Those associated with the project—parents, teachers, school principals, government agencies, participants and administrators—consistently have found "trout in the milk." It has been nearly 5 years since the first experimental class was formed. Since that time, 42 teachers have been through a teacher training program designed to prepare them for teaching in this project. Eighteen classrooms in six school districts in three states have been under the sponsorship of this project. Many observers of the program have set up their own version of the project without sponsorship or assistance from the Project ENABLE staff. Through all of this, the research has been meager in terms of hard data or classical research.

Except for the initial pilot program, none of the research done subsequently has dealt in hard data. In each of the various research attempts, experts have designed measures for factors involving self-concept, independence, attitudinal changes, interpersonal relations and concomitant effects in improved achievement. In each case the data took a form such as case study method, general inquiry method, teacher interaction, testimony and changes in teacher attitudes. But the group measures were not appropriate and the individual measures are difficult to put into meaningful terms.

The research data thus took the form of case studies, interviews, general inquiry techniques, projective measures, unobtrusive measures and subjective evaluations.

The chronology of the project is:

January 1966	Experimental Class Study
September 1966-67	Pilot project, 30 children with 2 teachers at a junior high school in a St. Louis suburb

September 1967- June 1968	Replication of pilot projects (2 teachers with 30 children)
September 1968- June 1969	Programs initiated in 5 schools in Missouri and Tennessee ranging from upper middle class to inner city
September 1969- June 1970	Continuation of 3 projects with 6 more programs initiated in- cluding 1 sixth grade class in elementary school
September 1970- June 1971	Addition of 4 elementary school classes to the project

The first class set up under this philosophy was researched along fairly traditional lines. Thirty seventh graders who formed the experimental group consisted of 18 boys and 12 girls representing the lowest achievers from a total class of 270 incoming seventh graders to a junior high school in a suburb of St. Louis, Missouri. A matched control group was selected from another junior high school in the same school district which represented a more traditional type school than the first control group.

The groups were matched by age, IQ, sex, achievement scores and perceptual deficits. The program was initiated at the start of the second semester. All participants were given pre-post achievement tests at the beginning and end of the one semester in the areas of reading and arithmetic. The results showed that the experimental group gained 1 year, 1 month in reading and 1 year, 4 months in arithmetic. The first control group gained 1 month in arithmetic but lost 7 months in reading. The second control group lost 1 month in arithmetic and lost 1 year in reading.

161

The really significant result of this pilot program was that the teachers found they could, in fact, completely individualize a class of 30 children to the point that there are 30 separate and distinct lesson plans for 30 children. A teacher could go an entire school year without ever addressing the class as a whole. Under these conditions group measures become relatively meaningless.

Research Report. A research team's analysis of the program activities to date indicate the following:

The Children—
Experienced obvious changes in attitudes characterized by their freedom of expression, comments, and lack of "fear" of their teachers.

Seemed to enjoy school, classroom atmosphere, and even their school work.

Developed and improved their social skills. (Especially in relation to one another and to the teachers.)

Seemed to understand that how much they learned or how far they progressed depended on their own efforts.

Seemed to work "harder" than they had in the regular school program.

Gained more than a full year's academic progress.

The Teachers—
Were able to assimilate the role of resource person and were able to individualize instruction to a large extent.

The Techniques—
Intrinsic motivation produced good results. No grades, progress reports, or other standard school rewards were given.

Tutoring appears to be beneficial for learning in a majority of the children.

The self-contained classroom with opportunities for frequent changes of activities is an important component of the program.

Personal attention by the teacher produces "positive" relationships with students.

Parent Comments. "Is enthusiastic—talks about school." "Wants to go to school—first time in ten years he hasn't hated school." "Bringing homework home now even though it isn't required." "Happier—gets along better with brothers and sisters, and with parents."

The Tutoring Program. The tutoring program was created so that the self-images of disabled learners could be built. Teachers noted that tutors, who previously lacked self-confidence, began to show a belief in themselves as they reacted to the respect they received from young children. The success that the tutors experienced coupled with the legitimate responsibility and trust given to them by teachers built their self-images. One, a tutor from the senior high school, epitomized this change.

> [He] *was nineteen years old, had no credits in high school and was reading at first-grade level. The counselor at his school called me to ask if I could take him in the junior high school because they had nothing to offer him at senior high. Murphy really wasn't prepared to teach very much, but he got hooked up with a fourth-grader and incidentally found that the boy couldn't tell time. Telling time was one*

163

*thing Murphy was good at, so he set about teaching the
fourth-grade boy. In a short time, Murphy had a time-
telling clinic going. He would teach a child to tell time
and then he'd find another one to start the process over
again.*

*In less than a month from the time Murphy was assigned
to us, we got a phone call from the counselor saying,
"Murphy's teachers want to know what you have done to
him. He has changed so dramatically that the teachers
can't understand it and would like to talk to you."*

*In brief, Murphy had been known to smile only twice in
the four-month period the teachers had had him. He kept
his chin on his chest and would not acknowledge the
teachers when he passed them in the hall, he had never
made a response in class, voluntarily or otherwise, and he
had never turned in a single homework paper.*

*The teachers now reported that in the past two weeks he
had been smiling almost continuously, he greeted them
in the halls, he had volunteered an answer in class, and
he had turned in assignments every day for the past week.
The high school teachers subsequently set up the opportunity for all of their classes to tutor in a nearby elementary school.*

The Problems

After hearing this program presented at a conference, a man stated,
"We've heard all the good things about the program. Will you tell
us what's bad about it?"

There are three things "bad" about it. The main one is that the
noninvolved teachers are likely to resent this special class in the

school. Giving students freedom in one class is regarded as a threat to many of the teachers who fear what will happen if children are not made to "know their place." In reacting to the threat, these teachers tend to undermine the program and make it difficult for the teacher involved in the program.

Another "bad" thing is the noise and disorder. Since teachers tend to be judged by their ability to *control* their class, the noise is upsetting. This is not so much because of actual distraction but because of the expectation of quietness and order.

The third "bad" thing is that the program upsets administrative procedures. The administrative conveniences of one hour per day for each subject, every child using the same book, and so on, becomes a real issue to office secretaries, custodians and central office people. One principal's evaluation of the class after a full school year was, "It's a great program for the kids because they really learn, but it causes too many scheduling problems." He didn't continue the program the next year.

Conclusion

The process of change is, at best, a difficult one with the difficulty generally in proportion to the quality of the change. Most innovations attempt to build a superstructure on top of existing programs. Improvement is the usual goal and most frequently consists of an extension of the existing conceptions. As an analogy, the usual approach to innovation represents rearranging the floor plan without changing the foundation.

This program represents changes in scheduling, curriculum, materials, discipline, interrelationships, processes, communications, evaluation and organization—*the foundation.*

The question of utilization of such a program becomes primarily one of a reordering of priorities. If things are to change for failing adolescents, they must also change for the schools (probably in direct proportion). If the school expects to be unaffected or only superficially affected, this program is not possible. If the school cares about what is happening to the bottom 10 percent of its adolescents, then it must put a priority on the kinds of changes necessary to accept a program such as this one.

The principles of learning which are widely recognized, though not widely practiced, indicate that this type of program should be as appropriate for young children as for adolescents and as appropriate for "smart" students as it is for "dumb" students.

Several years ago, Ray Barsh said in a convention speech, "There is a complete and utter void of anything being done for adolescents with learning disabilities." It is entirely possible that that statement is as true today as it was then.

A letter I received in the mail today from an intern teacher contained a sentence which seems appropriate to conclude with. She said, "I have found many recommendations for what to do with adolescents who have trouble in school, but I have found no one doing them." We're trying!

References

Combs, A. W. (Ed.) PERCEIVING, BEHAVING, BECOMING. 1962 ASCD Yearbook, Washington, D.C.: NEA, 1962.

Combs, A. W. **THE PROFESSIONAL EDUCATION OF TEACHERS.**
Boston: Allyn & Bacon, Inc., 1965.

Glasser, W. **SCHOOLS WITHOUT FAILURE.** New York: Harper &
Row, 1969.

FREEDOM, RESPONSIBILITY AND HUMANISTIC LEARNING

William F. Hendrix, Ed.D.
Principal, Amphitheater High School
Tucson, Arizona
        and
President, Arizona Association of Secondary Schools
Curriculum Board, National Association of
    Secondary School Principals

This article uncovers William Hendrix's approach to humanistic
education as he presented it at Amphitheater High School in Tucson,
Arizona. Dr. Hendrix is aware that individual differences do make
a difference; that awareness has led him to re-evaluate the school's
position to restructure the possibility for life and learning for his
students. His concern is that equal education for unequal children
will never lead to equal learning. Some of the changes in program
were facilitated by a need to open the campus to solve problems
of overcrowding. Dr. Hendrix used this atmosphere for change by
introducing many other changes. Most of these changes were based
on his belief that responsibility can only be learned through experience, and his belief that his students all had the maturity to begin
to learn responsible citizenship.

The article contains a lively description of a significant number of
new programs and philosophies recently introduced into Amphitheater High School.

M. B. R.

FREEDOM, RESPONSIBILITY AND
HUMANISTIC LEARNING

At what age does a person become responsible? When can he start to think for himself? When can he analyze the alternative solutions to a problem and come up with a logical conclusion? Does all this take place when he becomes 21 years of age? Or, could it be 17 or 18 years of age when the successful student finally gets out of high school?

The answer to all the above questions seems obvious—with the individual. Responsibility can be learned, and I contend we learn responsibility better by assuming it. Some people are not responsible citizens at 40 or 50. Some never reach a state of maturity. And yet, in the high schools of the country we still treat young people as though there were a magic day of self-determined behavior—the day of graduation! After this mystical day the young people are able to make choices on their own.

Not so at Amphitheater High School in Tucson, Arizona. The day of self-determination, the day of responsibility and freedom of choice comes much sooner. We talk about it with the junior high school students before they come to us. They arrive as freshmen students (ninth grade); they have the same freedoms and the same responsibilities as each of other citizen-students of Amphitheater.

We feel that we teach responsible citizenship more satisfactorily than any other subject—and, we don't even offer such a course.

Definition of the Problem

Simply stated, our problem is to find a means to teach responsible citizenship and provide freedom to learn in a humanistic environment; this is to be applied to each individual as he comes to us, whatever his educational needs might be.

171

Description of the Program

Most of us who work to effect a change in the schools realize that the American school curriculum and approaches to teaching-learning activities are deeply rooted. These roots are held fast with the soil of tradition and conventional approaches to learning. Security encompasses programs that have been tried before whether or not they worked, and fear of the untried or fairly new programs hinders innovation. Yet, Amphitheater High School *is* trying new programs and is accepting new points of view on the purpose and place of the school in the community.

The following paragraphs will describe some of the current programs and developments:

Open Campus. Amphitheater moved into the open campus concept as a means of solving an over-crowded school problem. With an extended day, one group of students would come to school first period and leave after the fourth or fifth period. The second group would come at the beginning of the second period and leave at the end of the fifth or sixth period, and so on until five groups had come and gone from school.

As new facilities were built the open campus remained. We continued to allow students to come and go with freedom of movement in the halls and around school during free periods and free time. An absence of hall monitors, either student or teacher, has existed. We continue to remind, teach, counsel and advise about the responsibilities of freedom. The students remind each other and display the pride of responsible citizenship. This is not all "a bed of roses"—it takes only one irresponsible person to "mess up" a restroom or participate in some other irresponsible act. But we hope and try to use this as a teaching opportunity toward acceptable behavior.

Relaxed Attendance Regulations. It seemed that the same small percentage of students continued to be absent frequently. Fake phone calls, forged notes from home plus parents who supported the truancy habit in their children caused us to think through our former attendance regulations. At one time we issued the "A," "B" or "C" excuses: "A" excuses allowed students to make up their work; "B" excuses were frowned upon but under most conditions missed material could be made up; but "C" excuses were unexcused and the students were not allowed to make up missed work. It was theorized that whether excused or unexcused the student should be allowed to study missed work and certainly reason should not be given a student to avoid make-up. We had trouble reconciling the time and effort taken to check notes and other justifications for being absent. Also, when students returned to school they missed more time waiting in the office. We concluded, in light of the philosophy of responsible citizenship, that this policy did not seem consistent.

Now students who have been absent no longer check through the office with an excuse from home. Telephone calls from home are no longer required; these calls are welcome, however. As a result of this change in policy, absenteeism dropped. In addition, time was used to greater advantage by the office personnel; they were free to call homes regarding unusual or prolonged absenteeism.

Freedom from Study Halls. The study halls that I have attended, monitored or observed have been an enormous waste of time for both the student and the teacher.

At Amphitheater High School students have freedom of choice. Places to study are available but no one is assigned to a study hall. The more formal library area is available as is the relaxed atmosphere in the cafeteria where students can study in groups, have snacks, visit or work individually. Many students study on the lawn under the trees or use an open classroom. Others go to the nearby public library.

Freedom to Take Partial Loads. Requiring each student to take the same number of units illustrates a point made once by Dr. B. Frank Brown when he stated that nothing was more unequal than giving equal education to unequal children. Many factors could cause a student to take only partial load: the need to work, home problems, inability to cope with the full program because of mental or physical capabilities. Whatever the reason, if a potential drop-out hangs on to even one course, he is not a drop-out; it is possible to work with him through counseling, whatever the need. If his need is financial perhaps the school can help through a placement program. If it is psychological, the counselors and teachers can work in this area. To hold on to a student part time is far better than to let him go completely.

Work Study Programs. Work study programs are valuable for a number of reasons. They give opportunities for employment for the student—an opportunity to earn while learning on the job, as well as at school. Because special attention can be given in designing a student's school program, he can work at an occupation in the community to ease the financial problems at home. Many of the vocational programs are planned to place students in jobs for experience. This same concept holds true in many student programs planned through the special education department.

Special Education Programs. Programs designed for educable special education students serve to bring these students into the full high school experience when possible. The special classes for these students are small (not over ten students) but some of these students function well in some regular classes, namely, physical education and some shop and vocational classes. As mentioned in the preceding item, some of the special education students are on vocational placement and they usually do well with the special attention and direction.

Upon completion of their high school work, they are granted an identical high school diploma—most certainly not a substandard or "Special Education" stamped one. The transcript records that courses were taken through the special education department.

Reading Center and Laboratory. We must accept all students as they come to us. Some have trouble reading, even though they are high school students. We, therefore, must attack that weakness. A diagnostic and treatment reading center aids in remedial reading, as well as increasing the rate of reading for other students who are interested in this program.

"Panther Pantry" (Breakfast at School). Some students do not receive breakfast before coming to school. The cafeteria opens at 7:00 a.m. for those who would like to come early, eat and study at the same time. The "Pantry" is open through the lunch hours.

Independent Study Programs. We feel that some of the most meaningful study and some of the most dedicated effort on the part of Amphitheater students and teachers comes through the independent study program. A complete paper—yes, a complete book, could be written around programs of independent study. For the most part the programs are patterned under the following general headings:

"Quest-Type" Programs for Development of Special Ability.
This pattern includes a variety of independent study activities for students who work almost completely on their own in exploration, extension, and refinement of special talents, aptitudes and interests not necessarily related to career choices.

Seminars Based on Independent Study. In this pattern the seminar is more than a class by this name, Instead, a group of individuals are engaged in independent study coming together frequently to share readings, projects, and research findings.

Job Oriented Independent Study. This pattern focuses independent study on preparation for a particular job, vocation, or career. The participants spend about 1 hour per day in class and laboratory at school and about 15 hours per week outside of school.

Change of Pace Programs of Independent Study. This encompasses students who have excelled in a specific area but need skills in another. A case in point: a student especially proficient in English composition, having trouble with hand writing, was put in typing. He did his composition work through his typing class.

Make-Up Studies. Often students do not complete required work to complete a course. At times this make-up is pursued through independent study. Quite often the counselor will work with the student and grant the credit on completion of the work. The thought behind this is that to repeat a full course because of a slight deficiency is not being fair to the student and well might cause him to "chuck" the whole thing.

Yes, at Amphitheater we encourage students to pursue almost anything by independent study. If there is no specific design, we will construct one. We have independent "probes" of short term (2 to 4 weeks), as well as independent "quests" of longer duration (5 to 9 weeks). We have long-term studies lasting the better part of a semester or longer. There is a lot of flexibility in this program.

University Work for High School Students. Some students want to pursue work at the University of Arizona while attending high school. The student may lack only a small amount of work for graduation from high school and want to get started in college. The student may be highly advanced in a high school subject or interest and want to pursue it at a higher level. The University of Arizona has been very cooperative in granting permisssion to these students to work in the university.

Student Council for Credit. The class in Representative Government has been highly successful. The class meets each day and has an extremely active program of student council activities. These young people become a powerful, dedicated, hard-working group as they pursue the work of the Student Council in their class of Representative Government. No minimum grade point average is required to be elected to this class and serve on the Student Council. By eliminating this restriction, better representation is possible and the council becomes, to a greater extent, the voice of the students.

Students Serving on Faculty Committees. The voice of the student is being heard loudly and clearly, either by design or by default. At Amphitheater High School students are now becoming a part of and participating effectively on faculty committees. They are serving also with parent-teacher groups. We have experienced remarkable success at having the students become a part of the "establishment." Their voices are clear and their thoughts, intelligent. They have participated in faculty seminars, faculty meetings and faculty executive committee meetings and they have performed with distinction. A greater involvement is in line for the future.

Expanded Programs of Vocational Education. In order to serve all students well, a truly comprehensive program of studies is needed. Usually the deficient area is vocational education. Greater emphasis is now being placed in the area of vocational education with an administrative objective in mind of having each graduate with a salable skill of some kind. We grant that often the skill is only a beginning place and that industry will have to continue to train. Briefly, some of the approaches to the growing program are listed below:

Expanded distributive education department and program.

Reorganization and expansion of agriculture department to meet the changing times with new cooperative programs in horticulture and agricultural mechanics with all members of the classes on placement in the community.

Expansion and reorganization of business education department—many advanced students on community placement.

Development of industrial commercial (cooperative) education program.

Reorganization of industrial arts area into industrial arts plus vocationally oriented approaches in many of the trade and industry areas.

Pilot Programs—Amphitheater High School is working closely with the Arizona State Department of Vocational Education on several pilot programs in vocational education.

Relaxing of Specific Graduation Requirements. The 8 years' study told us that students who were allowed to pick their courses and disregard the specific entrance requirements for the university did just as well in college, and better in most instances, than those students who were required to follow strictly the college entrance requirements. Yet, most high schools still have a large portion of the curricular program for every student graduating, loaded with specifically required courses. With the tremendous number of course offerings we must give greater flexibility to student's study programs. The specific list of graduation requirements is not necessarily the best for all. A shade of "equal program for unequals" shows itself here also. We have relaxed many of the requirements. Some are dictated by the state department of education. Too often in the past, students have been counseled back into school only to be placed into the very same situation that caused them to drop out in the first place. If we can help it—this won't happen now.

Results of the Program

To measure the results of this program, the attitudes of the students of the school must be evaluated. We could say that most of the students like the school; they are unafraid; they are usually well be-haved. These evaluative criteria are so subjective that I suppose they lose value. We could say, also, that we have not had riots or walk-outs but who can predict these things—let us not tempt fate! I feel that we can see the results of this program in the attitude, the pride, in the "head held high" and a courteous greeting as we meet the students in the hall. I feel we can see the results when the students rally 'round to correct a problem brought on by their peers. I feel that we can see the results in the responsible young citizens of Amphitheater High School.

Let me personally attest to it this way: If I had to choose my jury from a responsible citizenry, I would choose from the students of Amphitheater High School rather than from a cross section of any mature citizenry that I know. I feel that I would receive a more mature and fairer judgment.

JUST WHAT IS A TEACHER, ANYWAY?

Randy Huntsberry, Ph.D.
Assistant Professor, Department of Religion
Wesleyan University
Middletown, Connecticut

Myron Glazer, Ph.D.
Associate Professor, Department of Sociology
Smith College
Northampton, Massachusetts

The authors began active collaboration in 1968 when both were teaching at Smith College. This article describes their attempts to apply some of the characteristics of a T-group—particularly the peer group orientation and the freedom of discussion—to the college classroom. In the opening paragraphs, Dr. Huntsberry presents the rationale for the learning model which resulted. Much attention is devoted to the problem of helping students formulate models with which to order the information they confront. The major portion of the paper is made up of recorded dialogue by participants in classes where the program was tried. The dialogue seems a most revealing way of showing how the model worked and what aspects of the model were viewed as strengths and weaknesses by those involved in it. Some of the problems discussed include the need for more student and faculty orientation to the program, the confusion about the roles of students and teachers involved, and the necessity for dealing with conflicts that, with this approach to learning, are more likely to emerge openly than they are with "lecture learning." Participants in the dialogue are: Dr. Randy Huntsberry of Wesleyan University, Dr. Myron Glazer of Smith College and Rutgers University, Wayne Proudfoot of Andover Newton Seminary, Marlan Krebs and Paula Cortes from Smith College, Rick Nuccio from the University of Massachusetts, Nancy Hiromura of Mt. Holyoke College, Chris Palames of Wesleyan University, Ann Engebretson, Sue Ann Levin, and Laurie Effron, all of Smith College.

I am impressed by the sense of motion and aliveness that seem to characterize this way of learning. Perhaps because there was no attempt to conceal that the effort was an experimental one in which no one pretended to have the answers, there was less need for anyone to protect any one way of doing things. The comments of students indicate that the model gave them an increased awareness of the importance of learning how to learn, which seems to me one of the most crucial aspects of learning.

M. B. R.

JUST WHAT IS A TEACHER, ANYWAY?

It is usually very difficult to fix the precise point that a gnawing apprehension emerges into consciousness. Sometime during my senior year in college (1961) I finally admitted that I had gotten almost nothing from 4 years of hard work. I had diligently attended classes, taken copious notes, read 10 to 12 hours a day, learned to "psych" the examination system, and ended up Group II (magna cum laude). But after it was all over, I wondered if I had really learned anything!

After I became aware of the extent of my frustration, I began to re-examine my undergraduate experience in a desperate effort to salvage something of value from 4 years of effort. I soon realized that the Harvard experience had given me two important boons. First, I had developed a style of thinking, a point of view, as a result of many discussions with Winston White, a Ph.D. candidate at that time and resident tutor in sociology in my House. This continuing dialogue became my initiation into the sociological perspective and an arena for grappling with problems that interested me.

The second great educational force in my undergraduate life was the dining table bull session. These discussions, perhaps more than anything else, sharpened my critical faculty. Out of this re-examination of my undergraduate experience I realized that my education in the official structure had been a "bust" and that most of what I had learned came out of informal discussions with my tutor and my peers.

In my last year of Graduate school, I became a Teaching Fellow for my thesis director, Robert Bellah. For the first time I experienced the classroom from both the teacher's and the student's points of view. Professor Bellah had given this particular course 3 years before and I felt that his lectures were excellent. It came as a shock, therefore, to discover that many of the students didn't know what he was doing. Many long conferences with them vividly confirmed my undergraduate experience—lectures are not a particularly successful means of communication.

During this period, Professor Bellah suggested that I read a book called MICROCOSM: STRUCTURAL, PSYCHOLOGICAL AND RELIGIOUS EVOLUTION IN GROUPS by an old teacher of mine, Philip Slater. I had taken Professor Slater's Small Groups course some years before when he was lecturing on the material that later became the basis for the book. I had completely missed his point then. In MICROCOSM, Professor Slater describes the processes of group life which take place when the institutionally defined leader (the teacher) doesn't lead. As his title of Part One reads, Professor Slater is interested, among other things, in "The Evolution of Independence," in the "passive-to-active transition." By providing almost no structure and offering no approval or disapproval of the students' behavior, the teacher forces them to confront their dependency needs and to take responsibility for themselves and what they are doing. There are no lectures. Learning occurs through individual reading and group discussion.

Gradually, I began to wonder why some modification of the Training-Group model would not work on other kinds of problems besides group dynamics. Why couldn't any subject be successfully examined on this kind of peer-group basis? These thoughts were further reinforced when I learned that Professor Bellah was going to use this model for a course at Berkeley the following year in which the general topic would be the "faith and beliefs of the group members." Because I had a scholarship that required summer school enrollment, Professor Bellah convinced me to take the T-Group course rather than merely observe through the one-way mirror as I had originally planned. The experience of this course and the lively discussions I had with many of my graduate student friends convinced me that the T-Group model was worth a try. I still wasn't quite sure why

this model would be better than the lecture or seminar approach.
I only knew that I was dissatisfied with the traditional possibilities
and that the T-Group met two of the criteria which I had come to
associate with creative learning, discussion and a peer-group orientation.

I can remember one multi-section course during my first year at
Smith College in which the reading and weekly assignments had
been set before our first meeting. So, on the first day, I simply
walked in and took the only remaining chair; one befittingly at
the head of the table. The usual hush settled over the room, but
I sat silently. Some of the more empathic ones thought, "Poor
guy, he's too shy to start." Others thought I was praying. The
minutes passed by, and some began to fidget with their papers,
while others buried themselves in their books and notes. For
everyone the tension was approaching the breaking point. Ten or
fifteen minutes passed before one timid hand, puppetlike, was
haltingly raised. "Is it permissible to ask you a question?" she
puzzled, her voice faltering halfway through the sentence. I
mustered whatever poise I had left and as calmly as possible replied, "Why do you ask?" Her hand fell as if the string holding
it up had suddenly severed. We had begun!

We had begun to implement what I shall refer to as a kind of
cybernetic model for learning. It seems to me that the primary
problem is no longer access to sources of information and the
fixed truths implicit in them. Gone are the days when a student
more or less memorized the few books he chanced upon during
his lifetime. Rote memorization as the center of learning is dead—
our memories have cracked under the strain of too much information.

Not only that, we don't value memorization. Now we look to the
person who can make meaningful the information he has and thereby make viable choices and decisions. The main burden of education

185

has shifted from one of supplying information and fixed truths to one of finding or building images, patterns, models, or paradigms that will turn a chaos of information into some kind of meaningful order. The idea that there is such a thing as the truth just doesn't make sense. Models and information are in continual flux. In this context the human being is, as one student put it, like a computer— he needs a program to be able to both store and then meaningfully recall information. And, most importantly, new programs are being devised all the time.

The cybernetic model described here shifts attention away from the flood of information (facts) available to us and focuses on the patterns or models by which this information is ordered. Just as in a cybernetic system, vast amounts of random energy can be channeled and controlled by a device as simple as a thermostat, so the vast amount of information made available to us through modern communication systems can be ordered by relatively simple models. Instead of looking for what is objectively out there and repressing everything subjective, the cybernetic model takes seriously the dialectical relationship between the sources of information out there, and the ordering models formulated by the human mind. The modern student must be sensitive not only to information but also to models. He is forced to set a zigzag course between them so that new information may creatively inform his models and his models may be complex enough to order all the information. For information without controlling models leaves the student the unconscious and passive victim of the ebb and flow of the information to which he is exposed. Models without information, on the other hand, place the student in the sterile world of Platonic forms, alienated from the "nitty gritty" of on-going life. Only by maintaining a dialectical relationship between information and models can the student remain in contact with himself and his environment and, yet, at the same time, transcend them so that he might maximize his ability to make adaptive adjustments and, within the limits of the dialectic, be free.

As a way of illuminating both the strengths and weaknesses of the program described, what follows is a discussion by students and teachers who participated in classes where it was used.

PAULA: In our course on Latin America each person brought his own unique background and knowledge and from there began to build according to his own models. It is in this sense that I was at the same time helped and hindered. Having lived in Colombia most of my life . . . I do definitely have a certain viewpoint, that of the upper class, urban Latin American. Perhaps the most important and significant change was in the way I viewed the poor. I had originally thought of them being in their situation largely because of their own lack of initiative. . . Now I see the larger perspective. From reading George Foster's book, TZINTZUNTZAN, it became clear that the way of life of some peasants . . . is dictated by certain assumptions and values, primarily their image of "limited good." They believed that all good things exist in limited quantities and therefore someone's improvement is at the expense of someone else.

RICK: It seems to me that Charles Valentine makes the point most clearly in his CULTURE AND POVERTY: can not the poor be seen as humans trying to satisfy their needs as dictated by themselves and the larger society, using those resources that are available to them? It would appear that Oscar Lewis' concern that we view the poor as a subculture reflects a desire that the larger society not treat poverty as a condition of mere economic deprivation. While this intent is commendable it may also lead to a certain complacency on the part of the larger society just because it shows the poor to be really different from normal people—something the racist always likes to believe. The approach discussed by Valentine sees the poor essentially as people—people doing what they can with what they have; and what they have has been in the greatest part determined by others. I now believe that many people have mistaken a really astounding human talent for adaptation for a cultural distinctiveness so great that the larger society could not relate to it.

187

MICKEY: It is apparent from what Paula and Rick have said that they had to confront a good deal of material about Latin America. They certainly focus on some crucial issues. Paula's model based upon her Colombian background and Rick's model derived from his experiences in the United States seemed to have been challenged by Valentine's critique of Oscar Lewis and others working in this area. Yet I'd like to know a little bit more about the effect of the total class situation on your thinking.

NANCY: I still find it almost impossible to evaluate this course because my thoughts about it are constantly changing. Perhaps because I'm still partially bound by the traditional view of education, one of my main criteria for judging a course is the amount of knowledge I've gained from it. Although I believe that education should be a self-learning process (that is, that you come to your own conclusions through critically evaluating material rather than having cold facts thrown at you, only to be spit back on an exam), I still find myself wanting some concrete facts thrown at me . . . probably a result of conditioning from grade school and the definite lack of ability to read critically that I feel is due to my inexperience with this situation. As I look back on the material that we covered in the course, I honestly do not think I'd know what to say if someone came up to me and said, "What did you learn in Soc. 223 about Latin American society?" I'm probably sticking my neck in a noose and do not mean this offensively, but I don't think I'd be able to give concrete answers to that question. I think that basically the material simply helped to confirm the ideas I already had about Latin American society. Of course there were a lot of facts that I hadn't known, but my mind is in such a jumble that I can't concretely put my finger on them.

CHRIS: At this point I would tentatively suggest that groups do not facilitate learning. Creative intellectual activity is an individual endeavor, dialogue and criticism from others is valuable, but the heart of the matter is solitary thought and study. Groups tend to limit the individual's scope, subject him to pressures to conform, and waste his time with superfluous social ritual. What is needed is a method of facilitating true freedom to learn and work.

WAYNE: I feel very ambivalent about independent study. In my experience, students who have come asking for independent study programs have often been able students who want to avoid the social conflicts and negotiations which must go on between different members of a class and the teacher and which are an integral part of the learning situation. Such a student opts out of the social situation by choosing to do his own thing. He is above or is intimidated by negotiating his own needs and resources with those who bring other interests. Independent study also often involves a return to the student-teacher role in its apprentice-mentor form and risks the danger of the student having to conform to the expectations of one person, the teacher. Even where the teacher gives the student his freedom, the student is not required to check out his work or open it to public scrutiny in the very painful way that the classroom situation requires. In this way he is able to go through his schooling unscathed and untouched by his peers.

RICK: I feel inside of me the results of all sorts of emotional and intellectual confrontations that the class has provided. I believe that these visceral sensations are truly what the course means to me as a student and as a person, but I was afraid that they were too intangible to be worthwhile communicating. I still have that fear, yet I am more concerned that to neglect these confrontations would be much less than honest.

I have reread the first articles and minutes of our class and it did help me to see how far we have come and how much we have failed. Many of the concerns voiced about structure and progress were needless—we have progressed and learned in the traditional sense. The fears that all our discussions would become a series of tangents has been abated also. As students we have done pretty well; as people our record is poorer.

I said that what this course means to me was rather intangible. I suppose what I mean to say is that I don't know a lot more about Latin America than I did before I took the course. When I look back over the reading list I can recall countless discussions and readings which gave me understanding and thought about so many things. Racism for one. I realize how much I am affected by the disease and have seen its symptoms in others. I do not think that I have even started on a personal cure but I have warned myself to consider its subtle effects on all that I think and do. I have also been faced with the fact that people who have been to Latin America are hopeful, optimistic and even content about conditions there while I, who have never had the privilege of seeing the countries I love in some absurd, romantic way, feel a sense of crisis about their future. Who should I believe, a person who stands before me and says, "I saw it this way," or some book I read by someone who was there too? Considerations of **credibility** and perception which Tommy has pointed to in his minutes are crucial to anyone who makes a decision. The credibility gap between Father Bonpane and others in the class presented me with frightening questions I am still trying to answer. What this course has really provided me in terms of just Latin America is a feeling for people, the people I read as statistics on the **government surveys**.

There are many other things that this course has made important for me, but they are all very personal and perhaps have neither importance nor relevance to you. An exam that tested my memory of names, places and even concepts might find me wanting. But, whether through delusion or realization, I feel this course has made me less a memory bank and more a person; I think I could become knowledgeable without becoming a person and I am idealistic or naive enough to think that in trying most to be a person I may become both. Because of some of the things that happened to me in this course I will be able to learn, in all senses of the word, more in the future.

190

ANN: I was impressed both by how much we have accomplished and how much we have not accomplished in this course. In my reaction, though it may appear simple, I find implications of the great number of ways the course has affected me. Before reviewing the minutes, I was considering that, with respect to "facts learned," I did not feel I had very much concrete material at hand—as, for example, I might have if the course had been run in the traditional lecture style. I did not consider this a serious drawback—facts could be gathered through rereading and further reading—what was important was that throughout the course I felt I had successfully begun to develop a style of thinking, a recognition of my own point of view as being the outcome of a refining, discriminating process, a continuing dialogue between what I brought to the situation and new ideas. Then, in reviewing the minutes and attempting to recall my respective states of mind at the times, I realized that a facts-from-process separation was an artificial one. During the course we had encountered a great number of facts, but through our use of them they had ceased to hold their familiar form. They were not simply the pieces of information that I usually find compiled neatly from a series of lectures, but had served us as parts of larger con-texts. We had tried to interpret our facts, had tried to examine their implications, and, in retrospect, this process obscured their identity as isolated facts. My sense of a developing critical aware-ness and the attempt I see to order our information show me how much this course has accomplished.

What I think has not been accomplished reflects difficulties with the methodology, some of the class' attitudes and relationships, and the gap between results and my early expectations. Our diffi-culty in finding a common ground for beginning our discussions and our neglect in covering the basics before moving on to specifics and solutions show serious faults in our handling of the course. At various points in the minutes or during the discussions, a cry would come up for identification of role-players, basic institutions, and functions. Sometimes we would cover them (we paid special attention to them for a while after Mr. Glazer introduced a model for looking at social systems), sometimes we would return to them only after discussions had reached an obvious impasse. I think we were unaccustomed to laying a ground-work, it seemed artificial at first, and so in preparing for discussion and in beginning discussion, we did not give it priority consideration. Randy suggests beginning treatment of a topic by establishing common-sense models, by students discussing first the ideas they bring to a subject. This would have been valuable, I think, at the beginning of every one of our discussions. It would have prevented that haunting, "Where do we start?" feeling and the resulting, half-panicky attempts to begin anywhere. Our discussion seemed best when a book or comparison of writers' ideas served as a common ground. A more valuable common ground would be one built by the class, beginning with the basics and leading to a logically structured discussion.

When the class first began, when we were discussing Randy's and Duberman's experiments, I was excited and optimistic about a learning process which relied on the contributions of the students, the passive-to-active transition, the competition of ideas. For me, the course has succeeded to the extent that, as I mentioned before, I believe I have learned how to develop a style of thinking. Verbalizing my ideas and considering them in relation to others expressed have made me feel a responsibility for what I know, for continually re-appraising my point of view. But it could have been much more. If everyone had contributed consistently, everyone would have benefited.

RANDY: It is apparent from what Rick and Ann are saying that the strongest argument for peer-group learning is that it begins at the level of the students. This is not to say, however, that the level can remain stationary. To begin at the students' level merely ensures that the subject matter of the course will make contact with the vested interests of the students. Once this contact has been made, the discussions and readings which are selected as much as possible in response to the issues raised by the students will hopefully assist the students in their efforts to build more adequate models. We must first begin with what is *relevant* in order to progress to what is *adequate*. Irrelevant models usually occur when an instructor is insensitive to the needs of the students. Models presented by an instructor are almost inevitably based on a body of information far more extensive and complex than that possessed by the students. Since the instructor's models must be complex enough to order the information he possesses, there is a serious danger that they will be too complex and hence irrelevant for the students. If the students adopt these models, they do so on the authority of the instructor. And they are apt to remain bare skeletons which leave the students dangerously removed from the reality in relation to which the models originated. Often the model becomes a substitute for dealing with any kind of external evidence. For many students the model becomes reality and the dialectic between models and information, so necessary for dynamic learning, is lost.

MICKEY: I have an excellent example supporting that point. The Latin American course had been on for about 2 weeks and we were all struggling to get it off the ground. The students had read a number of general articles at my suggestion. These works were really at a fairly high level of abstraction which I had hoped would serve as a model into which the rest of the semester's material might be neatly placed. The early discussion showed that my thinking was way off. The students did not have the background for these models. The frustration was getting pretty heavy and I decided to take a couple of hours and present my own approach which I had found useful in ordering these diverse materials. The students' reactions were predictable. They were both relieved and unhappy that it had been I who had made the attempt to break through the log-jam. They felt that as a group they had failed to handle their first major challenge effectively, even while they appreciated my attempt. Even more important in this context was that my model did not turn out to be very much more useful than those which they had already read.

Again I had jumped to a level far more complex than what they needed. What had been useful to me was still irrelevant to them. This was made crystal clear by their response to a paper which I distributed only a week or two later. Here I dealt with a more straightforward and less abstract approach to the study of lower class Latin American groups. The model posed exactly the kind of questions they were into. They quickly decided to read a wide variety of studies on the comparative analysis of poverty. The class had really begun to move and to get a sense of itself as a problem solving group. They were no longer dealing with what others, whether authors or I, thought was important, but rather what they themselves had come to as a result of several weeks of groping.

It is interesting that this successful definition and handling of a problem increased the frustration of some of the students. In order to handle the poverty issue effectively they had to read a great deal of material. Obviously one semester is barely enough to scratch the surface. Some of the students felt that we neglected the other parts of the syllabus. They defined a successful course as one which completed the syllabus. Although most were aware that it is impossible to study Latin American society in one semester, they could not accept that their gropings were an integral part of the learning process. The tension remained between developing an effective group process and the goal of covering an appropriate amount of material.

RANDY: We really have to conceive of a "course" in quite a different way. We have to recognize that the syllabus, if there is one, is artificial, is a construct or model, and must be open and flexible.

MICKEY: This raised the question of whether there should be a syllabus at all. What I have done in my classes is to have a highly structured reading list. I think there is a great strength in that. The students feel that they are walled in and that it gives many a sense of support . . . In the first formal meeting you talk about the approach, and very quickly explain that a tremendous variety of things can be discussed. On the basis of my thoughts about this—and the evidence is in the pudding of that reading list—I'm suggesting a series of topics which I think makes sense. It helps those students who need some structure feel kind of good about it. But, if you look at the reading list you will see that there are more topics than could possibly be covered. As we go along, we must of necessity make some decision . . . That may be just too structured for the kind of thing that you've been thinking about.

RANDY: Even though I've usually used some sort of syllabus, I'm beginning to think that the course should begin not only with the problem of how we are going to operate but also with what we are going to study. I would like to see a syllabus develop during the course of the semester, or even several syllabae, with the necessary models to go with them. The course should be a movement toward a definition of the concern rather than deriving from a syllabus of my own. When I have issued a syllabus I have found that the students spend most of their energies trying to figure out what my conception of the problem is and what they ought to be doing about it. From that point on we have lost contact with the concerns of the students. I would rather try to come up with readings and other materials as our discussion and definition of our concerns progresses.

WAYNE: One function of the syllabus is to set before the students the resources and models for the course which the teacher has considered, and thus allow them to participate with him in choosing some of these resources. Without a syllabus the teacher has a store of books and information which is not known to the students and from which he pulls suggestions during the course of the class. If the syllabus is out in the open, then the teacher is not able to draw from a private store which can serve to heighten his authority. A syllabus helps to equalize the teacher and the student.

RANDY: But can the student really make sense of the syllabus and utilize it without implicitly, at least, accepting the teacher's definition of the course structure?

WAYNE: If the teacher has a conception of the possible resources and problems in mind he should try to make that available to other members of the course. That may involve more than just giving them the syllabus. He should explain what he brings to the course just as he asks students to articulate the questions and models which they bring to the course.

RANDY: Good point! But why can't the teacher participate in the first meeting on an equal basis with the others and simply make his concerns known in the same way during the discussion? It seems to me that if he has it all laid out, the students will tend to gravitate toward his conceptions of the problems and fail to articulate their own thoughts.

WAYNE: For the teacher to be using a Socratic method to try to elicit from the students directions which he already had in mind is dishonest. He should have a broader perspective on the possible problems and models in a particular course area because of his continued work on the subject.

RANDY: I certainly agree about the dishonesty of the Socratic approach, but aren't you assuming that the teacher's understanding of the problems and models is relevant to the students before that has been established? If the course topic is very narrowly defined to start with, then I would agree with your approach. But if the course is more open to definition, then the teacher has to put his preconceptions up for consideration just as everyone else. For example, in your nineteenth-century theology course, you could spend the whole semester trying to build a model which would be adequate to all of the currents of that period. You could begin the first meeting by making a chart or model of what the students thought about the nineteenth century and what they thought were important problems for them to consider. Each week a new chart could be produced on the basis of new readings and refinement of old models. Students could produce charts before class and then submit them for criticism in class. You, of course, would be able to introduce new historical figures and problems which a particular chart or model did not account for, driving the students to those resources. You also might be able to help the students refine their charts so that they would be more adequate to the data they are already trying to deal with. By the end of the semester all of you would have constructed one or more models and charts related to the nineteenth century and constructed a reading list relevant to these models.

WAYNE: The chart is a good idea, but we both agree that the teacher should press for his preconceptions just as anyone else. My suggestion has been that the teacher is often holding back these preconceptions under the guise of freedom and openness when he adopts a nondirective approach and omits his own position. This is a danger of beginning with no syllabus or no statement from the teacher as to why he chose the topic or area to have a course in at all. It makes sense for his preconceptions to be different because he has chosen a topic in an area which is of interest to him and which he thinks may be of interest to students. For example, I am planning to teach a seminar on "The Theory of Values." Preliminary discussions with students and colleagues reveal interest in literature which articulates values in our contemporary culture. I am also concerned that the students consider and struggle with different theoretical models and descriptions of valuing and use these to interpret contemporary values. I hope we can also revise the theories where they fail to account for the data discovered in our study of contemporary values. But at the moment I seem to be the only one who has this kind of vision of the course. My conception of the course was an investigation of different theoretical analyses of valuation. The material on contemporary values was to serve as data by which these theories could be tested and accepted or rejected. To the students with whom I talked the problem was not one of evaluating theories of value but rather of discovering and exploring contemporary values.

RANDY: I have come up against the same problem. I have always defined my courses in terms of using data to get at certain theoretical issues, but I have come to believe that this is the wrong order. Theory should be used to solve problems and deal with pressing issues. It should not be something for its own sake. It seems to me that you should approach the problem of theory by asking how is such and such a theory relevant to the problem of discovering and exploring contemporary values. If a particular theory is helpful in this task then it will become important. If not, it will be discarded. In this way you can begin with the students' interest in contemporary values and then help them penetrate more deeply through the use of value theory.

WAYNE: There are cases where theories can be studied for their own sakes in the sense that these are the phenomena with which the course is dealing. In the history of ideas specific ideas can be studied for their place in historical development, or for their esthetic value, and not only for their theoretical relevance.

MICKEY: There are a number of other crucial decisions we should bring up here. A lot of what goes on inside the class depends on the kind of preparation which goes on outside the classroom. All of us, I know, have relied very heavily on papers of one kind or another. In the second course that I was involved in, a class on Social Disorganization, I asked several students each week to prepare a paper in which they responded to the reading material. The papers were duplicated and placed on reserve in the library. They were read by all the students prior to the first class meeting of the week. The papers had a dual purpose. First, they provided the class with a set of observations and issues upon which to focus the discussion.

The papers, of course, could either be criticized or used to support the points which other people wanted to make. The papers also served to allow the quieter members of the class to make their presence felt other than through oral presentation. I must add that the papers served a third self-conscious purpose. I was determined to see that students did not neglect our course which utilized peer-group learning because of the pressures of more traditional courses which included regular assignments, mid-terms, term papers and the usual academic paraphernalia.

The papers were partially successful. It took a while for the students to accept and feel comfortable with the notion of writing critical and not reportorial accounts. Some students felt that while they benefited from writing the papers, reading them was often time consuming, tedious and repetitive. About halfway through the semester I suggested a somewhat new format for the class meetings which I think made the papers more useful. We spent the first hour each week primarily raising the questions which we would then discuss during a second and longer class session. The papers were then more helpful since they were now more directly related to raising questions. This new format also had the advantage of enabling us to decide before our 2-hour session the exact kinds of issues which we thought needed discussing. The students then had an agenda before the class met the second time.

We also utilized something which were called critical minutes. These included a summary account of what had occurred in the class and observations by the recorder as to the direction the next class meeting might take. These minutes were useful in reminding the participants of what had occurred and in giving everybody a sense that some important issues had been discussed. Students frequently leave discussion classes feeling that the conversation was useful but finding it difficult to remember exactly what had occurred. Later this problem translates itself into a sense that nothing useful has transpired.

WAYNE: I find that my assignment of papers embodies assumptions which conflicted with the structure of the course. I asked each student to write four papers at any time during the term on any subject in the discussion or reading material. I planned to discuss each of the papers individually with the student during the term. This assignment presumes that each student's problems and thoughts are his own and are to be discussed primarily with me. It was more conducive to a program of independent study or a reading course, and countered the peer-group orientation of the course. At one point I asked them all to write a short paper on Norman Brown's LOVE'S BODY and to make their papers available to all the other members to read. This was very good and increased the value of our discussion for that session. I now plan to use papers on common themes which are presented not to me but to the entire class.

MICKEY: I am really beginning to despair about the success we can have in a one course effort. Students are involved in so many other things that it is so easy to let a frustrating situation slide. I keep coming back again and again to the importance of going all out. I think we have to think about an effort in which the entire school is involved. How about a freshman semester in which all activity is directed toward resocializing incoming students? I see it as focusing on three major aspects. First, students should meet to confront their motivations for continuing their education. We realize how often they have worked in order to please others. Their goal is often defined as a high grade from the teacher and à pat on the head from the parents. Inner motivation and a real commitment of learning go by the wayside. The values of the faculty are also going to have to be brought under scrutiny. This is no easy task and will be very demanding of faculty and student time and energy. The second part of the program would focus on the students' ability to think and to examine material critically. It must be stressed that books, articles, and lectures are not simply to be accepted because they exist on some assignment sheet. Everything is doubted, nothing is sacred. Faculty and students together need to examine

200

carefully the assumptions, arguments and evidence presented. The third part of the orientation semester emphasizes student projects. A good deal of guidance by faculty and older students is essential here.

RANDY: I also think we need to think more self-consciously about the specific ways we might facilitate resocialization within the class-room too. Instead of forcing a student to perform verbally, we should have various other means of communication, especially non-verbal ones. I am beginning to think that various kinds of impro-visations during the early weeks of the course which are designed to produce trust among the class members will pay off in a greater ability of the class to perform whatever goals it sets out for itself. For example, when one of my classes became completely disrupted over the problem of racial confrontation, I suggested that we try a different means of communication. I had them all lie down on the floor and close their eyes. Then, nonverbally, they were slowly to begin to explore their surroundings. Of course, most lay without moving for a long time, in a way very similar to the blocks they had found verbally. But gradually some began to move their hands and after a long while some members touched. After about 40 minutes an intensity of relationship and communication had developed among most of the class members. Later they remarked that this had been the most important thing that had happened all semester. One white male student remarked ecstatically about how it felt to touch the afro-cut of one of the black students. One black male student and a white female student who had been rather hostile to each other through the semester felt they had achieved a new rela-tionship. To me, this simple improvisation was not only a deeply significant event in its own right, but set the foundation for being able to relate verbally once again and much more profoundly. We just have to introduce more than mere words into the classroom. I think that this "physicalization" of the classroom offers a very important way of helping students (and teachers) to escape roles and relationships which they have gotten themselves locked into. New media demand different roles.

WAYNE: At several points in my classes we have used similar physical exercises in order to express things which are not expressed verbally. Often just getting persons moving and touching each other in ways other than their normal modes of meeting provide stimuli for new feelings and experiences and for getting in touch with emotions which are circumvented in our normal conventions, but which underlie much of our language and argument.

MICKEY: That's the kind of thing that can make a great contribution when used by those who feel comfortable with it. My focus is still on the more straightforward forms of role-playing which can help us break out of the passive rut.

MARLAN: The thing that is good about role-playing is that it is not you, so much, but that you are in a role and you are not opening yourself up because you are somebody else during that period of time.

MICKEY: You are quite right. Role-playing can have at least two positive results. It can allow people to have freedom because they don't feel so personally on the line, and it can increase sensitivity as you try to take the role of the other person. Obviously, it's a natural for any kind of sociological study. It's fascinating, for example, to try to project oneself into the role of Bolivian peasants faced with the decisions of joining or rejecting Che's band of guerrillas. Or, taking it a little closer to home, to assume the role of a college president or dean faced with the dilemma of whether or not to call the police on campus during a student demonstration.

RANDY: I remember one class in which several students got into a tremendous argument over Vietnam. The principal parties were getting nowhere in the discussion. Each just shouted his pet arguments and slogans and hardly heard the replies of his adversaries. Finally, one frustrated student suggested that two of the principal antagonists switch roles. The radical student found that he couldn't get into the conservative's role at all. He was soon hooted down and replaced. The radical student simply had not taken the conservative's position seriously enough even to listen to his arguments. This revelation about his own attitude was probably one of the more profound lessons he learned during the semester.

MICKEY: If the students present their views in class and in papers, group members will very quickly get to know each other's positions. Conflict may very well develop among the students. The response to this conflict can result in an honest evaluation of competing models or in a reluctance on the part of students to expose themselves to any further disagreement and hostility.

RANDY: Then the problem is whether the students will "turn off," not because the course is irrelevant to them, but because the situation is too threatening. If the tension is too great the students will try to escape by any number of defensive measures, including, of course, dropping out.

If a discussion collapses as a result of interpersonal tension, regression to humor and triviality may play a therapeutic role. Without the possibility of regression the class, like any society, will probably disintegrate. The problem arises, however, when the class becomes fixated in its regression. If the fixation is not broken through, the learning process will come to a standstill. Real intellectual advance is highly correlated to the level of tension the group can tolerate without regression, or how fast it can bounce back from brief periods of therapeutic regression. Moreover, the tolerance level is itself correlated with the amount of unresolved interpersonal conflicts and hostility within the class. If the class is unable to deal with aggression among its members, then meaningful discussion and the tension which inevitably accompanies it will be avoided in an effort to preserve group solidarity and interpersonal tranquility. If the fear of overt aggression is deep enough it undoubtedly will disrupt the class effort to build and refine models.

Here again, the instructor may intervene. He can help the class become self-conscious about the interpersonal forces operating within the class and suggest how these forces might inhibit or facilitate their tasks. For example, in one of my classes the only male student happened to be absent one meeting. The class soon found itself strongly attacking a female member of the class. After a few moments it became apparent that the class was really building up for an attack on the male student with whom the female student had been closely identified. I finally proposed this explanation. Several of the students "confessed" at once and said that they had been afraid to attack the male student. This is not to say, however, that all interpersonal hostility suddenly disappeared. On the contrary, it was merely recognized for what it was and accepted. But by bringing these feelings of hostility to the surface the class found that it was better able to function in the future. Because the hostility had been openly acknowledged the students had more trust and confidence in each other. They now had all their interpersonal cards face up on the table. Many now felt secure enough to risk themselves and to contribute to the group effort.

SUE ANN: But I still have a question about what the role of a teacher in a class like this really is, or what it's supposed to be. I remember that we were talking about that in the very first session. I made that one comment about how we should think of you (Mickey) like any other member of the class. I can't think of a better way to say it, but I still feel basically that.

RANDY: Did it happen? Should it have happened? If it didn't, why?

SUE ANN: I don't know if that should happen. I don't know if that's necessary.

RANDY: Why did you think it was necessary then?

SUE ANN: If you're going to talk about breaking down subordinate relationships or authoritarian relationships, then they have to be broken down. On the other hand, in our class, those barriers weren't completely broken down and the class was still quite successful. I wonder if in your teaching this semester you have ever really felt that you have completely stopped assuming the role of the teacher in the traditional sense. Has that ever been possible for you?

RANDY: I think it's a mutual kind of thing. For some students I think it is completely broken down; whether the whole class makes it or not is another problem.

SUE ANN: . . . I'm saying that in certain environments, and with certain students you'd be working with, it would be completely necessary. Maybe it's not necessary here.

RANDY: Why wouldn't it be? Or why would it be? Let's get into that. You said it would be nice if Mickey was just like one of us. Now you seem to be wondering about that.

SUE ANN: I think that outside the classroom, in other things that have happened, it is very apparent to me that those barriers were never broken down at all.

MICKEY: Why should these barriers be broken down? In the class or outside the classroom, there are very real differences, and why should we fool ourselves that they don't exist.

SUE ANN: Well, I thought that one of the points of having a class like this was to start students thinking that they could have some responsibility.

MICKEY: Does that mean there is no responsibility if there are status differences . . . I assume the basis of this particular approach, as far as I'm concerned, is to say to students, not that there are no authority figures, and not that there are people who don't have expertise, or not that people aren't in a position to evaluate you . . . . You live in this kind of world.

SUE ANN: Well, I don't think that you should have any more special privileges than the students in the classroom.

MICKEY: What are special privileges? You mean you don't have a special privilege to come in with good ideas?

SUE ANN: No. Everybody has the right to come in with good ideas.

MICKEY: What other special privileges are there?

SUE ANN: Well, like the evaluation privilege.

MICKEY: That, I think, is a crucial one.

SUE ANN: . . . I wish I could find something more specific, but I just keep on thinking that if you really want people to be aware of alternatives to the present roles that they're playing like teachers and students, then they should be willing to go completely to the other extreme. I can't explain it.

MICKEY: I'll give you the ideal conception that I have. My ideal conception of what an excellent course is, is where I can feel free to say anything I want at any point with whatever force I want and know that if it hits home the students will accept it, and if it doesn't they will go on their merry way listening to other people . . . .

RANDY: Ideally, I would like to have a situation in which I would have no institutionally established prerogatives that the students don't have. If I am really knowledgeable and so on, then that would be the basis of my status in the class. But the rub arises at several points. I am responsible to the university for grading, for one thing. But more important, I take the initiative in setting up formal procedures for writing papers and even certain improvisation activities. There is no reason that students can't promote the same things, and, in fact, sometimes this has occurred. Nevertheless, I am usually the person who ends up suggesting paper assignments. Another way in which I feel myself separate from the students in the class was highlighted to me recently when several students wanted to "get high together." Though I might have enjoyed this under other circumstances, I definitely had the feeling that I was in charge of the class and would be legally responsible for such activity.

More than this, I think the teacher does have a positive responsibility to act as the "self-consciousness" of the group; he should attempt to help the students understand the nature of their intellectual *and* emotional self-interests. Only by first understanding where they are, will the class be in a position to work toward more complex, and hopefully adequate, models. Or, if the problem is not one of model conflict but of a scarcity of information and the concomitant existence of irrelevant models, then the instructor can suggest source materials which might provide the information needed to test and refine the models they already possess. Many students have never developed an ability to live with confusion and disorder and many have never learned to take responsibility for themselves. The rule of thumb I started using this semester was that I would participate to the same degree that I felt everybody else was. That is very difficult to pull off and I didn't make it a lot of the time, but what I'm driving at here is that if the members of the class are really doing their thing, if they are, as you say, saying the same things to me that they'd say to anybody else, then I feel free to participate in almost any way I want. But if I sense that something I said has suddenly altered the situation, if the group is either not ready or it regresses, then I back off again. A student once called my attention to the theory behind the relationship of the Zen master and his disciple, in which the Zen master combines perfect passivity with perfect activity so that when the student comes to him and delivers a response to the *Koan* he is working on, or when the student says anything to his master, his pure and perfect passivity-activity hears exactly what the student says and because it is such a pure reception his response is like a mirror image—a mirror is not a good metaphor but that is one that they use all the time—is the perfect response because it has been the perfect reception at the same time. So, it is activity then which is precisely and perfectly appropriate to the student's needs, because it is based exactly on what he had said. If the student is kidding himself about his state of "enlightenment," it is spontaneously, dynamically and actively responded to. Maybe one of the things the students should be, must be, getting out of this kind of approach is a greater sensitivity, a greater ability to really communicate, to really hear what the other person is saying and respond to that. That means that you are forcing less of your own preconceived hang-ups on the other person . . . . What I'm saying is that somehow what I want to do is put into the same environment both the passivity involved in the lecture system and the activity of the response that is not built into the lecture system.

LAURIE: Sitting here in Davis Lounge and seeing this class for the last time, I feel a certain affection for the people and the class. I feel as if the class has somehow been through something together that gives a certain closeness. That in itself is a novelty.

LEARNING IS BEING:
A COPARTICIPATIVE, EXPERIENTIAL
EDUCATIONAL PSYCHOLOGY COURSE

Karl W. Jackson, Ph.D.
Assistant Professor, University of Nebraska at Omaha
Omaha, Nebraska

Mary Sanders, B.A.
Student, University of Nebraska at Omaha
Omaha, Nebraska

Karl Jackson developed a course in educational psychology at Washington University in St. Louis, Missouri, wherein he incorporated some of the newest approaches in education. This course is unusual because the process and flow of the class itself serves as a living example for the academic content. Decision-making and goal-setting were determined democratically from many available alternatives and students were actively involved in getting the information they found useful for themselves.

The students responded with enthusiasm to learning more about themselves and felt hopeful that they could be more effective as teachers when they were comfortable in an understanding of themselves.

I am excited that people are now trying such a course with new ideas that are challenging to the present structure of education.

In this article Karl Jackson and a student in the course, Mary Sanders, have combined a thorough theory section with sections of narrative from the course and descriptions of specific class exercises used to facilitate learning.

    M. B. R.

LEARNING IS BEING:
A COPARTICIPATIVE, EXPERIENTIAL
EDUCATIONAL PSYCHOLOGY COURSE

> *It was a typical day in our educational psychology class.* ***We***
> *were sitting in ten circles, five of us in each as usual,* ***rapping***
> *while we waited for class to start.* *Karl (our instructor) came*
> *in, and as usual several people went up to talk to him about*
> *various pressing matters.* *After a few minutes it was time to*
> *start.* *Karl looked up at the clock and picked up the 3" x 5"*
> *feedback cards from last week.* *In a few seconds the class*
> *was silent, waiting expectantly for him to begin . . . .*[1]

The Origin-Pawn Game.[2] Karl began passing out blank pieces of
paper. He asked each of us to think back to when we were in the
sixth grade and to play the role of a sixth grade child for the next
few minutes while he played the role of a sixth grade teacher.

In that role he began: "During the next few minutes you'll have
an opportunity to do something creative with the paper. You
might draw a picture, make something, write a poem, or whatever
you like. These are just some ideas. I'm hoping you'll do whatever *you* want to do, working alone, in pairs, or whatever. If
there's something else you'd rather do right now, I hope you'll do
it instead."

---

[1]This "quote" describes selected portions of class #4 (March 3) from the perspective
of an imaginary participant observer. We composed it with the help of notes and
comments made by students in the class and our own memories of the class and
similar experiences in other groups. The description is accurate with respect to basic
feel and content, except that the vignette lecture presented at the end condenses comments made in the class over several weeks time.

[2]This version of the game was developed for the class by the senior author. Its pre-
cursors were similar games described by Kuperman (1967), Shea (1969), and Shea
and Jackson (in press).

I enjoyed watching the class for the next few minutes. The group hesitated for a minute or two, and then people began to work playfully. Soon the class was in a jovial mood, and I watched with amusement and pleasure as they began doing things with their papers. Some talked and laughed, either working together or sharing. Others were soon lost in deep concentration, apparently oblivious of those around them. I was surprised to see that three or four people seemed disconcerted by the assignment and just sat thoughtfully or watched others.

John[3] immediately made a paper airplane and let it go at the teacher. He grabbed it deftly in mid-air and sailed it back. The people watching laughed or oohed with admiration. Many didn't notice since they were deeply intent on doing their own thing. Linda was drawing a picture of the teacher, with huge piercing eyes. Bob was making a figure. Karen was writing a poem. From time to time someone would finish, and either show his production to a seatmate or the teacher, or just sit and enjoy it. The teacher seemed to be aware of the three or four people who seemed to be stuck, sitting uncomfortably doing nothing or pretending to do something, obviously embarrassed that they couldn't think of something to do.

After helping one boy to solve a mechanical problem in the design of his paper truck, the teacher read a girl's poem with obvious pleasure, and responded to her frustration about the wording of part of it by suggesting that she consult Barbara, an editor of the school newspaper and poetess, for advice. As the girl walked quickly over to Barbara for help, the teacher turned casually to the first of the "stuck" people. Tom, the oldest in the class, and the most resistant to the "new" methods, sat silently, looking down at his blank paper in stunned embarrassment. The teacher spoke to him quietly for a few minutes. Tom began to look more hopeful, and as the teacher moved away he began to draw, hesitantly at first, and then with determination . . . .

[3]All names in this section are fictitious with the exception of Karl, John (Colburn), and Theresa (Greenberg).

212

All this, and much more, happened in about 15 minutes. At the end of that time the teacher (Karl) said he had to go to a meeting and that a substitute teacher would be coming in to take his place while he was gone. The class continued its creative activities for a few minutes until he came back and introduced himself as the substitute teacher.

"Now children," he said in a loud, almost angry voice, "take everything off your desk but a pencil or pen."

Several children grumbled, and he responded with: "There'll be no more talking or noise in this room. If you have something to say or a question to ask, raise your hand." With a straight face, he went on, "And there'll be no more smoking or gum chewing either!"

The class laughed when he said, "No smoking," but quickly subsided into submission when they saw that he was deadly serious. It was at that moment that I began to hate the teacher.

"What you need," the teacher said, "is an exercise in following directions." He handed out blank sheets of paper, and began.

"Now, the key to this exercise—and to being a good student—is to do exactly what I tell you. Now raise your right hand."

One student raised his left hand maliciously. The teacher responded sarcastically with, "Young man, don't you know your right hand from your left? Put your left hand in your lap and raise your right hand. I'll have no insubordination in this class!"

The boy did as he was told, although he was visibly angry.

"Now, put your hands in your lap and sit up straight," the teacher continued. He paused for a moment, glancing around the room, finally stopping with one girl, staring at her angrily. She was slouched in her chair with her feet on another chair. When she didn't respond to his glance, the teacher reprimanded her and forced her to sit up straight with her feet on the floor.

He went on with, "Take your pencil in your right hand and draw a horizontal line about 3 inches long at the top of your paper. Now put your pencil down and put your hands in your lap."

He continued to give very explicit, step by step directions, controlling every movement the class made and constantly keeping them under surveillance for possible deviations. At first the class was interrupted from time to time by laughter, and students smiled knowingly at each other. As time went on, however, a strained silence fell over the room.

One girl raised her hand. The teacher appeared to see her hand, but failed to call on her. At several points he asked the children to hold up their drawings. Each time he would compliment one child's drawing, and ask those who had not followed directions carefully to correct their drawings. The first time, for example, he told Sally that she had done a "very good job," asked her to hold up her drawing for everyone to see, and demanded that all drawings be corrected to be like hers. Sally seemed mildly embarrassed and irritated when complimented. This was true of most of the students he singled out, although Tom seemed pleased when he was complimented. He was one of the few people who seemed to enjoy the exercise.

The teacher's instructions must have been ambiguous, because people kept getting the drawing wrong. As the exercise continued I noticed more and more tension arising in the class. As I realized that, I also got in touch with my own anger. I could hear Mr. Simpson, my own fourth grade teacher, saying, "Open your geography books. Now turn to page 37. Johnny, answer question number one. Now turn to page 42."

214

I came back to the present with a start and tried to understand what the other people in the class were feeling. Many of them looked frustrated and angry. Some seemed bored. Some carried on surreptitious activities on the side. The class remained quiet, but the silence was electrically charged by the end of the 15 minute period spent on the exercise. Finally the teacher just walked out of the room.

At first there was surprised silence. Then the class exploded. Everyone was talking all at once. One boy ran to the door and slammed it shut behind the teacher. Mary savagely ripped her piece of paper apart and others followed suit. The class seemed completely out of control, frenzied. Several people were obviously afraid of the hostility being expressed around them. A couple of students sat in silence, stunned. Theresa, one of our discussion leaders, stood at one side of the room, frozen into hurt immobility. As I looked closer I saw that there were tears in her eyes. She looked as if she were really hurting, but couldn't just let go and cry.

Karl came back into the room, and the class became quiet again, with people going back to their seats. John looked around, then, incredulously, at himself seated in his chair, and exploded with, "You dirty son of a bitch!" When he saw how hurt Karl was by this he said, "Oh, I know it's not you, Karl, but . . .!"

Karl walked over to Theresa and put his arm around her, comforting her, and I could see that he was as emotionally affected as we were.

He then gently suggested that we form five groups to discuss the exercise with the help of a discussion leader.

Discussion of the Origin-Pawn Game. Karl and the four student discussion leaders guided the discussions in the five groups. In my group we focused on feelings during the two parts of the game:

215

toward Karl in his two roles, toward the two products, and toward ourselves. Near the end we talked about what was different about Karl's behavior in the two roles and about the relationship between this game and education.

Most people hated the second part of the game, but enjoyed the first part. Feelings during the first part were mostly in the happy-joyful range, while feelings in the second part were mostly frustrated or angry.

Reactions to the frustrations of the second part of the game varied. Some people withdrew into a mechanical obedience, but thought a lot about other things. Their attention was divided between the task and unrelated phantasies. Other people stayed angry throughout and shared phantasies of hurting the teacher or smashing something.

Most people really enjoyed creating something during the first part of the game. Many had been attending so carefully to the task that they didn't even notice some of the funnier moments, as when Karl caught John's airplane on the fly.

Almost everyone liked Karl in the first role, but disliked him in the second role. Mary even said that she was still angry at him and was afraid to trust him anymore. This feeling came out even more clearly when the group responded to the question: "How do you feel about the two pieces of paper—the ones from the first and second parts of the game?" Bill summarized the general feeling when he said, "I was proud of my poem, and I'm going to take it home with me. But that second thing, that grotesque—it's not mine—it was yours (looking at Karl). I took great pleasure in tearing it up. Frankly, it was like tearing you up. I own the poem, you own those scraps of paper."

One girl in our group seemed surprised at all these reactions. She had found the second part of the game much more enjoyable than the first and liked the product just as well as the picture she had drawn during the free part. She reported being uncomfortable in the first role. She said, "In the first part I just couldn't figure out what to do. I kept trying to catch your (Karl's) eye to get some suggestions. I liked the second part because the task was clear. I was angry at the class for being so childish when he left the room." When asked how she felt when complimented for her work during the second part of the game, she said, "I was proud to have done a good job."

Her last statement led to a heated discussion by two other people who had been complimented during the second part. I never understood their feelings completely, but it was clear that they had been irritated by Karl's compliment, and embarrassed. Sam said, "I was insulted and angry, and somehow uneasy, too."

At one point in the discussion Mary said she was proud of herself for refusing to go along with Karl in the second part of the game. Others shared their disappointment and anger with themselves for obeying his directions without question. John was obviously embarrassed because of his own obedience when he said, "Why did we let him do it?" and "Why did we go along with him?"

Jack responded by pointing out that Karl's controlling behavior was typical of his own educational experiences, and that he had learned (the hard way) to obey. This led to a brief discussion of the differences in Karl's behavior in the two roles and of the relationships between the game and people's actual experiences in school.

The group seemed to agree that Karl was "authoritarian" in the second role, but couldn't come up with a label for his behavior in the first role, except that it was "OK!" Almost everyone in our discussion group had experienced situations like the second part of the game in school. In fact, the group seemed to agree that, as a basic rule, that's the way school is, even the university. Karl interrupted just as this conversation got under way and spoke to the whole class during the last few minutes of the period.

Origin-Pawn Vignette. I'd like to take a few minutes to try to summarize some of the things you've said this afternoon, and to share some of my own feelings and thoughts about this exercise with you.

Most of you had sharply contrasting feelings during the two parts of the game. You reported being motivated—turned on to the task— during the first part; but the second part seemed to leave you unmotivated—turned off. Several polar dimensions of experience seemed to differentiate the two states.

First, the basic feeling tone seemed to be positive in the first half, and negative in the second half of the exercise. You used words like pleasure, happy, and joyful to characterize the first experience, and words like frustrated, irritated, angry, bored, and afraid for the second experience. Second, your level of commitment to the task seemed to vary from a high level to a low level. This difference was reflected in differences in attention and concentration. Most of you became engrossed in the task during the first part. Your concentration was evident. In the second part many of you reported distractibility, divided attention, conflict, and a low level of concentration on the task. The difference in commitment was also evident from your activity level. As a group you seemed to be highly energetic during the first half, but passive during the second half. Finally, you seemed to have a sense of ownership in the first, but not in the second part of the exercise.

These motivated and unmotivated states seemed to be associated with perceptions of freedom and constraint, respectively. During the "free" condition you were able to choose your own objective, medium, and pace. During the "constrained" condition I made all the choices for you. DeCharms (1968) has developed terms to describe these perceptions, depending on who is in control of the behavior. In the first condition *you* were in control and *you* originated your own behavior. In DeCharms' terms, you felt like an *Origin*. In the second condition you were constrained; your behavior was determined by the teacher. You felt, DeCharms would say, like a *Pawn*. This game is called the *Origin-Pawn Game*.

Massive evidence indicates that when a person feels like an Origin he is much more productive and happy than when he feels like a Pawn.[4] This means that a student who feels like a Pawn is not likely to learn as much or enjoy school as much, as a student who feels like an Origin.

Many of you reported that most of your educational experiences have been more like the Pawn condition than the Origin condition. That has certainly been true of my own experience. What happens when a student is treated like a Pawn over a long period of time— for years? It seems that such a student (and I was such a student) tends to become passive, not able to do things on his own, afraid to challenge himself, authority, or the system. He tends to learn to see himself as powerless, at the mercy of external events and people. He no longer requires a Pawn situation to constrain him. He becomes constrained as a person, and his belief that his behavior is controlled by external forces becomes a self-fulfilling prophecy. At the extreme, a person of this personality type may be called a Pawn. One interesting thing about such a person is that he no longer feels upset or angry when someone controls or manipulates him. He is, in fact, more comfortable being directed than doing things on his own. As a learner he is rigid, inhibited, unprepared to deal with our

[4]See Kuperman (1967), DeCharms (1968, in press, in preparation), and Deci (1971) for an introduction to some of this evidence.

rapidly changing and unstable world. In addition to becoming dead as a person, he may develop a generalized aversion to school, and even learning itself. This aversion may put him in an avoidance-avoidance conflict (avoid school versus avoid punishment for withdrawing or acting out) which leads to numbness and a reduction of awareness, and ultimately to either apathy or violence within the classroom.

A person who has experienced years of Origin experiences, on the other hand, develops in a different way. Such a person learns to see himself as the locus of choice, control, and evaluation of his behavior. He believes that he makes the choices, and that the effects of his behavior are determined by him. He is highly autonomous, independent emotionally and intellectually. He is able to cope with rapidly changing, unstructured situations, and to seek and process new information on his own, as needed to deal with a rapidly changing world. We label this idealized personalized type an Origin. Origins, by the way, tend to behave quite differently than Pawns in the O-P Game. They tend to approach the first part of the game with confidence and pleasure, and to be very resistant and hostile toward the director in the second part of the game.

What specifically leads to Origin or Pawn experiences, and, over time, to Pawn personality types? My behavior in the two roles I played is a key to answering this question. All teachers and parents influence their children/students; but they do so in different ways. In the Origin part of the game I allowed you to do your own thing, providing guidance and help only when it was clearly needed. In the Pawn part of the game I controlled most of your behavior. These two broad strategies of influence are called "Allowing" and "Controlling." Evidence indicates that they lead to Origin or Pawn experiences and personality types.[5]

[5]See Kuperman (1967) and DeCharms (in press) for data which supports the assumption that allowing and controlling leadership styles lead to Origin and Pawn experiences, respectively. Data reported by Jackson (in preparation) suggests that these leadership styles,

The teaching styles associated with Origin-Pawn experiences and personality types seem to have major implications for education. We'll explore them further as the semester progresses.

I personally hate to be or see others treated like Pawns. As the course continues, I'll try to help you examine the features of teacher behavior which produce these different experiences. I'm hoping that after today the concepts of Origin and Pawn will help you to be more sensitive to these different experiences in yourself and in others, and will help you to organize your experiences on these dimensions. I hope you'll let me know how your experiences in the various parts of this course fit along the O-P dimension. One of my objectives in this course is to treat you like origins and to help you to feel and live as origins. To do this, I need your help in the form of feedback.

I'm hoping that you'll add this dimension to your thinking as you fill out the feedback cards for today (passes out 3" x 5" cards on which students write their feelings and comments about the day, and suggestions and questions). I've put several copies of DeCharms' paper, "Origins, Pawns, and Educational Practice," on reserve and hope that you'll read it in preparation for our next class.

The Problem. The Origin-Pawn Game was a key input in the course. It is also an introduction to the problems I tried to solve through the course.[6]

employed by mothers, are associated with Origin and Pawn personality types in their children DeCharms and Koenigs (in preparation) report similar relationships between free and constrained classroom climates and student Origin-Pawn scores.

[6]This paper is written from different perspectives. First there is the imaginary participant-observer perspective. Mary and I cooperated in writing those sections, with me (Karl) taking primary responsibility for the preceding sections and Mary taking primary responsibility for later sections. Second, a few portions of the paper are written from an "objective" perspective. Mary and I share responsibility for them. Finally, other sections are written from a personal perspective. Mary and I took responsibility for writing different portions of the paper in a first person "I" format. We'll identify who is speaking in these sections. I (Karl) took major responsibility for The Problem, Overview, and Objectives and Plans, and write from a first-person perspective in these sections.

A few years ago I began a systematic examination of Origin and Pawn experiences, and the conditions under which they occur (Jackson, 1968). As I began to identify the conditions under which I personally felt like a Pawn, I realized that many of them were within the context of my role as a graduate student. I had only recently realized that much—even most—of what I was asked to do as a graduate student had little value for facilitating my intellectual or personal growth, and that my graduate school experience was only an extension of similar experiences in college, high school, and grade school. Now I found that I could begin to isolate the features of the situation which disappointed me so much. First was the conflict I experienced so often between doing what I wanted to do and what I was asked to do by the program and my professors. Second, I was often frustrated and left with that lonely feeling which comes from not being heard, accepted, and prized when my work, and even my whole person, was ignored, misunderstood, or categorized by my professors.

I was hurt and afraid when I realized how Pawn-like I was, how easily I had bought into the expectations of the program, how afraid I was of doing things on my own, how sensitive I was to criticism, and how much irrational fear and emotional deadness characterized me. Later I realized that I had become a production-machine, valuing myself only on the basis of my products and their evaluation by others, rather than for myself. I characterized myself as a gold-star man; and I was afraid I wouldn't be able to break out of the system which I had internalized.

When I looked around me I saw that most students seemed to be Pawns in someone else's game; and later I realized that many faculty members were also, having merely substituted publications for gold stars. When I realized how much damage they and I had suffered from the educational system, I was violently angry. After awhile the anger was complemented by fear that they and I would stay locked in (and up), by sadness at seeing their deadness and my own, and by deep despair as I realized the magnitude of the problem and felt my own helplessness to change myself or them and our mutual situation.

These feelings, and a blind faith that at least I could help myself, somehow gave me the courage to translate my theoretical understanding of motivation into a program designed to help me grow as a person and shed some of the straitjackets my family and the system had built into me. As I began to see myself progressing, albeit slowly and painfully, toward becoming the open, emotionally rich, spontaneous person that I wanted to be, I began to develop hope that others could travel a similar path, and that the scars left by our social and educational systems need not be permanent. After awhile I even began to hope that the systems themselves could be changed.

Just before I began planning this course I wrote: "I have developed a deep and personal commitment to increasing degrees of experienced freedom in the world; a commitment to help create situations in which people can grow and learn in such a way that they actualize their full potential. I will begin by attempting to improve our deadening educational system, in whatever small way I can."

When I was given an opportunity to teach this course I challenged myself to develop a design and relationship with the class which would provide a living and workable alternative to traditional education. I knew that if the course were to be successful it would first have to undo the damage that so many of the students would have sustained in their 14 or 15 years of education. Then it would have to help the students learn how to apply the educational principles and skills that I would be using to help them, so they, in turn, could help solve the larger problem.

As I looked forward to the course, all the feelings and thoughts and experiences I've just described came back to me. The sadness and fear I felt when I thought of those students who were as debilitated as I had been—the despair, the anger at the system—all these came back, along with a fear that I wouldn't be able to avoid doing it to them, too. These feelings plus little tendrils of hope were my problem—the problem which led to the construction and implementation of this course.

I've shared the problem from a very personal perspective to show you that the problem was not exclusively an intellectual one. It was a problem posed by the deepest of personal feelings—the most human part of me as a person.

Overview

My planning for the course was guided by a conceptually vague, but affectively and analogically clear, image of the attributes of a person well prepared to deal with our rapidly emerging world, and a similar image of the attributes of a person who could help others become so prepared. My first task was to try to objectify these images into a set of concrete course goals and to evolve an action-plan for attaining them. The next section of the paper, Objectives and Plans, summarizes the results of this process.

Objectives and Plans

I've struggled during the 15 months between when I began to plan for the course and now with an attempt to objectify the tacit knowledge (Polanyi, 1958) or recipe knowledge (Garfinkel, 1967) which guided so many of my decisions and activities in teaching the course. I had relied heavily on those intuitive feelings which said, "This course of action is the best one—it feels right." These feelings were a result of subjective understandings developed in my own self-directed personal and intellectual growth program, in my apprenticeship as a motivation and human-relations trainer, in my trial and error teacher-skills development experiences, and in my years of developing research skills as an educational-social psychologist. This section is an attempt to share the objectives and broad action plans aspects of that knowledge as I've managed to explicate it to date. The next section describes what actually happened and is our attempt to share recipe knowledge of the every-day events of the course.

Mr. Edward Psychologist. An image of an "ideal" educational psychologist served as a guide to the selection of course objectives and action plans. The broad objective of the course was to allow students to become more like Mr. Ed Psych by developing some of his skills, and to decide whether they wanted to go on to become even more like him by sampling some of his typical experiences.

Ed has a core set of personal-interpersonal attributes which he brings to bear when he wears his various hats (i.e., learner, teacher/counselor, theoretician, applier of knowledge, researcher). Development of these attributes and skills was an implicit objective of the course, so I want to share them with you.

Ed is autonomous, creative, curious, open, and flexible. He has an accurate, well-differentiated, and accepted concept of himself, and is sensitive to the ways in which his attributes, including typical feelings and needs, affect his work. He is good at abstract conceptualization and symbolic manipulation, but is also able to bridge the gap between ivory tower and real world. He is relatively non-dogmatic, nonbiased, and nonparochial; so he avoides supporting any one narrow philosophical, methodological, or theoretical point of view. Finally, he is interpersonally sensitive and is effective in interpersonal communication.

Ed has specific attributes and skills which are associated with his various hats and which roughly correspond to the first five course objectives:

1. He has high level capacity and desire for self-initiated intellectual and personal growth (learner hat).

2. He has high level capacity and desire for helping others become autonomous learners (teacher hat).

3. He is able to actively recall some of the major concepts, principles, methods, data, and theories generated by educational psychology and has some familiarity with those he cannot actively recall (conceptual/theoretical hat).

4. He is able to select, design, and implement research (research hat).

5. He is able to apply educational psychology principles and findings to real life situations (applier of knowledge hat).

In addition to the five objectives implicit in the above attributes, I tried to help the students pursue their own objectives and to design the course in such a way that they developed an affection for the subject matter—so that they would be likely to pursue it further in the future. The sixth explicit course objective—maximize unity or freedom experiences—was intended to help these things happen.

The remainder of this section elaborates the six course objectives and means established for attaining them.

Objective 1: Enhance capacity and desire for self-initiated intellectual and personal growth. I remembered the experiences and characteristics I had had when I first realized how Pawnish I had become and contrasted them to the experiences and characteristics that I had now. I had changed a great deal. Now I had successfully separated the process of learning from meeting system requirements; and this allowed me to do what was needed to please my professors and graduate school without confusing it with skill development or meaningful learning. This had freed me to learn how to design and implement meaningful learning experiences for myself. I had become a self-starter, eager to grow and learn under my own steam, fully capable of doing without courses or unsolicited guidance from outside. I had become my own school and was experiencing all the pleasure and care of learning which comes with being an autonomous learner. I wanted to share these newly found experiences and attributes with my students.

Schaefer's words helped me to conceptualize this objective:

> *There is considerable agreement among educators at all levels that the basic purpose of instruction is to prepare the individual for further learning. Education is intended to be a dynamic rather than a static affair—open-ended and continuous rather than closed and finite. Its aim is agreed to be not accumulated segments of information and knowledge but the conceptual tools, the modes of thought, and above all, the disposition for a life-long pursuit of knowledge. The measure of the learned person is not years of formal schooling nor units collected in colleges, but capacity for continuous intellectual and personal growth . . . .*
>
> *But while it may be agreed that the primary purpose of formal instruction is to develop the capacity for self-initiated learning, such a goal is exceedingly difficult and elusive . . . .* (Schaefer, 1968)

I formalized the first objective in these words: Facilitate development of capacity and desire for self-initiated intellectual and personal growth.

Making the Objective Concrete. Several concepts and measures are related theoretically and empirically to a high level capacity and desire for self-initiated activity. They include a positive self-concept

(Wylie, 1961) or a high level of self-esteem (Coopersmith, 1967);
a creative learning style (Rosenberg, 1968), "abstract" conceptual
ability (Harvey, 1969), self-actualization (Maslow, 1962), a high
level of ego development (Loevenger, 1970), and a high level of
moral development (Kohlberg, 1964).

These concepts have one thing in common: all presuppose a high
level of intellectual and emotional autonomy. Three concepts have
been related to such autonomy in a large number of studies. An
autonomous person would be likely to be "internal" on Rotter's
(1966) internal-external control of reinforcements dimension, have
a higher than average level of n Achievement (McClelland et al.,
1958), and be near the Origin end of DeCharms' (1968) Origin-
Pawn variable.[7] I decided to focus my efforts to "enhance capacity
and desire for self-initiated intellectual and personal growth" by
attempting to enhance internal responses and n Achievement and
Origin behavior.[8]

Means for Goal Attainment. Shea and Jackson (in press) and
Jackson and Shea (in press) review a number of studies which indicate that individual motivation and motivated performance can be
developed via motivation-training programs.

Basically, the training course employs four training principles:

*1. Participants are trained to carefully examine themselves—
their behavior, their needs, and their feelings.*

---

[7]Rotter's questionnaire provides a measure of the degree to which a person believes that
he (rather than his environment) is in control of his reinforcements. McClelland's achievement motive scoring system is used to score TAT stories and provides an indication of the
intensity of a person's disposition to compete with a standard of excellence. Plimpton's
(1970) scoring system is also used on TAT stories, and assesses the degree to which a person sees himself as an Origin.

[8]A pre-post control group research design was developed to assess the success of the course
in attaining these and most of the other objectives. Data analysis is being done now and
will be reported in a later paper.

2. Participants are trained to be aware of the thoughts and actions of "motivated" individuals and are helped to learn how to think and behave like those individuals.

3. Participants are trained to set realistic goals that they can responsibly achieve.

4. Participants, in a group setting, are supported in their attempts at personal change . . . . The training course is composed of well over twenty "psychological inputs" (Shea and Jackson) that are designed to facilitate motivation change based on the four principles outlined above. (Jackson and Shea, in press, p. 17)

These inputs consist of game-like activities, role-plays, scoring and interpretation of motive measures, vignettes (short presentations of theory and data), brief readings, written exercises, group discussions focusing on self-examination and skill development experiences.[9]

Motivation training helps participants focus on questions like: 1. "Who am I as a motivated person?" 2. "What is a highly motivated person like?" and 3. "How can I change to become more highly motivated and successful?" The training is built around working assumptions about the answer to question 2.[10] These are summarized in the motivation syndrome, a set of attributes of the highly motivated person:

He has a well differentiated, accurate, and accepted concept of self.

[9]A more complete description and explanation of motivation-training appears in Shea and Jackson (in press). My adaptation of it to this course is briefly characterized in the description of the first half of the "Class."

[10]See Shea and Jackson (in press) and Jackson and Shea (in press) for data supporting most of these assumptions.

He is aware of his own feelings, needs, and motives.

He is future (goal) oriented.

He thinks like a highly motivated person (uses the n Achievement intensity subcategories in his thinking).

He is a moderate risk-taker.

He seeks and utilizes feedback and other useful information from the environment.

He takes personal responsibility for his own behavior.

He is an autonomous person.

I decided to use motivation-training to help students develop internal control of reinforcements, achievement motivation, and Origin behavior. Motivation-training is usually performed in a retreat workshop setting in a small group (16 trainees maximum) over a period of several days. I had to adapt the training so that it could be done in 10 or 12 contact hours spread over a period of 5 or 6 weeks in a class of 50 or 60 people.

Three other means were used to facilitate attainment of this objective. First, students were asked to practice being autonomous learners by meeting the "process-requirement" in each aspect of the course. In each case they were asked to establish their own objectives, means, and mode of evaluation and then to implement their action plan. Second and third were the leadership training and the coparticipative/experiential process aspects of the course (see below). They provided the student with additional motivation-relevant experiences which would help them differentiate their own feelings, needs, and motivational properties and take more and more responsibility for their own learning.

Objective 2: Enhance Capacity and Desire for Helping Others Become Autonomous Learners. The ultimate objective of any teacher-training program is to facilitate growth and learning on the part of school children. I assume that the most important thing children can acquire in school is a capacity and a desire for self-initiated intellectual and personal growth. The second course objective was to help my students learn how to help their students develop this capacity and desire. In short, I decided to help my students become Origin-trainers.

DeCharms (in preparation) found that teachers who had experienced basic motivation-training and leadership training and who implemented motivation-training inputs in their classrooms were successful in enhancing achievement motivation, origin scores, and autonomous behavior on the part of their students.[11] DeCharms and Koenigs (in preparation) also found that trained teachers had more Origin-producing classroom climates than control teachers. Alschuler (1968) reports similar results, and my own experiences and observations as a motivation/leadership trainer, I decided to use leadership training to develop Origin-trainers.

No adequate explication of behavioral objectives was available as I planned the course. I want to share the results of my own attempt to translate the personal recipe understandings I had developed as a motivation-trainer into concrete objectives.

Most therapists and trainers agree that people who try to help others grow may be ineffective or dangerous if they do not have a high level of emotional autonomy or ego strength themselves. Motivation-trainers agree that motivation-training is implemented most successfully by people who have experienced it themselves. For these reasons the basic motivation-training program used to attain the first course objective was an indispensable precursor to leadership training.

[11]Their students also accelerated in academic achievement, realistic goal-setting, and ego development, and were less often tardy or absent.

231

Most teachers seem to have a relatively high level of power motivation. The need for power (n Power) is defined in terms of influence. A person who has intense desire to control, advise, impress, or influence others is likely to have a high n Power score (Winter, 1968). Power motivation is not necessarily a bad characteristic. A teacher may satisfy his power needs via various strategies of influence, some having a negative impact on the student, others being very helpful. The strategy of influence I used in the "Pawn" part of the Origin-Pawn Game was one which seems to produce Pawns (Jackson, in preparation). I call this a "Controlling" strategy. The strategy I used in the "Origin" part of the game was one which seems to encourage the development of Origins (Jackson, in preparation). I call this an "Allowing" strategy. Both strategies satisfy a person's power needs, but the "Allowing" strategy is obviously preferable to the "Controlling" strategy.

A first subgoal toward developing Origin-trainers was to enhance student capacity and desire to use an "Allowing" strategy of influence.

Even if the students became more autonomous learners themselves and developed a general disposition to treat others as Origins, they might have trouble translating their understandings into action in the classroom. I decided to pursue a second subgoal by attempting to enhance their capacity and desire to apply what they had learned in classroom settings.

Making the Subgoals Concrete. The strategy of influence a teacher uses to satisfy his power needs is revealed directly in his interactions with students and could be shaped directly through behavior modification (Tharp and Wetzel, 1971). I decided not to do this for two reasons. First, I believe that behavior modification may sometimes create Pawns (see DeCharms, 1968, 1970, in press), and I did not understand the conditions under which that might occur well enough to be sure that I wouldn't be working at cross purposes to use it.

Second, I believe that a person's typical strategy of influence is a reflection of more central aspects of the person which cannot be economically changed through behavior-specific operant conditioning. The teacher's basic interpersonal orientation, for example, is more central to him as a person than is his specific behavior, and unless it is consistent with an allowing-helping style no amount of behavior-specific conditioning will produce a permanent change in him.

Even more central than basic interpersonal orientation is interpersonal motivation. If a teacher's motivational structure is consistent with a highly controlling-helping style and an authoritarian leadership style, it will be very difficult to change his behavior without changing his motivational structure.

Thomas, Goleman, and Goldstein (in press) have developed a scoring system for **n** Power which differentiates between two types of power motivation. Socialized (**s**) power is consistent with an allowing strategy of influence, and personalized (**p**) power is consistent with a controlling strategy of influence. A high socialized power score reflects an intense desire to influence others—but it is a desire expressed in helpful, rather than controlling ways. A high personalized power score reflects the same intense concern with influence—but the concern is expressed in highly controlling, manipulative ways.

Two people with the same total **n** Power score may manifest their power motivation in markedly different ways. One may have a high **s** power/**p** power ratio, corresponding to an allowing strategy of influence, while the other has a low **s** power/**p** power ratio, corresponding to a controlling strategy of influence. I decided to focus my attempt to enhance capacity and desire for using an allowing strategy of influence by taking it as a concrete objective to help the students enhance their **s** power/**p** power ratio.

The ideal way to determine whether a student is able to apply what he has learned in a classroom is to observe him in a classroom. Since this was impractical I looked around for a good measure which would give an indirect indication of whether students in the class were able to apply what they had learned. I found nothing that was unambiguously related to motivation training and allowing behavior; but Teaching Situation Reaction Tests (T.S.R.T.) seemed to tap into many dimensions of that behavior and was reasonably well validated, so I decided to use it.

The second concrete sub-objective then was to enhance T.S.R.T. scores.

Means for Goal Attainment. A few recipes for helping people develop an allowing strategy of influence were available to me from past experience as a motivation/communications/human relations trainer-apprentice. The same procedures were also designed to facilitate transfer into actual classroom behavior, but I decided to complement them with additional inputs designed for that purpose. Although the procedures were to be intertwined in actual practice, I will discuss strategies of influence training and applications training separately.

Allowing Strategy of Influence Training. I decided to use techniques of three kinds here: 1) leadership training, 2) communication training, and 3) student role sensitivity training.

1. **Leadership Training.** DeCharms, Collins, Jackson and Shea (1968), DeCharms (in press; in preparation), and DeCharms and Koenigs (in preparation) cite evidence which suggests that leadership training (Shea and Jackson, in press) helps participants develop a more allowing strategy of influence, presumably as a function of an increase in the **s** power/**p** power ratio. Leadership training of this kind is focused around the question, "How can I motivate others?", and is always coupled with individual motivation training (see above) in one package. It uses processes similar to those used in individual motivation training.

The classic Lippet and White (1943) study of leadership serves as a basis of one of the inputs (the squares game, see class #8 p. 261). A discussion of the three strategies of influence or leadership styles used in that study will clarify the objectives of the training. The authoritarian, democratic, and laissez-faire strategies seem to send messages which affect the child's autonomy. These messages, in the form of metacommunicational statements of relationship (Watzlawick, Beavin, and Jackson, 1967) make statements to the student about the distribution of control in the student-teacher relationship, and hence about the degree of autonomy the teacher trusts him to manifest. These messages are important because the student becomes autonomous as a person and a learner to the extent that he sees himself as the locus of control in his life (see Jackson, in preparation).

Some messages which seem to be sent from the three leadership roles are:

Authoritarian:
"You are a child; I must take care of you." "I don't trust you to take responsibility for yourself—or for me." "You are incapable of taking care of yourself." "I don't value you as a person, although I may accept you if you do the right things (what I tell you to)."

Laissez-faire:
"You are an adult; you can take care of yourself." "I trust you to take responsibility for yourself—but not for me." "Take care of yourself." "I don't love you for what you are—but I may accept or recognize you if you do something spectacular that pleases me."

Democratic:
"You're an adult; with help you can take care of yourself."

"I trust you to take responsibility for yourself and for me."
"You are capable of taking care of yourself; but I want to
work *with* you." "I value you as a person. I love you for
what you are, not for what you do."

The authoritarian leader places the locus of control in himself
and tells the child that he is not capable of taking responsibility.
Just the opposite is true of the laissez-faire leader who allows
the child to take responsibility for himself, but also trusts him
to take some responsibility for him (the leader). Obviously the
democratic leadership pattern is more likely to encourage autonomy than the other two. The laissez-faire pattern, however, also
seems to place a lot of responsibility in the child, and seems at
first glance to fall in the allowing category.

The messages have import at another level, which probably has
an impact on the child's autonomy. The amount of warmth or
concern expressed to the child probably affects his autonomy
as well.[12]

The laissez-faire leader seems to send the message, "I don't care
about you," which may come through as, "I don't love you for
what you are—but I may accept you if you *do* the right thing."
This is the pattern which seems to produce the acceptance-
anxious child (Rosenberg, 1968). Such a child seems to value
himself only in terms of his products, especially products which
will be valued by others. His self-esteem seems to be contingent
on *doing* rather than *being*. In the sense that he constantly
seeks to impress others by his works, he is "external."[13]

[12]See Rosen and D'Andrade (1959), Winterbottom (1958), and Jackson (in preparation)
for indirect support of this assumption.

[13]During my own "gold-star man" period I was such a person. I still suffer from some of
the negative effects. My guess is that a large proportion of Ph.D.'s and professional people
are acceptance-anxious.

The democratic leader seems to send contrasting messages with a contrasting impact. The democratic message seems to be: "I love you because you're you, not because of what you do." An implication of this message is that the student can safely choose his own point of view or course of action and express or pursue it, but need not produce in order to be loved. I believe that this allows the student to learn for the pleasure of learning.

Leadership training, then, attempts to help participants develop an allowing or democratic helping style. When they in turn use this helping style, the impact on the student allows him to *be*, rather than *do*, and his natural curiosity and developing autonomy are expressed in learning.

I decided to adapt this form of training to the classroom. It was previously done only in small group, intensive retreat workshop settings; but I was determined to develop a design for implementing it in 8 or 10 contact hours during the middle 4 or 5 weeks of the course with the entire class (50 or 60 students).

2. **Communications Training.** Page (1971) describes a model of interpersonal communication which seems to summarize many of the ideas of Rogers (1964) and others. The model provides an alternative to the absolutistic, categorical, judgmental, supportive mode of communication typically used by authoritarian teachers; so I decided to try to share it with the students in the class.

3. **Student Role Sensitivity Training.** Borofski (1969) has developed a game called the High-School Game which allows the student to explore the feelings of students of different IQ levels in authoritarian, democratic, and laissez-faire classes. I decided to complement similar exercises in the leadership program with this game in order to give class participants an

237

opportunity to further develop their sensitivity to the feelings of students.

Other facets of the course would complement these three means. Individual motivation training would supply key personal knowledge, understanding of motivation, and the leadership conditions under which various motivational states would occur. The use of small peer groups for discussions within the class and discussion sections would allow leaders to emerge and get feedback. The overall coparticipative design of the course and the behavior of the instructor and discussion leaders would provide a model of how allowing and democratic helping and leadership strategies can be translated into classroom action. The coparticipative design would give the students an opportunity to apply democratic decision making skills. Finally, the experiential/self-examination approach used in the class would help the students in the course to become reflexive (Gouldner, 1970), that is, to see and examine themselves from a third person perspective. This would help them continue to grow and learn as leaders in the future.

Applications Training. I decided to use indirect and direct methods to help students prepare to apply an allowing approach.

1. **Indirect Methods.** Alschuler (1968), Rogers (1969), and DeCharms and Koenigs (in preparation) suggest that a democratic classroom climate, an open classroom structure, and experience-based learning facilitate motivation. These process-level aspects of classroom operation actualize the democratic/allowing influence strategy and constitute indirect forms of autonomy-training. I decided to model these by using them in our class. Specifically, I wanted to use classroom processes the students could apply later in their classes: a) peer group learning, and b) experiential learning, and c) coparticipation. I thought that by experiencing these processes students would be in a position to apply them later in their own classes.

a. **Peer Group Learning.** Traditional classes are composed of one group (the whole class) with one leader (the instructor). I planned to use a variety of group structures and leaders, with special emphasis on five-person groups led by emergent student leaders. I wanted to use these small peer groups for several reasons. First, they require that each class member take responsibility for his own learning (Huntsberry, 1971). Second, they encourage students to take an active, rather than a passive, learning role (Dewey, 1962). As a result of speaking more, they have more opportunity to clarify their ideas and feelings by translating them from subjective into objective realities (Berger and Luckman, 1967). This also allows them to get feedback from others, which encourages the development of a reflexive attitude (Gouldner, 1970). It allows them to refine their models of reality by comparing them to other models presented by other group members, thereby forming models which fit the reality structure of the world better (Huntsberry, 1971). These groups also make learning central to the student as a person, because it occurs within the context of meaningful relationships (students become close friends quickly in this type of design), and because there is less threat due to surveillance by an authority figure. Finally, each student has much more power to control the course of events, which means that the locus of control is much more in his hands (DeCharms, 1968). All of these features of small group process enhance learning and the development of initiative and motivation on the part of the students.

b. **Experiential Learning.** The traditional class is mostly made up of lectures, with occasional discussion. Lectures establish a relationship in which the lecturer is in control of classroom events and the students are passive rather than active learners. In that sense they fit the authoritarian leadership model. Experiential learning (Rogers, 1969) and learning by the enquiry approach (Suchman, 1966) provide an alternative which actualizes the allowing/democratic influence strategy by using a variety of processes (games, role-plays, small group discussions, skills development exercises, etc.) which allow the student to be an active learner and take responsibility for guiding at least part of his own learning. I decided to use this approach throughout the course, so that students would become familiar enough with it to apply it in their own classes.

c. **Coparticipation.** The coparticipative design of the course (see below) would provide still another model which students could apply in their classrooms.

I knew that peer group, experiential, and coparticipative learning (see below) would work best in an atmosphere where open, honest, feeling-level, here-and-now communication was the norm. I planned to be "real" with the students and to use the communications model (Page, 1971) consistently to encourage such an atmosphere.

2. **Direct Methods.** I knew there would not be time to provide much direct application practice, but I decided to at least give the class an opportunity to write out and discuss a motivation-training design using allowing process principles, and to apply the communications model in role-plays of classroom discipline problems.

Objectives 3, 4, and 5: Develop content knowledge in educational psychology; develop research skills; develop application skills. These three objectives are heavily emphasized in most educational psychology courses, with most of the emphasis placed on the first one. I decided to place all three lower in priority than the two objectives

240

discussed above. Objectives of these three types are so common-
place in educational psychology courses that I will not burden the
reader with an extended description of them, or my rationale for
them. My general plan of action was to ask students to read extensively in key educational psychology areas to concretize what
they had learned in brief papers, and to apply and strengthen their
learning by writing criticisms, comparisons of points of view or
approaches, applications to a personal or classroom problem, or a
description of how what they had read related to their own experience. I planned to minimize lectures and use a lot of class time
in discussions in which students discussed and clarified their concepts,
or in role-plays or similar application exercises. I also planned to
offer them an opportunity to develop simple research skills by asking them each to do a small observational study in a classroom, and
summarize it in a research report. Finally, I planned to set aside
one-fourth of the course for individual projects, so that each student
could pursue his own personal objectives. I anticipated that many
students would use this as an opportunity to read more extensively
in some area, do research, or try to apply their knowledge in a real
life setting.

Objective 6: Maximize unity experiences. What are the optional
conditions for creative learning? By answering this question I hoped
to have some guidelines for designing the course. From my own experience, and observations of others, I had developed the belief that
learning and creativity seem to be optimized under certain experiential conditions or states of being in the world. Mary and I call these
experiences "unity experiences."

The following quotes point to and tentatively define what we mean
by unity:[14]

---

[14]These experiences correspond to those characterized by Koch (1956) as B-States,
DeCharms (1968) as Origin-states, and Jackson (1968) as freedom experiences.

Unity as a Motivated State. What is it Like to "Be Motivated?"
The words that we use in describing the state of "being motivated" are packed with energy—words like "drive," "desire,"
"concerned," and "engrossed." When we are motivated we are
"turned on"—so actively concentrating on what we're doing
that all else fades into the background. We are deeply committed to the task at hand, free of conflicting thoughts or pre-
occupations, polarized and unified toward a specific objective.
Present thoughts are translated immediately and smoothly into
action.

Unity as Surrender. *In surrender man becomes totally involved
undifferentially and indistinguishably; with himself, with his act
or state, and with his object or partner.* (Wolff, K. H., 1964,
p. 45)

Unity as Wholeness. *Your best is done . . . when you scarcely
know that you are exerting yourself, when you are least conscious of the effort . . . the cooperation of the whole of you
. . . resides in the fact that the whole of you is bent to the
task . . . when a man is fully conscious of what he's doing,
there is too little of him left to do it. You put the whole of
yourself to work only when part of you is not watching you.*
(Curtis, 1962, p. xvi)

The experience of unity characterized in these quotes seems to be
associated with creative learning. Some aspects of unity which seem
to enhance such learning are: 1) a wide scope of awareness (open-
eyeness); 2) an openness to new information (nondefensiveness and
freedom from rigid sets for construing or interpreting the world; 3)
spontaneous generation of new modes of seeing, categorizing, interpreting, theorizing about the problem at hand; and 4) easy and
effortless integration of new material. In the light of these, I believe that a person who is experiencing unity is engaged in a high
level of creative learning.

I decided to try to enhance learning in the course by trying to maximize such experiences.

Making the Objective Concrete. Unity experiences seem to occur when self-acceptance is at a high level, i.e., when we feel free to "be" without feeling compelled to "do" something in order to prove ourselves to ourselves or others. I suggested earlier that democratic organizational systems send more prizing (Harris, 1969) messages than authoritarian or laissez-faire systems. According to the line of reasoning presented above, this means that they are more likely to encourage "being," unity experiences, and creative learning. Learning under this condition seems to be effortless, pleasure-filled, and highly efficient. I adopted as a working assumption the notion that unity experiences (and the creative learning which accompanies them) will be maximized in a democratic or coparticipative process.

Coparticipation in Education: Theory

From a theoretical point of view, the situation that students are attacking when they express boredom or charge that a class is irrelevant is one in which the locus of choice and the locus of control for the events in the course are placed in the instructor. There is an increasing body of evidence which indicates that people who are forced to pursue goals selected by others, and who are not at least partially in control of the process which leads to the attainment of those goals, feel frustrated, dominated, and uncared for. They find it difficult to commit themselves to the goals chosen by the "master," and tend to see them as irrelevant. In the phraseology of DeCharms (1968), they feel powerless, like "Pawns."

Students often argue for the opposite situation mentioned above—that is, they argue that the students should make all the choices and control all the ongoing activities in the classroom. They would thereby be Origins, and the teacher would be the Pawn, feeling left out, useless, manipulated, and controlled.

243

A proponent of Origin-Pawn theory might argue that if students are to feel like Origins they must be completely in control, and if teachers are to be Origins, they must be completely in control. This implies that with respect to experiences of mastery and competence, life is a zero sum game, in which one person in any pair must always be the master and the other must be the slave.[15]

A Third Alternative: Coparticipation. I don't want to accept either extreme situation because both parties in the interaction feel uncared for. Neither feels maximally free, because neither can trust the other.

The major principle upon which this course is designed is the principle of coparticipation. In the situation of mutuality or coparticipation, the locus of choice and control is distributed between the students and the teacher. The goals for the course, and the form in which the class is to be run, are selected by students and teacher together. In such a situation both students and teacher feel like origins, in control of their fates (although they don't feel as much in control as under the previous conditions), and they also experience warmth, respect, trust, and consideration from their counterparts.

Means for Goal Attainment. Actualizing a coparticipative approach is not easy. The course introduction went on to describe the overall course design and how it was intended to overcome obstacles to coparticipation.

Coparticipation in Education: Application in the Design of This Course

Difficulties in Creating a Coparticipative Course Design. It is easy to design a course in which the teacher calls all the shots, or even

---

[15]The reader should note that DeCharms and his co-workers have never made such an assertion, and that they would undoubtedly find it incompatible with their basic humanistic point of view. Nevertheless, this position is the ultimate logical consequence of Origin-Pawn Theory as now conceived.

244

one in which the students call all the shots. But it is extraordinarily difficult to design a course in which coparticipation (mutual choice and control) is the rule. Six basic problems make such a design difficult to construct.

1) We said first that students and teachers are not ready for full coparticipation all at once, because they are accustomed to a different system, involving different kinds of relationships and responsibilities, and that a too sudden introduction of coparticipation would violate the background expectancies of all. Several features of the design should facilitate the development of the new classroom roles and responsibilities, without requiring them to be fully present all at once. The somewhat structured lesson-plan of the class will relieve the student of the responsibility of designing his own major learning experience all at once. Finally, the clear delineation of available alternatives and procedures which is presented here should help simplify the transition into the new system for all of us, and help us create our new social reality (Berger and Luckman, 1967) quickly and efficiently.

2) We are not well equipped with the communication and cooperative skills necessary for successful coparticipative education. The design incorporates several opportunities for developing these skills. The goal-setting sessions between staff members and individual students will be useful here, as will the goal-setting and progress evaluation and sessions in the discussion sections. The many hours we will spend talking together in classes and discussion sections will also help in sharpening our skills. Class participants will receive some focused practice in developing leadership and communication skills, and those who so desire may participate in an encounter discussion group. The staff will do everything possible to foster open, honest, two-way communication, and an atmosphere in which we can all give each other feedback which will help us develop skills.

245

3) We assert that the individuality of students poses a problem for our design. We want to allow each student to design his own program. The individual learning experiences, the many alternatives to the class and the many discussion-section choices should help each student express and satisfy his individual educational needs.

4) The large class size posed very complex administrative problems for a coparticipative design. The carefully specified procedures, and the larger than usual staff, overcame this problem.

5) The instructor would not have time to conduct a fully coparticipative design alone. The development of a new educational role—the discussion leader—has helped overcome this problem. Four carefully selected and specifically trained students will share the administrative and other responsibilities of the instructor. They are the key to the success of the design (Jackson, 1970 a, pp. 4-11).

6) The sixth problem, that of meeting the curricular requirements of the department, has been resolved by constructing half of the course (the class) in such a way that those requirements will be met in it. In addition, the entire course design should generate experiential data relevant to all three major content areas (Jackson, 1970 b, pp. 1-2).

The Design of the Course

Three Aspects of the Course. The three aspects of the course are the class, the discussion-section, and the individual project. These aspects of the course will require, respectively, one-half, one-fourth, and one-fourth of the time each student spends on the course. All three aspects are coparticipative, but the locus of choice is intended to lie more in the overall GIE curriculum and the instructor than in the students for class activities, to be equally shared between discussion leader and students in the discussion section and to lie more in the student for his individual project. The locus of control is distributed about half and half between students and instructor, or between students and discussion leader in the class and discussion-section, and is placed entirely in the student for his individual learning experience project.

Students were able to choose from a variety of alternatives for each aspect of the course and alternatives to participation in the class were available. Within the class there was a great deal of freedom for individual expression, as indicated in the following introduction presented to the students: You will be able to choose among five discussion-leaders, on the basis of their personal descriptions of what they would like to do in their section. Within a discussion section you will work with your discussion leader to select, design, and implement your section's activities.

You will be able to create almost any kind of individual learning experience for yourself. Your project will be coparticipative at the point of goal-setting and at the point of outcome evaluation, inasmuch as you will be asked to discuss your individual learning experience goals with your discussion leader and will be asked to somehow communicate your evaluation of the outcome to him; but you will take full responsibility for implementing your project yourself. You will be able to share your project with other students if you like, whether by telling them about it or by working on team projects.

Finally, you are free to construct any alternative or set of alternatives to any portion of the course, or to the whole course, within only a few minimal content and process constraints.[16]

Process Requirements of the Course. Each of the three aspects of the course has a basic process-requirement: a procedure of

[16]Content constraints hold only for the alternatives to the class portion of the course.

coparticipative goal-setting, progress-sharing, and outcome evaluation sharing.

The process requirements have been institutionalized in the course for three reasons: 1) they are (theoretically and in terms of existing evidence) a very good way to maximize commitment, productivity, and enjoyment on the part of the student; 2) they will allow him to examine first-hand in terms of his experience, the processes involved in autonomous activity within a coparticipative educational system: and 3) they will allow the staff to share their information, skills, and interests with the student, and to share his project(s) with him.

The Management System Employed in the Design. The typical university classroom seems to be based on a seriously maladaptive management system. At the extreme this system is rigidly hierarchical, with a relatively authoritarian teacher at the top and Pawn-like students at the bottom. Very little coparticipation occurs, even between students.

The course attempts to approximate a "participative group" management system (Likert, 1967). The participative group system uses group decision-making and overlapping group structure, attempts to keep all possible communication and influence channels open, and keeps everyone informed of everyone else's activities. The structural properties of the system are based on the concept of linking-pin group membership. This means a thorough interconnection of the parts represented fairly to facilitate coparticipation.

Three task groups are involved in this structure: 1) the staff, composed of the instructor and the discussion leaders, 2) the middle management group, composed of the five discussion leaders plus one participant from each discussion group, 3) the discussion groups, each composed of a discussion leader and about twelve or thirteen participants.

248

Ideally, at least one participant from each of the other four discussion groups would participate as a linking-pin member in each discussion group.

The Course

This section is a description of the course itself. It is divided into five subsections: 1) how the course began, 2) the class, 3) discussion sections, 4) individual projects, and 5) how the course ended. Heavy emphasis is placed on the class, since it was the core of the course, and in order to provide a descriptive recipe for those who would like to develop a similar course.

How the Course Began. I (Mary) remember feeling both excited and somewhat uncomfortable when I read the very honest and human introduction that the instructor had written:

> *I am a social psychologist in the making. I am trying to become a good teacher, applied researcher, and trainer. A keen desire to further understand human freedom and constraint, and the conditions under which they occur, guides much of my research. I am hindered in the process of becoming a competent social psychologist by various fears and actual or imagined inadequacies, and helped by above average intelligence, persistence, and careful planning. This is my twentieth year as a student. After grade school I was mostly bored or angry in the student role. Most of my student experience after high school has been in what felt like pretty controlling and stifling situations. I have often felt unseen, unheard and uncared for in the student role. I am frustrated and/or bored when others are consistently superficial with me, or only pretend to hear me; and I am unhappy with myself when I am unable to be open about myself, or when I am unable to hear someone who needs to be understood. I'm scared of the bomb, people who don't hear me but have influence over me, and*

being rejected. I hate the Vietnam war, dishonesty, cruelty
and people who don't feel they are obligated to meet their
commitments. Overall, I am a rich man—rich with a striving,
struggling, but meaningful present, and rich with the prospect
of becoming more competent, developing a more balanced
life, and growing more as a person in the future.

Even after two class meetings I was confused and lost about what I
would do in the course, but I was developing somewhat of an understanding of what the course could offer and what it would be like.
I felt that I might really like it.

From Instructor Perspective. I (Karl) expected the course to require
more initiative and responsibility than most students were accustomed
to. They would be required to make major choices and set major
goals for themselves.

It would also employ learning processes which might be frightening
at first, e.g. self-examination exercises, small group discussions, role-
plays, and so on. Finally the focus would be as much on emotional
(affective) learning as on intellectual learning. As a result of these
things I expected students to go through an initial stage of confusion
and low level anxiety. I expected these feelings to be expressed as
hostility toward me and the course design.

I planned to smooth entry into the course by 1) circulating a
written course introduction on the' first day, 2) planning the first
"classes" so that they helped students move gradually into the processes and issues of the course, 3) soliciting as much feedback as
possible from students and discussion leaders, and flexibly evolving
the class design in the light of the feedback, and 4) paying special
attention to management of the anxiety level. I hoped that these
things would help the class move to a lower anxiety level by the
third or fourth week of class.

The Class

Originally this section was a description of what occurred class-by-class. The material has been condensed for this chapter to include the following topics: hammer analogy, class theory, class democracy, class games, administration reaction to class, and student self-evaluation. To maintain some perspective of the timing involved we have indicated from which class the material came. For instance, (6) indicates material from the sixth class meeting. Mary is primarily responsible for the class material and it is written from her perspective.

The class consisted of twelve 2-hour weekly meetings and the outside work assigned in them. Three of the course objectives were pursued in oscillating cycles throughout the course: 1) develop content knowledge in educational psychology, 2) develop research skills, and 3) develop application skills.

Hammer Analogy. Karl explained that creativity can be inhibited due to anticipated evaluation. (7) As he said that, I was thinking of the discussion I had with Karl a few days earlier. We were talking about what happens to kill creativity as people grow up, what perhaps had limited mine. He used an analogy that really got to me:

> *As soon as Tommy is born, he begins exploration. Perhaps one day, when he is two, he decides to explore the ground by tasting it. Mother tells him that he* can't do that. *One day, as a five-year old in kindergarten, Tommy draws a picture of a house and trees, a picture that he really likes—the house is purple, the sky is orange, the trees are blue and the grass is yellow. Teacher tells him that his picture is* wrong— *the sky is blue and the grass is green, etc. In the fourth grade he writes a story about his dog and is told that he didn't do it the way he was* supposed to *and must do it again. Inside Tommy's head a hammer is growing, a hammer made up of*

251

*the expectancy that he will feel hurt or be rejected or be
"bad" if he does something that is "different" or unique.
In high school he ignores the hammer for a little while
and writes a poem instead of a paper for English class.
Bang—the hammer falls on his head and he gets a failing
grade because a paper was required; and furthermore the
"form" of the poem was bad. Finally Tom enters college*
knowing *that skies are always blue, grass is always green
and learning is doing what you are told to do. Creativity
is either hiding from being hammered on, or has been
hammered to a point of almost total nonexistence.*

To be able to get in touch with and use creative powers it is helpful to brainstorm first and then go back to choose and evaluate alternatives.

A conflict may arise between an intrinsically meaningful goal and an extrinsically meaningful goal (adequately capturing one's feelings in a poem versus writing a poem which has the correct "form"). It may also be between an intrinsically meaningful goal and a goal which was once extrinsically meaningful, but which has become internalized. For example, one may want to express one's negative feelings about a class to one's teacher, but may also have a built-in expectation that such expression would bring punishment from the teacher, and therefore have a learned goal of keeping quiet to avoid punishment. The result is not only conflict, deadness, and lack of spontaneity and creativity in that area. It may also generalize to the point where deviancy from the current dogma and accepted ways of doing things is so deeply feared that it is as if the person carries a little authority figure around in his head, and is hit with a hammer by that figure for even thinking deviant thoughts. When this happens, as I believe it often does in American education, the person becomes a cripple.

252

We tried to design this course in such a way that it would help the students lose the hammers in their heads as quickly as possible. Creative and spontaneous growth and learning cannot occur at an optional rate until the hammers are gone. Only in their absence can unity experiences occur.

Class Theory. We moved into the main exercise of the day, the scoring of T.A.T. tests for n achievement. (3) Through a short talk by Karl last week and through the readings assigned for last week, the class had had some exposure to scoring n achievement. This week people would really get a chance to understand n achievement and its scoring by a group scoring process. Using a scoring manual[17] each member would take a turn reading his story and then scoring it with the whole group through a mutual decision-making process. The manual was to be used as a guide, but when it was inadequate the group was to make an arbitrary decision and write it down to be used as a criterion for future scoring problems. This process would help each individual develop his understanding of achievement motivation while it produced a fairly reliable score for him.

After people had scored their T.A.T.'s, Karl asked them to take some time to process what had happened in the group, focusing on how effective the group had been in completing the task and maintaining individual morale.

Karl then spent about 10 minutes trying to tie together ideas about achievement motivation—what the scores meant, what the motivation syndrome was and what highly motivated people were like. He used a profile of scores for businessmen to help people understand where their scores put them in a comparative way.

As I looked around I saw that many people were embarrassed about their low scores. One or two people challenged the validity of the

[17]Behavioral Science Center

scoring system, almost angrily. Karl responded by hearing their embarrassment and anger and explaining that the scores could best be used as a source of information. Each person would have to decide how to interpret it, in the light of his own experiences and his understanding of the way the test was developed and validated.

Karl asked people to write down their scores, their feelings about them, and their ideas about how they fit with their pictures of themselves as they really were and as they would like to be.

He then pointed out that one pathway to enhancing our achievement motivation was to learn to use the scoring categories in one's thinking. He suggested that everyone test their understanding of the scoring system by writing another story, as high on n achievement as possible. After the stories were written he asked us to score the story, multiply by six, and compare our scores from now and before. Almost everyone had shown that they knew the concepts well enough to write a high n achievement story. The class as a group seemed relieved.

Class Democracy. The class was arranged to make use of a coparticipative design. This questionnaire was designed to lead to revision of the class if desired.

Questionnaire (4)

1. Would you prefer to continue with our current "class" design during the second half of the semester, or would you prefer to break into three groups, each using a different approach to the same subject matter?

   Check One:

   Current Design ___

   Three Groups ___

2. If we broke into three groups, which group would you prefer:
   a. Staff-designed reading, discussion,

   Check One:

   a. _____

254

brief paper writing group.
b. Participant-designed reading, discussion,   b. _____
brief paper writing group.
c. Instructor-designed experiential learning,   c. _____
reading, discussion, brief paper writing
group.

(7) Karl suggested that we switch to an examination of the question, "What is wrong with the class so far?" and then to, "What can we do to change the class?" We would do this by dividing into small groups and then brainstorming. Karl gave two words of advice: say anything that comes into your head without censoring or evaluating it, no matter how wild it might sound; and don't criticize anyone's ideas. The class broke into groups and began writing their thoughts about "What is wrong with the class so far?" on newsprint. Then they did the same thing with the question, "What can we do to change the course?" Finally each group put its newsprint full of thoughts in the front of the room for everyone to see. It looked as if a few people were anxious about sharing these "criticisms." Some of the faults listed were "less structure—let the groups decide time limits—interests will vary," "bigger classroom," "redundancy of material," "we've only learned one theory and way of looking at things—DeCharm's and Jackson's course should be the title of the course," "Karl is a lousy lecturer, technically." Some suggestions were, "being in smaller groups," "more solution-oriented work," "more role-playing," "turn out lights with music in the background," "more practical experience," "majority rule," "less written work," "hear ye, we, the members of groups local 5 demand that the grading system be decided earlier in the semester!"

The class also designed their own goals for learning and their own criteria for evaluation.

Karl began the body of the fifth class session by modeling a triad goal-setting discussion. Theresa was the "listener" who tried to tune into what the "goal-sharer" Karl was saying, hearing not only the thoughts but also the feelings, and also trying to help by clarifying and concretizing goals. Bob was the "process observer" who made process comments and other helping comments as needed. Karl talked about one of his goals, that of finishing his dissertation. As the class began to understand what a triad goal-setting discussion was, the modeling was stopped. Karl then asked the class to complete the final phase of the basic motivation sequence by discussing their goals in triads with two other people whom they felt comfortable with, using the model he had demonstrated. After a few minutes, each person switched roles until everyone had a chance to play all three. A help in this would be the goal-setting manual people had filled out during the last week.[18]

When the triads were finished, Karl moved to a process of trying to apply motivation and Origin-Pawn concepts to the classroom. First everyone wrote their answers to 1) What is an Origin? 2) What is a Pawn? 3) How can a teacher help a student to become more of an Origin? These answers were handed in. Then Karl suggested that every triad combine with another triad to form a group of six and discuss how grading or evaluation systems could be handled to help students become more motivated Origins in their classroom. He stressed that this problem included not only the creation of an Origin evaluation system but also the creation of an Origin classroom.

Karl handed out a "Proposed Procedure for Developing an Evaluation System for Grading Purposes," and asked everyone to read it for the next class.

---

[18]Instructor's note: The goal-setting manual was a deeply significant event for many students in the class. Several students who had major goal-conflicts or were upset and afraid of confronting the necessity of taking responsibility for their own future came in to talk to me.

After class I read through the feedback cards. A few people had disliked the goal-setting process. One person, for example, wrote: "I *hate* those goal sheets! They were totally annoying and I feel they are useless. I am *very* unmotivated."

The next day I read the "Proposed Procedure for Developing an Evaluation System for Grading Purposes" which suggested that the evaluation system help with two decisions. It suggested that the credit/no credit decision be made on the basis of whether the student had completed all the required work and included a proposed list of requirements for our consideration. For the decision about what grade a person would get, it proposed a democratic system for evolving a set of criteria and procedures:

Given the assumption that it is your responsibility and right to design and implement your own grading-system, the staff feels that it is our responsibility to facilitate your process of doing so in any way we can, without trying to influence you toward any particular outcome, or participating in the final vote. We propose the following steps to help you generate a grading system, and to allow you to explore experientially the basic issues in evaluation.

1. Generate basic issues in class for discussion later.

2. Discussion of basic issues in discussion sections, as a part of the regular routine, or separately, as your group decides.

3. Discussion section formulate a concrete proposal or set of proposals, rank-ordered in terms of preference.

4. Discussion section select one or two people to represent group and see that their ideas are embodied in the final alternatives. This person may or may not include the discussion leader, at your option.

5. Representatives meet with the staff to share proposals and pool them into a set of alternatives that can be voted upon. (Staff function here is facilitative only.)

6. Proposed alternatives will be typed up and distributed, with ballots, to all class members.

7. Class members will vote for the alternative they prefer.

8. Representatives will count the ballots and transmit the results to the members of the course.

Discussion sections desiring to propose changes in the procedure outlined are asked to do so when the grading issue is discussed.

Some key issues, probably overlapping those we will generate in class and relevant to your discussion as you evolve your proposals follow: 1) What is the purpose of a grading or evaluation system? 2) How can such a system facilitate learning? 3) How can such a system inhibit learning? 4) What are the advantages and disadvantages of staff evaluations? 5) What are the advantages and disadvantages of self-evaluation? 6) What is the most growth-producing evaluation system? (Jackson, 1970 d)

As he had handed out and explained the proposal for a grading system procedure, Karl had asked each discussion section to spend time in the next week or so to discuss both the procedure proposal and the grading system per se. They were charged to approve or disapprove the procedure (if they disapproved, they were to suggest an alternative), and then to formulate a comprehensive grading system proposal.

Class Games. To insure the learning that results from personal involvement, Karl evolved and borrowed some games for use in the class design. The Origin-Pawn exercise described at the beginning

258

of this chapter is one example. At the second class session I noticed people going out and back into the room one by one. I was really curious about what was happening so I asked Bob, one of the discussion leaders, who told me there was a ring toss game in the hall. It was used in three different situations to help people examine their risk-taking strategies, a part of the motivation syndrome. He explained that after everyone was finished throwing four rings outside the room it would be brought back into the classroom and everyone would play once more. Finally, a scaled monetary incentive would be added and anyone who wanted to play could do so for a dime.[19]

The small group discussions seemed to be nearing an end and the discussion leaders brought in the ring toss game. It was fascinating for me to see the different reactions of people. Sue stood only 3 feet from the peg, smiled at the class and dropped on all four rings. Joe stood all the way back at 21 feet and just threw them, missing them all. Tim paced back and forth until he found a place that looked tough but comfortable, turned to the peg with much concentration and threw his rings, getting one on.

After everyone was through participating we moved into five groups to discuss the experience. The discussion leaders and Karl guided the discussions. We focused on the experience first, and then on the different approaches to risk-taking manifested in the game. Some people had challenged themselves by throwing from a moderate-risk position. Most of these people had been in a "motivated state" in the sense that they had been conflict free, polarized toward getting the rings on to test their own ability without showing much concern for the impressions they were making on the group. These people had not been affected by moving from a private to a public version of the game or by the money incentive. Other people stood either

[19]See Shea and Jackson (in press) for a detailed description and explanation of the ring-toss game and other games, discussions, and lecturettes in the individual motivation and leadership training aspects of the course.

very close to the post or very far away. They seemed to be more concerned with making a good impression on the group than getting the rings over. It was as if they didn't enjoy tossing the rings for the sake of exploring their own abilities or developing their skill. They seemed to have used the game as a means of getting indirect acceptance (Putney and Putney, 1964) from the other people.

Karl summarized some of the different ways people had approached the game, and the experiences they had reported. Then he pointed out that people with high levels of achievement motivation tend to take moderate risks, and challenged us to use our behavior and experiences in the game as a source of information about ourselves as motivated people.

Stephanie brought out some blindfolds and informed us that we were going to have a blindfold walk. (6) Half of the class would be blindfolded and half would be guides. Everyone would go and explore outside. I was really excited about the idea. When people had their blindfolds on we moved out. Down in front of the library John, a guide, was grabbing Sue every few seconds as she tried to explore. He kept on insisting that he would help her and finally led her away. Joe was leading Tim, although Joe seemed to be just wandering around and talking to everyone else. I felt a twinge of pain as Tim wandered off into a tree with Joe standing talking to Ray. Tim sounded pretty angry and a little shaken as he told Joe to get over to him. Lisa and Harriet seemed to be enjoying themselves running around on the grass and talking to other people. They were trying to see if Harriet, who was blindfolded, could recognize directions and people without seeing them. As I got closer to them, Harriet tried guessing who I was. Lisa gave her help when she needed it and after a few seconds she guessed correctly. In a little while it was time to go back to class. There Karl focused on different experiences that people had had in their roles and pointed out that too much help or too little help from the guide created different feelings from just the right amount of help. He suggested that people's experiences in the game could be used as a source of information about themselves as leaders or as autonomous explorers.

Before he gave the next assignment Karl summarized some of his own feelings as they related to the idea of loosening the reins. "Loosening the reins" (DeCharms, in press) refers to the process in which a teacher *gradually* allows students to take more and more responsibility, being careful not to give them so much all at once that they are paralyzed with anxiety, and yet giving them the responsibility when they were ready for it. Problems often came up for the teacher during this process.

These problems boiled down to fears—fears that if the class were trusted to do its own thing and express itself openly, members might reject the teacher or choose to "go away," leaving him feeling alone and useless. There was also the fear that a person would, if he ventured alone, fall or even hurt himself. Then there were fears of losing control or being rejected by other staff members because the class chose a course of action inconsistent with the curriculum. These problems might keep teachers from sharing control with students—from allowing students to be Origins. But if teachers could own the fears and then take the risk of loosening the reins anyway, they would be helping Origins grow.

Karl read the following directions to the whole group: (8)

> *In a moment I'm going to give each group a task to perform. Each group is to make five complete puzzles out of the materials I'll give you. The objective is to complete the puzzles before the other two groups do. Each of you will be given a packet of materials to use in your group's puzzle.*
>
> *Before we start, let me make two rules of the game clear. First, you may not speak during the task. Any kind of non-verbal communication, however, is O.K. Second, no member*

may take a puzzle piece from another member without
his (nonverbal) permission . . . i.e., no grabbing. Each
group should pick a leader now, and I'll give the leader
additional information.

Then each group of five nonverbally picked a leader who was sent
for instructions. After the leaders had returned, the game began.
Since I was the outside observer in general, I also was an observer
for one bunch of three groups. As I walked around looking at the
different groups beginning their puzzles, I felt like laughing. The
first group I watched was Lisa's group. All four of the members
were busy trying to figure out the puzzle. Lisa was staring around
in space, looking as if she was enjoying a beautiful day in the park.
When after a few minutes she put her head down on the floor and
closed her eyes, the nonverbal reactions of the other members
seemed to suggest that they were irritated. Kathy tapped on her
shoulder and hummed a "Come on, you're our leader," noise. Lisa
sat up and just shrugged her shoulders. At that point, I moved on
to another group. Just as I sat down to watch Bill's group, the
leaders were called out again. Everybody waved goodbye to Bill
and continued working. They all seemed to be enjoying themselves
although they looked frustrated with the puzzles. Harriet was hum-
ming little songs absentmindedly as she passed pieces to others and
received pieces. When Bill got back, he signaled that he had some
new information. Everybody clapped, and then, together, they
started to figure out what the information was and how it would
help.

I got up to go and watch the third group and passed Lisa's group.
They had succeeded in moving the circle in such a way that they
totally excluded her physically. She looked a little lost. I approached
the third group, Joe's group, and almost decided to go back to one of
the other two. Joe had crawled into the middle and was doing the
puzzle himself. Phil looked as if he was ready to hit John. Dianne
was outside of the group staring at what other groups were doing.

262

The only one who looked even somewhat comfortable was Tom. As I got back to Bill's group I heard Phil shout, "Bastard!" and throw the puzzle pieces all over Joe.

Finally the game was over. We reformed into larger discussion groups and the discussions went on for a long time. When they were finished, Karl explained the "Squares Game" and the three different forms of leadership—democratic, laissez-faire, and author-itarian.

Each of the leaders chosen by the groups had been given a leader-ship role to play. In my group, Lisa had been asked to be laissez-faire, Joe had been asked to be authoritarian and Bill, democratic. They had all been given the same information and had been asked to deal with imparting that information according to the leadership role that had been assigned them. He pointed out what happened under the three different leadership conditions. The key point that interested me was that the democratic groups finished first, and had more fun than the other two. Karl then discussed motive arousal under the three leadership conditions (achievement motivation arousal in the democratic, affiliation and power arousal, respectively, in the laissez-faire and authoritarian groups).

Karl noted that we could look at discipline through a role play situ-ation that he and the discussion leaders had created. (9) It was a role play of what might happen between two students and a teacher and a principal who were both "hung up" on control and "appear-ances" during lunchtime. Tom played the boy who *had to* see his girlfriend because they had had a fight the night before. Lisa played his girlfriend who was in the lunchroom where Tom was not supposed to be. Kathy played the teacher-lunchroom proctor who was con-cerned with keeping up the "appearance" of order at all cost. Joe was the principal who didn't really care what happened as long as he continued to be looked on as a "good" principal with no problems in "his" school. It seemed like the people who were playing the roles had trouble really getting into it, maybe because the class was laughing a lot. After the first four people were finished, other people tried it. Then everyone divided into groups of six with at least one participant from the role plays and, using a discussion guide which stressed examining the feelings and needs of each role, the groups talked about what had happened. It seemed like a lot of people were getting something helpful out of the whole thing.

During the eleventh class we all went outside to take part in the High School Game (Borofski, 1969). It was a role play situation of a high school in which the whole class took part. People were either teachers, deans, the principal, or students. Within the student roles, each student was given an IQ which he was "stuck with." The teachers had classes, and students went from class to class. The three teachers played authoritarian, laissez-faire, and democratic roles, respectively. Each teacher gave grades or points to the students in their classes, but the amount of points a student could get was restricted by his IQ. That was the structure, for the most part. What happened after that was determined by each player. Most of the class found this a really valuable and enjoyable experience. I came to understand more about what a student must feel like, why he might do some of the things he does, and I also got a startling look about the way I had approached learning, especially during my first 12 or 14 years of school.

Administration Reaction to the Class. The administration of the Department of Educational Psychology gave some negative feedback to Karl on his approach to learning, curriculum, and evaluation. Several students had reported to a department administrator that they were alarmed by the course introduction and the structure (or lack of it). There was concern about the use of students as discussion leaders and about the possibility that they might have power to influence grades, as well as confusion about the evaluation procedures which had been suggested. As a result of this feedback, Karl issued a statement clarifying the roles of the discussion leaders and making clear that they had no discretionary powers. He also assured the administration and students that the course would cover the content areas discussed in the catalogue.

As a result of the controversy about the class content and procedures, some students expressed their concern that the class model be continued by formulating a petition which was read at the close of the semester. The petition read, in part:

We, the undersigned, would like to express a strong desire to see certain aspects of Educational Psychology 405, Section 1, incorporated into the course which will be taught next semester. This course, which is based upon a theory of experiential learning, seems to be of great value to those of us wishing to go into fields of education, psychology, etc. which by their very nature require self-awareness and self-knowledge. This theory of learning seems to deviate from the more traditional approach of teaching Educational Psychology.

Two basic elements of Mr. Jackson's course—the coparticipative approach from which comes peer-group learning and the three-part design of the course (a 2-hour class, a discussion group with student discussion leaders and individual projects) have established a compromise between the demands of the curriculum and individual desires. These two basic elements have allowed us, as students, the necessary freedom to influence course changes and to pursue our individual interests. The idea of experiencing, within the classroom, actual incidents that will confront us in the future has been extremely beneficial. It has helped to create an atmosphere of friendship and trust within a class of sixty people.

Student Self-Evaluation. At three times during the semester the students evaluated themselves and the course in writing. Space considerations do not permit inclusion of their statements here. The questions used to guide their evaluations were "Why do I want to take this course?" and "What do I want to get out of it?" They followed the same basic process that they had used to look at "Who am I?"—writing, discussing in pairs, and finally discussing in small groups. A majority of people prefaced their answer with some form of, "I signed up for this course because it was required . . . ."

Instead of taking a midterm exam, everyone filled out a manual during the sixth class session. The manual (Jackson, 1970 e) was designed to 1) help students summarize and objectify the more differentiated self-pictures that they had developed in the first part of the course, 2) help them assess their progress in the class to date, and 3) help the staff evaluate its effectiveness to date. The manual was divided into four sections: 1) Who am I? 2) Strategies of Influence, 3) Goal Progress-Reports, and 4) Course Evaluation. Each section began with a brief statement and a series of guiding questions followed by blank pages for student responses.

I (Mary) went to Karl's office during the next week (13) to read the final evaluation manuals. They contained self-examination and personal planning sections designed to help the students apply what they had learned during the last part of the course to their own lives. Completing these sections was the final assignment for the class portion of the course.

Self-Examination Section

This section had eight parts. Each part began with a statement and a few guiding questions written by Karl; the student was asked to respond by writing in the manual. Part 1, for example, was introduced with:

Who am I as a creative innovator? Our brainstorming session during class 7 gave you an opportunity to take a look at the degree to which you were free versus inhibited in generating and sharing creative ideas. Write a paragraph below describing yourself as a creative innovator. These guiding questions may help you:

1) How free do I feel to express unusual or unpopular ideas in a group?

2) How spontaneous am I?

3) What could I do to become more free to express myself in a group and more spontaneous?

Part 2 of the evaluation manual focused on interpersonal communication skills; Part 3 on coparticipation skills. Part 4 asked the students to answer the question, "Who am I as an applier of theory?" Part 5 asked, "Who am I as an establisher of educational objectives, means of attaining them, and modes of evaluating the outcome?" Part 6 was introduced with: "Who am I as an astute observer of groups and classrooms, from the experiential point of view? Retrospecting on your experiences in the High School Game, how effective were you in seeing the real objectives or people in high school settings (students, teachers, administrators)? How could you become a more sensitive and accurate observer of such groups?" Part 7 asked, "Who am I as a change agent?" Part 8 focused on "Who am I as a potential teacher or helper of others?"

Figure 1 shows one student's final discussion-section evaluation:

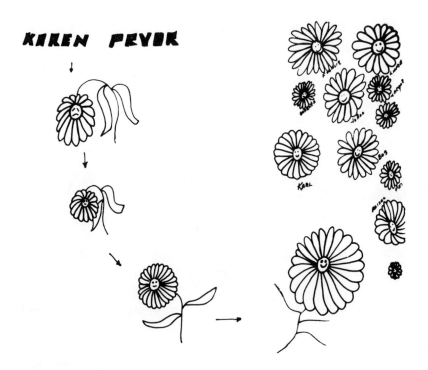

FIGURE 1. Karen Pryor's Final Discussion-Section Evaluation

Discussion Sections

Students spent about half of their time working on the class portion of the course or an alternative. The other half of their time was equally divided between a discussion section and an individual project or their alternatives. These two nonclass aspects of the course were made possible by the student discussion leaders.

The discussion leader role was defined for students in the class via the following written statement:

> *Discussion leader qualifications, responsibilities, and authorities are presented below. You are encouraged to suggest any changes you like in their responsibilities and authorities.*

Qualifications. The student teaching assistants were selected from among the students in last semester's course. They have at least as much content knowledge of educational psychology as the typical person who has completed the course. They are not *"experts"* on educational psychology content, nor do they purport or need to be. They are still learning, like you, the instructor, and every true scholar. They are *trained* to perform their functions and fulfill their responsibilities in the course. They are qualified to play the facilitative role they've been assigned.

Responsibilities. Each student teaching assistant has the following responsibilities: 1) to guide and facilitate the processes of his or her discussion section, 2) to help students who want to adopt an alternative to the discussion section to select, concretize and implement that alternative, 3) to help students select, concretize, and implement their individual projects, 4) to play a facilitative role in the class as needed, 5) to act as a full coparticipant in the middle management group when it meets, and 6) to advise and help the instructor in fulfilling his responsibilities for the course as needed.

Authority. Each discussion leader has been assigned authority commensurate with his or her responsibilities. This includes the authority to act as a full coparticipant in staff, class middle management, and discussion groups, and the authority to be sure that his or her discussion section and individual members of his or her section to meet the process requirements of the course. It includes the authority to find and allocate resources for the discussion section and its individual members. It includes the authority to

accept whatever responsibilities the discussion section
wants to assign. (Jackson, 1970 b, p. 3, 5)

Process Requirements Within the Discussion Sections. Each discussion section was to formulate its goals, means, and mode of outcome evaluation on the first day it met. The discussion leader was to take the responsibility of writing these out in a one-page description and the staff to reproduce them and circulate them among the discussion sections.

Alternatives to Discussion Sections. Two classes of alternatives could be selected in lieu of one of the five discussion sections. Any group of students could design a discussion section of its own, without a staff discussion leader, or any of the alternatives described below could be substituted by individuals for discussion section participation. In the former case, a staff member was to be assigned to the discussion group as an adviser and the group was to be required to keep him informed of its activities by fulfilling the same process requirements as those in the regular discussion sections. Individual alternatives to discussion section participation included:

1) Attend a weekend "T" group, encounter group, communication workshop, psychodrama workshop, or teacher skills development workshop, or the equivalent, and complement that experience as needed with readings and/or writing.

2) Read and summarize any six books from the reading list or any other six books related to educational psychology. Summaries must be in writing.

3) Read and summarize any educational psychology textbook.

4) Do a field or library research project.

5) Do something else which fits your goals and needs better than any of the above.

Individual Learning

The following statement about individual learning experiences
appeared in the course introduction:

> *Each student will design an individual learning experience for
> himself, with the help of his discussion leader. Any project
> or experience is acceptable, as long as it meets the process
> requirements of the course. Any of the listed alternatives to
> the discussion section, for example, would be acceptable proj-
> ects. You may work individually, in pairs, or in small groups.
> You may attend a second discussion section in lieu of the in-
> dividual project. You may also combine your individual learn-
> ing experience with an alternative (or alternatives) to one of
> the other aspects (or both of the other aspects) of the course.*

As for the other aspects of the course, a process requirement procedure of goal-setting and planning, midsemester program report
and final evaluation was specified in detail as well.

Each student relied upon his discussion leader to help him formulate, implement, and evaluate his individual learning experience.
Usually this process began with an initial individual meeting, after
which the student completed the first phase of the process requirement by writing out his goals, means, mode of evaluation, and
mode of sharing. The discussion leader then read this statement
and helped the student clarify and elaborate it before moving into
action. During the semester the student used his discussion leader
as a resource person, and at the end of the course shared the outcome of the project with the discussion leader.

A wide variety of learning experiences was selected by students
in the course. The following brief characterizations, taken from
the midsemester information-sharing booklet, illustrate this diversity:

271

1. *Motivation—tutoring.*
2. *Readings—studies of teaching, learning, adjustment; problem of low-income children.*
3. *Observations of high school counselors.*
4. *Tutoring with motivational change techniques.*
5. *Variations in child motivation—free settings versus school setting.*
6. *American Indian educational problems and recommendations.*
7. *Attending Rosenberg's clinic for teachers.*
8. *Wide range of readings.*
9. *Setting up innovative music program in which child makes his own instrument; getting grant to finance program.*
10. *Rapid reading program for GED tutee.*
11. *Couples communication workshop.*
12. *Deaf education research paper.*

How the Course Ended—Looking Back and Ahead

Leaving or closing any group which has become close and in which people have grown and shared together is always sad, and sometimes traumatic. There was no artful plan for an "ending," although there were several opportunities for all of us to punctuate our experiences together. We would like to share part of Karl's parting statement with you, along with Mary's feelings about the end and the beginning. Here are a few excerpts from Karl's statement:

> *If I could turn you on,*
> *if I could drive you out of your wretched mind,*
> *if I could tell you I would let you know.*
> —R. D. Laing
> (THE POLITICS OF EXPERIENCE, 1967, p. 138)

> *I sit at my desk wondering how I can tell you what I know.*
> *I'm very tired and discouraged now, after hours of trying with*
> *only limited success. I am troubled by the realization that I*

cannot tell you all I wanted to tell. I can only share a few specifics with you, and tell you here my experiences as a teacher trying to accept that you will go away. Regrets about the things I'd like to have done better plague me, along with a deep satisfaction over the overall course of events between us. As I think of you in the future I am curious, in some cases joyful, and in some apprehensive. I am not frustrated because I failed. I don't think I failed, but I am frustrated because I now care about you enough to want more for you than I could give in the time we've been together.

One way for me to punctuate this statement and the course is to give you my overall reactions to the course. I've learned a lot from it, intellectually and emotionally. I've enjoyed it—though it has often been painful for me. I'm happy that many of you also found it useful. I hope to develop what we've done into a better course in the future. Overall, I'm happy because I see the course as a "beginning" for me and for many of you.

Mary recaptured some of the feelings she had at the end of the course in these words:

Looking back on the last day of class is as strange to me as looking back on the first day, but for different reasons. I was afraid on that last day, afraid of life as I had been on the first day, afraid that the life I felt growing in me would stop growing, afraid that the growing desire and ability to really learn would disappear, afraid that the autonomy that I was developing would shrink back into pawnishness, afraid that Karl and other people that I cared about would go away and I would never see them again.

I (Karl) sit a year after the course ended, looking back and ahead. On June 1, 1970, I received a memo from the director of the institute in which I had taught the course:

> *I wanted to express my deep appreciation for the outstanding job you have done with Education 405 this year. Attached is a memo which I recently received from several of your students.* [This was the petition the students had submitted to the administration.] *I'm not sure what I'm going to do with my copy of it, but I do believe it will be useful in future efforts to incorporate your techniques into the course on a regular basis.*

The dean of the college officially legitimated the discussion leader role and thanked the discussion leaders for their efforts. A few excerpts from his letter to each discussion leader follow:

> *In view of the innovative and, I gather, successful nature of your activities, I should like to record your appointment as Honorary Discussion Group Leader for the spring semester . . . Among these opportunities which higher education must more fully investigate is the use of highly qualified undergraduates in discussion sections. Your willingness to participate in such an endeavor is to be commended and I should like to express the appreciation of the College of Arts and Sciences for your contribution in this regard.*

I (Karl) have learned a great deal from teaching this course. I learned that it could be done, and that I could do it; and this has given me the courage to explore new approaches to teaching and organizational development during the last year. Somehow the overall process has also cooled my anger toward existing educational institutions and educators. Instead I now feel a new determination to help them understand and grow, complemented by a genuine appreciation for the strengths and beauty hidden within them, waiting to be nurtured to full flower.

Mary and I realize that this course was based on many assumptions which demand further empirical test. The theory section of the paper reflects a number of these and we are planning to test some of them in the near future. We need all the help we can get, and hope that others will provide us with feedback and will research some of our important assumptions.

Finally, a note of optimism. We believe that motivation training would become unnecessary if our public schools were operated coparticipatively. Motivation training is in a way a rehabilitation technique, and such rehabilitation would be unnecessary if the damage weren't done in the first place. There are many signs which indicate that a revolution is beginning in American educational practice, and that the movement which embodies that revolution is rapidly expanding. Mary and I are hopeful that this movement will be successful, and are dedicated to making it so. We believe that learning is being and that being is learning.

The authors are indebted to George Brennan, Lee Sa Beth Jackson, and Peter Lippincott for their comments and suggestions during the preparation of this paper. The senior author is also indebted to Theresa Greenberg, Stephanie Reass, Bob Yeum, and Cheryl Zwick for their help as discussion leaders during the course we describe here.

References

Allen, Colburn, Daniels, DeCharms, Elkins, Temlinson, Van Wessen, Wirth. Report of ad hoc committee on undergraduate education. Unpublished report. Washington University, St. Louis, 1970.

Alschuler, A. S. "How to Increase Motivation Through Climate and Structure." Technical Report #8, Achievement Motivation Project, Harvard University, 1968.

275

Amidon, E. J. and Hough, J. B. **INTERACTION ANALYSIS AND THEORY RESEARCH AND APPLICATION.** Reading, Mass.: Addison-Wesley, 1962.

"A scoring system for need for achievement." Unpublished manual. Behavioral Science Center. Cambridge, Mass.

Berger, P. and Luckman, T. **THE SOCIAL CONSTRUCTION OF REALITY: A TREATISE ON THE SOCIOLOGY OF KNOWLEDGE.** New York: Doubleday, 1967.

Borofski. "The High-School Game." Unpublished manuscript. Harvard University, 1969.

Bridgman, P. W. **THE WAY THINGS ARE.** Cambridge, Mass.: Harvard University Press, 1959.

Brown, R. **SOCIAL PSYCHOLOGY.** New York: Free Press, 1965.

Buch, R. **JONATHAN LIVINGSTON SEAGULL: A STORY.** New York: Macmillan, 1970.

Coopersmith, S. **THE ANTECEDENTS OF SELF-ESTEEM.** San Francisco: W. H. Freeman, 1967.

Curtis, C. P. It's Your Law. In C. P. Curtis and F. Greenslet (Eds.) **PRACTICAL COGITATOR,** Third Edition. Boston: Houghton-Mifflin, 1962.

DeCharms, R. **MOTIVATION IN THE SCHOOLS** (in preparation).

DeCharms, R. Origins, Pawns and Educational Practice. In Lesser, G. S. (Ed.) **PSYCHOLOGY AND THE EDUCATIONAL PROCESS.** Greenview, Illinois: Scott, Foresman and Co. (in press).

DeCharms, R. **PERSONAL CAUSATION.** New York: Academic Press, 1968.

DeCharms, R. "The Making of Pawns in the Classroom." Paper presented at American Psychological Association meetings, September 1970.

DeCharms, R., Collins, J., Jackson, K. W., and Shea, D. J. "Can the Motives of Low-income Black Children Be Changed?" Symposium presented at the American Educational Research Association meetings, Los Angeles, California, February 7, 1969.

DeCharms, R., and Koenigs, K. Origin-Pawn Classroom Climate Measure and Associated Research. (Research in progress, to be summarized for publication) In DeCharms, R. **MOTIVATION IN THE SCHOOLS** (in preparation).

Deci, E. L. Effects of Externally Mediated Rewards on Intrinsic Motivation, **JOURNAL OF PERSONALITY AND SOCIAL PSYCHOLOGY,** 1971, **18**(1), 105-116.

Dewey, J. **THE SCHOOL AND SOCIETY.** Chicago: University of Chicago Press, 1916.

Dreikers, R. and Grey, L. **LOGICAL CONSEQUENCES.** Now under the title **A PARENT'S GUIDE TO CHILD DISCIPLINE.** New York: Hawthorn Books, Inc., 1970.

Garfinkel, H. **STUDIES IN ETHNOMETHODOLOGY.** Englewood Cliffs, N. J.: Prentice-Hall, 1967.

Gibson, J. T. The Learning Process. In **EDUCATIONAL PSYCHOLOGY: A PROGRAMMED TEXT.** New York: Appleton-Century Crofts, pp. 217-276, 1968.

Gouldner, A. G. **THE COMING CRISIS OF WESTERN SOCIOLOGY.**
New York: Basic Books, 1970.

Halsti, O. R. Content Analysis. In Lindvey, G. and Aronson, E.
(Eds.) **HANDBOOK OF SOCIAL PSYCHOLOGY,** Second Edition, Vol.
II. Reading, Mass.: Addison Wesley, 1969.

Harris, T. A. **I'M OK—YOU'RE OK. A PRACTICAL GUIDE TO TRANS-
ACTIONAL ANALYSIS.** New York: Harper and Row, 1969.

Harvey, O. J. "Belief Systems and Education: Some Implications
for Change." Unpublished manuscript. Boulder, Colorado: University of Colorado, 1969.

Holt, J. **HOW CHILDREN FAIL.** New York: Dell, 1964.

Huntsberry, R. "Peer-Group Learning." Unpublished paper.
Smith College.

Jackson, K. "Addendum to Course Introduction for Educational
Psychology." Unpublished paper. Washington University, St. Louis,
1970 b.

Jackson, K. "A Proposed Procedure for Developing a Grading System." Unpublished paper. Washington University, St. Louis, 1970 d.

Jackson, K. "Child Rearing Correlates of Motivation in Low Income
Black Middle School Children." Doctoral dissertation. Washington
University, St. Louis (in preparation).

Jackson, K. "Course Introduction for Educational Psychology."
Unpublished paper. Washington University, St. Louis, 1970 a.

Jackson, K. "Degrees of Freedom: Presteps to a Phenomenological Description of Experiences and Conditions of Freedom and Constraint." Unpublished manuscript. St. Louis, Mo.: Washington University, 1968.

Jackson, K. "Midsemester Progress Report Manual." Unpublished paper. Washington University, St. Louis, 1970.

Jackson, K. "Motivation for Success: Future Planning Manual." Unpublished paper. Washington University, St. Louis, 1970 c.

Jackson, K. "Review, Prospectus, and Final Evaluation Manual." Unpublished paper. Washington University, St. Louis, 1970 f.

Jackson, K. and Shea, D. Motivation Training in Perspective. To appear in Nord, W. **CONCEPTS AND CONTROVERSIES IN ORGANI-ZATIONAL PSYCHOLOGY**, Pacific Palisades, Calif.: Goodyear, 1971.

Koch, S. Behavior as "Intrinsically" Regulated: Work Notes Towards A Pre-Theory of Phenomena Called "Motivational." In M. R. Jones (Ed.), **NEBRASKA SYMPOSIUM ON MOTIVATION**. Lincoln: University of Nebraska Press, 1956.

Kohlberg, L. The Development of Moral Character and Ideology. In M. Hoffman (Ed.), **REVIEW OF CHILD PSYCHOLOGY**. Russell Sage Foundation, 1964.

Kuperman, A. "Relations Between Differential Constraints, Affect, and the Origin-Pawn Variable." Unpublished doctoral dissertation. Washington University, St. Louis, 1967.

Laing, R. D. **THE POLITICS OF EXPERIENCE.** New York: Random House, 1967.

Likert, R. **THE HUMAN ORGANIZATION: ITS MANAGEMENT AND VALUE.** New York: McGraw-Hill, 1967.

Lippitt, R. and White, R. K. The "Social Climate" of Children's Groups. In R. G. Barker, J. S. Kouning and H. F. Wright (Eds.). **CHILD BEHAVIOR AND DEVELOPMENT.** New York: McGraw-Hill, pp. 485-508, 1943.

Loevinger, J. and Wessler, R. **MEASURING EGO DEVELOPMENT.** San Francisco: Jossery-Bass, Inc., 1970.

Maslow, A. **TOWARD A PSYCHOLOGY OF BEING.** Princeton, N. J.: D. Van Nostrand, 1962.

Massiaus, B. G. and Zevin, J. **CREATIVE ENCOUNTERS IN THE CLASSROOM: TEACHING AND LEARNING THROUGH DISCOVERY.** New York: John Wiley and Sons, Inc., 1967.

McClelland, D. C. Achievement Motivation Can be Developed. **HARVARD BUSINESS REVIEW,** 1965. (Reprinted by Behavioral Science Center, Cambridge, Mass.)

McClelland, D. C. Business Drive and National Achievement. **HARVARD BUSINESS REVIEW,** July-August, 1962, 99-112.

McClelland, D. C., Atkinson, J. W., Clark, R. A., and Lowell, E. L. A Scoring Manual for the Achievement Motive. In J. W. Atkinson (Ed.), **MOTIVES IN FANTASY, ACTION, AND SOCIETY.** New York: Van Nostrand, pp. 179-204, 1958.

McClelland, D. C., and Winter, D. G. **MOTIVATING ECONOMIC DEVELOPMENT.** New York: Free Press, 1969.

McDonald, F. J. The Self-Concept. In **EDUCATIONAL PSYCHOLOGY,** Second Edition. Belmont, Calif.: Wadsworth, pp. 432-441, 1965.

Morris, V. C. **EXISTENTIALISM IN EDUCATION**. New York: Harper and Row, 1966.

Neil, A. S. **SUMMERHILL: A RADICAL APPROACH TO CHILDREARING**. New York: Hart Publishing, 1960.

Olson, J. Ready for the "Goal." Cambridge, Mass.: Behavioral Science Center, 1966.

Page, W. R. An Innovative Program for School-Alienated Adolescents. **EDUCATIONAL THERAPY**, Vol. 3, Seattle, Washington: Special Child Publications, Inc., 1972.

Plimpton, F. H. "O-P Manual: A Content Analysis Coding System Designed to Assess the Origin Syndrome." Unpublished paper: Washington University, 1970.

Polanyi, M. **PERSONAL KNOWLEDGE**. Chicago: University of Chicago Press, 1958.

Postman, N. and Weingartner, C. **TEACHING AS A SUBVERSIVE ACTIVITY**. New York: Delacorte Press, 1969.

Putney, S. and Putney, G. J. **NORMAL NEUROSIS: THE ADJUSTED AMERICAN**. New York: Harper and Row, 1964.

Rogers, C. "Some Elements of Effective Interpersonal Communication." Talk presented at the California Institute of Technology, Pasadena, California, November 9, 1964.

Rogers, C. R. **FREEDOM TO LEARN: A VIEW OF WHAT EDUCATION MIGHT BECOME**. Columbus, Ohio: C. E. Merrill, 1969.

Rosen, B. C. and D'Andrade, R. The Psychosocial Origins of Achievement Motivation. **SOCIOMETRY**, 1959, **22**, 185-218.

Rosenberg, M. B. "Basics of Communication." Unpublished manuscript. Community Psychological Consultants, St. Louis, Mo., 1968.

Rosenberg, M. B. **DIAGNOSTIC TEACHING.** Seattle, Washington: Special Child Publications, 1968.

Rosenzweig, S. Personality. In **ENCYCLOPAEDIA BRITANNICA,** Vol. 17, Chicago: William Benton, pp. 694-699, 1969.

Rotter, J. B. Generalized expectancies for internal versus external control of reinforcements. **PSYCHOLOGICAL MONOGRAPHS,** 1966, **80.**

Ruch, F. L. **PSYCHOLOGY IN LIFE.** Seventh Edition. Glenview, Illinois: Scott, Foresman and Co., 1967.

Schaefer, R. Preface. In L. Smith and B. Hudgins (Eds.) **EDUCATIONAL PSYCHOLOGY: AN APPLICATION OF SOCIAL AND BEHAVIORAL THEORY.** New York: Alfred A. Knopf, 1968.

Secord, P. and Backman, C. **SOCIAL PSYCHOLOGY.** New York: McGraw-Hill, 1964.

Shea, D. "The effects of achievement motivation training on motivational and behavioral variables." Unpublished doctoral dissertation. Washington University, St. Louis, Mo., 1969.

Shea, D. and Jackson, K. "Motivation Development Training with Teachers." In R. DeCharms (Ed.) **MOTIVATION IN THE SCHOOLS** (in preparation).

Smith, L. M. and Hudgins, B. B. **EDUCATIONAL PSYCHOLOGY.** New York: Knopf, 1964.

Stein, W. J. Exploiting existential tensions in the classroom. **TEACHERS COLLEGE RECORD,** 1969, **70**(8), 747-753.

Suchman, J. R. Building skills for autonomous discovery. **MERRILL-PALMER QUARTERLY**, 1966, **7**, 147-149.

Tharp, R. G. and Wetzel, R. J. **BEHAVIOR MODIFICATION IN THE NATURAL ENVIRONMENT**. New York: Academic Press, 1969.

Thomas, M., Goleman, D., and Goldstein, R. Scoring manual for personal and social power concerns. To appear in forthcoming book edited by D. McClelland.

Travers, J. F. Measurement and evaluation. In **FUNDAMENTALS OF EDUCATIONAL PSYCHOLOGY**. Scranton, Penn.: Intext Educational Publishers, 399-462, 1970.

Watzlawick, P., Beavin, J. and Jackson, D. **PRAGMATICS OF HUMAN COMMUNICATION: A STUDY OF INTERACTIONAL PATTERNS, PATHOLOGIES, AND PARADOXES**. New York: Norton, 1967.

Winter, D. G. "Scoring manual for n Power." Unpublished paper, 1968.

Winterbottom, M. R. The relation of need achievement to learning experiences in independence and mastery. In Atkinson, J. W. (Ed.) **MOTIVES IN FANTASY, ACTION, AND SOCIETY**. Princeton, N. J.: Van Nostrand, 453-478, 1958.

Wolff, K. H. On "surrender." In W. G. Bennis, E. S. Schein, D. Berlew, and F. I. Steele (Eds.). **INTERPERSONAL DYNAMICS: ESSAYS AND READINGS ON HUMAN INTERACTION**. Homewood, Ill.: Dorsey, pp. 44-52, 1964.

Wylie, R. **THE SELF-CONCEPT**. Lincoln, Nebraska: University of Nebraska Press, 1961.

WELSH TEACHER DEVELOPMENT CENTER: EDUCATIONAL PROGRAM

JoAnn C. Anderson, M.A.T., M.S.
Principal-Director, Teacher Development Center and
     Demonstration School
Rockford, Illinois

Sections of this article were prepared by these staff
members at the Teacher Development Center:
Joyce Holmberg, Margaret Schmidt,
Clare Almquist, Beverly Lindsey,
Betty Piotrowski, Nancy Sandberg,
Grace Donewald, Greg Houston, and
Randall Larson

This article is composed of separate presentations, reports and descriptions submitted by the staff at the Teacher Development Center. It provides a perspective of many of the programs there.

The contributors are JoAnn C. Anderson, principal-director of Welsh Teacher Development Center, Joyce Holmberg, Margaret Schmidt, Clare Almquist, Beverly Lindsey, Betty Piotrowski, Nancy Sandberg, Grace Donewald, Greg Houston, and Randall Larson.

The presence of democratic classrooms and individualized instruction as stated policy at a school within the public school system is very encouraging to me. I would like to see such alternatives to traditional modes of education in every school system.

Some of the selections in this chapter explain the philosophy at the Teacher Development Center and others describe specific programs and methods for carrying out the philosophy.

M. B. R.

WELSH TEACHER DEVELOPMENT CENTER: EDUCATIONAL PROGRAM
JoAnn C. Anderson

The purpose of the Welsh Teacher Development Center and the heart of the issues which relate to the Center directly are the individualization of instruction—or the concept of continuous progress—and a democratic learning climate.[1]

Recently someone stated that men of today are not really any better equipped to paint, in detail, the face of the future than men of the past were able to forecast our world of today. But we do know today that across the face of the future will be written the word "Education." It used to be that an education made it perhaps a little easier for one to become wealthier, or to gain more automatic status or respect from one's fellow men. But as the children of today become adults, education will be needed for survival.

At the same time, the quality of our educational systems will be directly linked to the professional competency of our teachers. And so today, we are offered opportunities in our profession to increase our competencies on the job. Other professions likewise offer similar kinds of training experiences to their people, and industries do this as well for their employees.

This, then, simply stated, is the purpose of the TDC—to offer on-the-job training for Rockford's elementary teachers. Teachers within the Center have opportunities to become familiar with new and exemplary methods and materials which will help them to plan a program of continuous academic progress for each child.

Beyond this prime purpose, we have other goals. Major among these is to provide a system which enables our teachers to share what they

[1]First given as a speech at Court Street Methodist Church, Rockford, Illinois, in April, 1968.

287

have learned with other teachers who request such sharing. This is the reason for our teachers returning to other Rockford schools at the end of the year. Also, because we have in-service classes and Center visitations for other teachers within the district, and because we talk with them and ask them to complete post-visit opinionnaire cards, we learn from them. The master teachers and I comb these cards and listen to comments; we pay close attention to what they like or approve of, what they dislike and believe is not worthwhile, or what they question. This provides a kind of continuing evaluation of our work and points the way to constant changes in the program at the Center. The personnel at the Center have no monopoly on good ideas, successful educational programs or familiarity with new materials. We try to encourage the many excellent teachers throughout our system to share with us too.

Turning to the concept of continuous progress, the best way to describe this is to show graphically the range of achievement in arithmetic in the sixth grade at Welsh.

Achievement Levels
Sixth Grade Welsh School
Iowa Tests of Basic Skills: Administered Fall, 1967

Achievement Levels	Math Concepts	Reading Comprehension
3rd	I	III
4th	⦀⦀ ⦀⦀ II	⦀⦀ ⦀⦀ I
5th	⦀⦀ ⦀⦀ ⦀⦀ ⦀⦀ IIII	⦀⦀ ⦀⦀
6th	⦀⦀ ⦀⦀ ⦀⦀ ⦀⦀ ⦀⦀ ⦀⦀ ⦀⦀	⦀⦀ ⦀⦀ ⦀⦀ ⦀⦀ II
7th	⦀⦀ ⦀⦀ ⦀⦀ ⦀⦀ ⦀⦀ IIII	⦀⦀ ⦀⦀ ⦀⦀ ⦀⦀ ⦀⦀ ⦀⦀ ⦀⦀
8th	IIII	⦀⦀ ⦀⦀ ⦀⦀ ⦀⦀ I
9th	I	IIII

This illustration is typical and occurs all over Rockford and throughout this country. It is not unusual. Too often we quote "average figures" when looking at achievement levels. But, when we look at an average, we know that half the children are below this point and half are above.

Understanding this wide range of achievement, we minimally have two options. We can place all children in the same textbook and see to it that all children cover the same amount of pages each day. On the other hand, we can use diagnostic tests, past records, and teacher observation of each child in specific learning situations to determine what skills and concepts he has mastered and what tasks he needs to do next. There are liabilities and assets to each plan.

If we place all children in the same book on the same page, all children will have covered the same material. The teacher's job will be much easier—at least superficially. Reporting to parents can be in purely objective terms—so many right equals an **A**, so many a **B**, and so on. Communication and coordination problems are cut to the bone. There will be no ambiguity about assignments; children will understand that they have a specific book to cover that year.

If, on the other hand, the continuous progress concept is decided upon, we definitely increase the teacher's task in planning. We will have problems of communication and coordination. But we also will maximize learning for each child because we take him up each step of the ladder, giving him tasks appropriate for his mental development and his achievement level. We will help each child to firmly grasp basic skills that are considered important.

When we work with the continuous progress plan we also will have more time to work with the average child because we will not have categorically lost the slow learning child and the fast learning child. Both the slow and fast learning cause problems in the traditional system because they become frustrated, bored and angry—for different reasons, but the result is often the same. So, while superficially, it would appear that the task is easier for the teacher to keep all children together on the same lesson, she will have many more problems keeping each child interested, enthusiastic, and involved in school. I'm sure you know that the reason most often given by dropouts for leaving school before acquiring a diploma is lack of interest in school.

At the Center we have chosen to develop a total program of working toward a continuous progress plan, believing that this is the way we help each child to grow and learn basic skills and knowledge.

The problem is complex, and during this first year we have in many ways come to grips with this kind of complexity, finding ways which will cut down on the teacher preparation time for such a program.

Before I leave this concept I would like to emphasize that we never have sent all children to junior high school with the same skills nor have we sent them to junior high school all ready for seventh grade work. Research tells us that the more the teacher is able to enrich the learning experience for the children, the greater the spread will be among pupils in her classroom. For years good teachers have been coping with a spread in achievement and by coping with it, have increased that spread.

Thus, the focus of the TDC is to help teachers to do a better job of meeting the educational needs of each boy and girl within a group. We do this within a learning climate that we call "democratic." This term is misleading, as most terms or labels are. Also, there is really no such thing as a *purely* democratic climate, but we use this term because it describes our emphasis.

When we speak of a democratic climate we are speaking within this context.

Children have rights and responsibilities. As they grow up, both increase. Children must learn that when the rights of one child interfere with those of another, his end. One of the major rights and responsibilities each child has is to learn. This means that adults have some obligations and so does the child. We do not ask the child in the skill subjects what he wants to do as much as what he needs to do. Each teacher helps the child to undertake appropriate study and activities. Appropriateness is based on the goals of the school, as decided by the Board of Education, and the elementary school teacher's training and education, as well as on the needs of the child.

At the Center discipline is also individualized. Our goal is to help each child, in as much as possible, to become self-disciplined. Structure, controls, freedoms, and choice of activities vary according to the issue, the maturity level of the child, and his demonstrated ability to function within certain kinds of limits.

There is a misconception that in elementary schools, or in junior high schools, standards, structure, and control are simply set by command—with magical expectations—that this will solve all of the problems in relation to the individual child and to all children. Rather, they need to be determined by a careful evaluation, on-going observation, and change of tactics.

We do have control, structure, limits, and consequences (these are not *bad* words—they are *good* words), but in relation to the individual child. Some rules and regulations are for all children, but at the same time some children require more control or less, can handle more flexible limits or must have very firm ones. We structure these as much as possible so that we maximize the learning experience of the child. Many of you would, I am sure, be surprised at the amount of time we spend helping teachers to establish good structure. You know, the major reason that teachers fail in their first year of teaching is because of their inability to set a learning climate.

Structure and control do not, however, mean lock-stepping or regimenting whole classes of children. It also does not mean that anything goes.

We try to structure in a way so that each child stays learning-oriented. We don't gain one thing in moving towards our goal if the end result of discipline is to make the educational experiences for the child so painful that it interferes with the learning process. It is almost universally accepted that if people approach an experience with enthusiasm, they take more from it.

At the same time, I have strong convictions that not maintaining an appropriate level of control can be equally damaging to learning opportunities for children.

Big task! Just think for a moment of all the children you know, and how differently each behaves.

We have not just chosen this democratic climate on the basis of a hunch, but on the basis of research. Research has looked into three basic kinds of climates. In actuality, none would be a pure example of any one of the three, unless very specifically set up that way for a specific purpose. The three are laissez-faire, democratic, and authoritarian or autocratic. Each has, by and large, specific kinds of results which one can predict.

In the laissez-faire climate in which the children have complete freedom to do as they wish with no attempt by the teacher to appraise or regulate what is going on, aggression will emerge and there will be very low morale. This happens because of idleness, poor work, a lack of a respected adult and stated goal. A lot of frustration occurs.

In the authoritarian climate in which the teacher decides everything—goal, activities, work partners—the general outcome will be a high degree of aggression, a stoppage of work the minute the teacher leaves the room or when she is not around, and a great deal of scapegoating. Out of this climate comes, by and large, displaced aggression which results in such things as vandalism.

In the democratic climate the teacher states the broad goal, and ways of reaching it are discussed with students with the assistance of the leader. The teacher gives suggestions, knowledge, and general resource material necessary to reach the goal, but the children have some decision-making in ways to reach the goal or choice of work partners. The result of the democratic climate is a high interest in work, even when the teacher is not there; pleasure from work and jobs well done; and friendliness with other children and adults. Within this climate learning and creativity are maximized.

Of course, there is no question that many talented people have emerged from an authoritarian system. One must decide if for the world of today and tomorrow the authoritarian or democratic system will produce, by and large, more of the kinds of people we need; which system will produce fewer criminals, dropouts and people generally oriented negatively toward society.

At the Center we are helping children work toward *self*-discipline, *self*-control, *self*-responsibility, believing that our work will require people who are adaptable and able to function purposefully without an authority figure standing guard. We also know from predictions being made about the future that our children are going to have to engage in a lifetime of learning. To build a school system that makes them despise learning, books, and study will not help our society nor these children individually.

Has our school system up to the present given us all of the excellence we require in this country? Will a maintenance of the status quo help us to meet some of the challenges that are facing us now: high urbanization, atomic energy turned toward destruction or toward growth

293

and health, progressively reduced relative distances between peoples and countries, changing value systems and changing family structures, and a bombardment of propaganda not just negatively oriented, but directed toward shaping people's behavior appropriate to the generic values?

I cannot tell you that the TDC has all of the answers or any of them. The program must stand on its own merit. Two years from now we shall have some data to look at beyond our initial attitudinal data which looked very good, and several years from now as the TDC children move to junior high school and senior high school and on to college, we shall have more answers.

I would like to say this, because I feel it so strongly and I think that you will agree: Whether we are idealists or pragmatists, we realize that, in our world today, there can be no one expendable child. If there is, this one dropout or school failure may not just live his own life, but may grow up to direct, in many blatant and subtle ways, our lives and the lives of our children.

TDC SLIDE-TAPE PRESENTATION SCRIPT
Joyce Holmberg

Education is like a flame. You can give it away without diminishing the one from which it came.

This symbol of the Teacher Development Center signifies the transfer of learning within the Center from one teacher to another, from teacher to child, and from child to child. In fact, everyone at the Teacher Development Center is a learner. We find excitement in learning the most effective educational techniques and learning concepts.

Sometime you, too, may have felt the loneliness of the teachers' role in the closed door classroom. Here at Welsh, we have found that a professional climate for sharing problems and solutions can make the light of education illuminate a thousand dark corners.

The TDC is not an event—it is a process of education in which *our teachers* are working toward the same goal *you* have been working toward for many years—guiding children toward independent scholarship within the framework of a democratic school and classroom.
In America, we stress the worth of the individual. For democracy to succeed, the individual must succeed within himself. To impart the flame of knowledge to this individual, we must develop with him a program of individualized instruction.

The Center approaches the individual child by combining three learning methods: independent learning, individualized learning, and personalized learning. Independent learning allows the child to make his own decisions; prepares him to assume the responsibilities of a free man. Individualized learning is guided by the teacher who acts as the decision-maker and determines what the child should do next. The common theme beneath both of these approaches is the personalization of learning: the realization that although all children have certain traits in common, each is motivated in a unique way. To individualize instruction, to catch the beat of that different drummer in the breast of each child, this is what the Teacher Development Center is all about.

Rockford's Superintendent of Schools, Dr. Thomas Shaheen,[2] has emphasized that the great problem in education today is not the lack of innovative ideas and exemplary programs, but the lack of implementation of such programs throughout the majority of school districts. Here at the Teacher Development Center, Rockford teachers are combining the old with the new to stimulate educational progress.

[2]Now Superintendent, San Francisco Unified School District.

Our TDC classrooms are housed in old buildings. Most of the more than forty elementary school buildings in Rockford are also old. For the Center program to be effective, it must be applicable to the realities found in most of our older buildings.

Just as the buildings which house the Center program represent the district as a whole, so do the children. Welsh School is located in a middle income neighborhood. All children who live within the Welsh boundaries may attend the Center. The students are a cross-section of the community.

In addition to the old, we have added something new—eight master teachers and seven factor principals from the Rockford district who spend part of each week at the Center with a view toward implementing the Center's program in their home schools, and a team of University consultants working here on a part-time basis.

We have temporarily borrowed twenty-four teachers from other schools in Rockford and have renamed them teacher-interns for their 1-year stay at the Teacher Development Center.

So, we have something old, new, borrowed, and blue: some bright blue-eyed children.

The Center is committed to encouraging each teacher-intern, master teacher, and factor principal to understand his or her individual strengths and weaknesses so that all might reach their top potential.

There is only one sure way to gain status at the Center, and that is to be a learner.

The Center, as symbolized by the passing on of knowledge, seeks to develop interpersonal relationships between administrators, teachers, and children. Let us first see how the master teacher and intern work together, remembering that each teacher is also a unique individual and is motivated differently than other teachers.

296

The basis for the master teacher's relationship with her three assigned teacher-interns is worked out in a seminar situation once every 2 weeks. These sessions allow the team to work out their educational philosophies and to think through their needs in terms of resource materials and equipment.

The master teacher monitors the classrooms of her interns and follows up her visits with a report to each intern. It is the responsibility of the intern to self-assess her teaching methods in response to the master teacher's reports.

Closed-circuit television tapes were made of the Center staff in classroom situations prior to the start of the school year. In viewing these tapes and consulting matrixes made on their behavior with children, the staff members made further self-assessments of their teaching effectiveness.

The master teacher also helps the interns to learn new techniques. Inductive teaching methods, reporting to parents and diagnostic testing and interpretation are some of the practices stressed by the master teachers to their interns. Master teachers also substitute for their interns one half day each week so that the intern is freed to learn to use new equipment and study new materials, or visit other classrooms in action at the Center or throughout the school district.

Master teachers are learners too. Several times each week they attend classes given by University consultants. In subsequent years, the master teachers will be expected to take over some of the responsibilities of the consultants.

It is the intern-teacher's responsibility to work toward a personalized learning program for each child within her classroom. She must also give her class the basic skills for which we are responsible in the elementary schools. One of the first steps for the teacher is child study, and for the young child as he begins school this is the teacher's major responsibility. The teacher learns to understand the child as she observes him, and as she develops, uses and interprets diagnostic tests designed by the Teacher Development Center staff. On this basis, as well as on the basis of information teachers have always collected, we decide what learning the child is ready to undertake and what his interests might be. We can then motivate him to move in accordance with his abilities and development. We gradually increase his responsibility for learning and his rights in learning. As the child moves into the middle elementary and intermediate years, we encourage him to do more self-assessing, more pacesetting, as well as giving him more content options. The teacher acts as a guide and a resource person, helping the child to self-assess his needs, skills, knowledge, and values.

Working together, master teachers, the teacher-interns, factor principals and University consultants are evolving a program of individualized instruction applicable to every elementary school in Rockford. The theory under which we work is old and teachers will recognize that there is nothing new in understanding individual differences. At the Center we believe, however, that only in the 1960's have we come to have the technological know-how and the educational materials to do the job that teachers have been attempting to do in Rockford for perhaps the last 30 years. The added features of our program: language masters, listening stations, commercial tapes, programmed learning materials, as well as a variety of approaches in reading, are here primarily to aid the teacher in changing his role.

The autocratic role, where the children are always told what to do, has been replaced by the democratic role where the teacher aids and encourages the child to accept responsibility for learning. On the other hand, children do not rule the classroom. Instead, they learn to operate within the rules and boundaries of a democratic school; freedom for the mind rather than freedom of behavior.

Whatever happens in accordance with our goals, happens because we set a climate in which the child trusts the teacher and the teacher trusts the child. This is the real key to the Teacher Development Center. The teachers and the children have a right, as Dr. Shaheen would say, to seek, to search, and to blunder.

At the end of 1 year in the Center, our twenty-four teacher-interns are assigned to one of the seven factor schools. They go to these schools as classroom teachers in order to spread the philosophy and program of the Center to the staff members who are interested in pursuing this kind of program. These interns will offer help to those people who wish to move toward more independent, individualized and personalized learning. At the same time, the interns will be looking to some of the staff members in the factor schools for help in further developing programs and techniques begun this year. Whether or not we are successful will depend upon the degree in which all elementary school teachers in Rockford can contribute to one another through this open door policy.

The day school began we had a visitor from England's educational system. That day she helped us to understand one of the reasons why the American educational system has such potential. She said that the greatest thing that happened at the Center that day was that we opened our doors to enable each teacher in our system to question, to share and to change.

Education is like a flame; you can give it away without diminishing the one from whom it came.

DEVELOPMENT OF INTEREST CENTERS AT WELSH TDC
Clare Almquist

Why Use Interest Centers?

If one of our goals is personalization of instruction, we must begin in the primary grades to provide opportunities for each child to make choices. Only as he makes choices and learns the importance of following through with his choice will he gain in his ability to use his time and energies well.

With the use of various interest centers in the classroom, the children are allowed some choice of activity, and they assume responsibility for keeping a record of how they have spent their time. Although some written work may be required, only a few children remain at their desks at one time, lessening the need for countless ditto sheets. Once the program is set up and the children learn how to use the centers well, the teacher will find herself freed from the age-old task of finding enough seatwork for "the other children."

However, if the goal of the teacher is to have a "you can hear a pin drop" classroom, she will not want to set up interest centers, as there is apt to be more noise, as well as more movement and action.

How will the use of interest centers aid in the personalization of instruction?

1. There is a greater variety of activities to satisfy the needs of more children. They are given the opportunity to create new meanings out of old, by putting together in rearranged forms what they alone have to offer. (Variety)

2. Each child makes a choice of how *he* wishes to spend *his* activity time. (Involvement)

300

3. Children share in the setting up and care of the centers. (Responsibility)

4. Each child is responsible for his own behavior as he works at the various centers. He must learn to control his impulses and channel them into productive activity. (Self-direction and self-control)

5. There should be no one right response in all of the activities. Children are encouraged to use their own ideas, to create with words and materials. Creativity often begins where "knowhow" ends. (Creativity)

6. Skills learned, such as writing and math, are put to use in the interest centers. (Application)

7. Children have a reason for moving around the room, meeting some of their need for action. (Purposeful movement)

8. Continuous and consistent evaluation with the children is important, both as a group and for the individual child. (Self-evaluation)

Arrangement of the room should be planned to allow freedom of movement toward and around the centers. Each center should be individually introduced to the children so that they will better understand the purposes of the centers and their responsibility in the use and care of them.

We realize the importance of setting expectations for good work habits, and holding to those expectations if full use of the centers is to be enjoyed. We recommend beginning simply with a few centers and adding centers gradually as the children are able to handle their independence and have learned to choose between those few activities that have been provided.

After the initial experience of working with many centers, the teachers will be more alert to those that challenge and more conscious of those where there may be a lack of interest. This will call for an evaluation by the children and the teachers to see where changes need to be made. Part of the usefulness of the centers is teaching self-reliance, which will be enhanced as the children recognize their needs for materials and can take care of these materials independently.

LIBRARY-LEARNING CENTER
Margaret Schmidt

The goals of the Library-Learning Center are in accordance with the goals of the TDC: to provide opportunities for children to learn in accordance with their unique needs, interests, rhythm, and learning style. At the same time, the Learning Center director and librarian have encouraged children to become responsible for their own learning as much as possible—to be self-disciplined rather than obedient: "What do I need to do?" rather than, "What are 'they' going to tell me to do now?"

The Learning Center is an avenue for widening and deepening children's interests because of the freedom of selection and the excellent range of materials.

Job Description: Learning Center Resident Teacher

Under the administrative direction of the director of the TDC, the resident teacher in charge of the Learning Center is to assume the following responsibilities:

> To create, administer, and evaluate a Learning Center which is in accordance with the philosophy and goals of the Teacher Development Center. Explicit goals for the Learning Center will be a part of this program.

302

To translate this program to paper so that it may be used by other administrators in the Rockford system as a guide to the establishment of Learning Centers in their school buildings. The program must be in keeping with the policies of the Rockford Board of Education with regard to the elementary school curriculum.

To develop a system of working with individual and/or groups of intern teachers in cooperation with resident teachers in order that each intern teacher grows in his competency of material/program/equipment selection beyond the basal program to meet the individual academic needs of individual youngsters.

To correlate her efforts with those of the librarian, particularly in the purchase and selection of library books and visual aids which would be appropriate to the needs of the children. Effectiveness in choosing materials is evidenced by the interest of the children in reading and borrowing books for home.

The Learning Center was set up in the following order:

First Week

Physical arrangement of furniture, equipment, and materials.

Preparation of individual folders for each student and clerical work necessary to organize new materials, books, and so on.

Scheduling of Learning Center time for each child in third through sixth grades; each classroom teacher was consulted.

Recruiting and staffing of Center with volunteer aides.

Second Week

The librarian and Learning Center director held orientation sessions with each class of children: proper use of card catalogue, method of withdrawing books, use of resource materials.

At this time a policy was established that any teacher might send not more than three students from his class at the same time to use the library facilities of this space. This policy has resulted in the steady use of the library with no overcrowding during the year.

Third Week

The director held 5-minute interviews with each child to determine his choice of work and to provide materials relevant to that choice.

Fourth Week

Learning Center was in full operation.

There seemed to be two scheduling possibilities for the Learning Center: 1) a specific time for a complete class to attend the Center or 2) approximately eight students from three different classes being scheduled at a specific time 4 days each week. Alternative 2) was chosen, believing that this plan was more in keeping with the nongraded goals of the TDC. At the same time, this plan would enable the teacher to have a smaller group of children to work with in the classroom several times each week. This plan was also more practical because a wider range of materials would be in use by this multi-aged group of children.

Teachers were encouraged to use a flexible plan in sending youngsters to the Learning Center so that the reduced class number would be meaningful educationally to the teacher, and when children were absent, substitutions could be made. At the same time, the teachers were also encouraged to have all children make use of the Center.

Below are listed the questions asked of each child before he was initially scheduled into the Center:

1. List your school subjects (*all*, including gym, art, music) with your favorite as #1, next favorite #2, and least favorite at the end of the list.

2. List your school subjects according to difficulty—the hardest as #1, the easiest at the end of the list.

3. Name the subject in which you need the most help. Is there any skill within a subject in which you would like help? (For example, arithmetic seems easy, but you would like to know more about Roman numerals, fractions, etc.)

4. Write a paragraph explaining exactly how you would like to spend your time in the Learning Center.

A corps of ten mothers was recruited by the Learning Center director to assist in the Center. These mothers assist largely with library work, checking out films and materials by students and teachers, and occasionally by setting up equipment for use by the children. They aid the child in learning how to correct his own work and generally function as assistants to the children and in clearing clerical work for both the director and the librarian.

The only problem with this corps is that not enough mothers are available because of full-time employment elsewhere, children still at home, transportation problems, and the illnesses of school-age children. The aides the Center has been able to recruit have proven invaluable, and have helped the Center to become effective. Largely due to their attention to detail and record-keeping, the Learning Center director and librarian believe that materials and equipment are kept in much better shape and costly items are not lost or misused.

The staff was encouraged to explore the Learning Center and to consult with the Learning Center director about the special needs of children and the special materials available to the teachers to enrich classroom programs and to help children grow in the skill areas at their own unique rate of growth. The Learning Center director can help teachers to diagnose learning problems and to program materials which would help the child. The teachers simply cannot do this before school, at noon, or after school because of the overwhelming amount of in-service work being conducted for these people in formal in-service courses.

TEAMING PROGRAM—KINDERGARTEN AND FIRST GRADE
Beverly Lindsey

One of the Welsh TDC innovations in vertical organization the second year of its operation was the teaming[3] of two teachers from the kindergarten, one teacher from the first grade level and one resident teacher. The program emerged as these four teachers worked and talked together about how to provide programs and a learning environment which would be relevant to each child. Each of the teachers involved believed that the self-contained classroom was not allowing each child to meet his unique developmental needs.

The teachers decided to organize ten learning centers within the three rooms. They moved on the premise that this specialized use of space and staff would enable them to provide a program of

[3]This teaming approach has been expanded successfully to groups of 1-2, 2-3, etc. in subsequent years of the program.

greater challenge and depth for each child, and would allow instruction to be more individualized, giving the children greater opportunities for self-motivation and decisionmaking.

As the teachers set up the learning centers, they planned for each child in terms of the amount of structure needed. Those able to set their own goals were free to do so, and those children seen as needing more security and limits were given these.

Ten interest centers were formed: art, woodworking, home economics and guidance in one kindergarten room; music, math, science and physical education in the other kindergarten room; language experiences in the first grade room; building blocks on the stage in the gymnasium. Each center was staffed by one of the teachers (on a rotating weekly basis) and by fifth and sixth grade students and a volunteer future teacher or a volunteer mother.

The program is organized in such a manner that each child selects the center in which he wishes to work—1 hour each day for the kindergarten children and 2 hours each day for the first grade children. A child may work in the same center more than one day if he desires or if he has a continuing project. The balance in programs is provided by having the children at their home base for the rest of the school day, meeting the curriculum requirements of the district and state.

There have been many exciting learning experiences for students and teachers. The children have grown in their ability to assume varied kinds of responsibilities: selecting activities, staying with the selections made, finishing projects begun, cleaning up, caring for varied materials and equipment, and moving from one room to another through the corridors of the school with very little noise or confusion.

The children also have adjusted well to the three classroom teachers. There has been no tendency to follow their own teacher or even question which teacher would be in a specific center.

As they make their choices for a center, it is evident that the children really want to know what they are going to be able to do in that center, what they will learn, and what kinds of materials there will be. Social relationships have not seemed to influence choices; at the same time, peer relationships seem to be enhanced by the desire to work with someone in order to accomplish tasks.

The teachers endeavor to provide opportunities for real work experiences in the centers. The teachers are in agreement that concept development appears to be at a higher level with this group of children, and because of the need to read and perform arithmetical operations in order to accomplish tasks, children appear to have greater interests in learning skills.

The teachers have noted several learning styles among the children and this has many implications for these children moving into first and second grades.

The teachers have taped interviews with the children, video-taped children working in the centers, had conferences with parents not only to explain programs but to obtain feedback from the children, and have had feedback from the aides working in the centers.

Evaluation reports and checklists of developing skills are sent home to the parents at periodic intervals.

The teachers believe that they have learned a great deal about providing a relevant education for each child and wish to continue their work as a team. Several questions have arisen and need to be answered:

Is it possible to start this program earlier in the year, and if so, what would be the gain, if any, in skill, knowledge, and attitude development?

Ideally, the program would flow through the first 4 years of school. Can this be done effectively?

Are there children who do not benefit from this type of program? This year this question has been answered, "No."

A methodology for effective evaluation needs to be established. (cognitive, affective, and psychomotor domains)

Can scheduling methods be made easier and more effective?

Are the aides being used in the most effective manner?

The principal of the TDC believes that this program is probably one of the major contributions to come out of the Center's 2 years of operation. The plan seems to capture the true essence of individualized instruction, providing an education which is relevant to *each* child. Further than this, the interest of the children in learning to read, their enthusiasm toward school, and the wholesome peer relationships appear to be highly unusual and atypical. This may, indeed, be one of the TDC's major contributions to the children of Title I schools. These children are using the school, and in many cases bombarding their teachers for more and more reading materials.

A TDC PROGRAM OF CONTINUOUS PROGRESS: FIRST GRADE
Clare Almquist

At the Teacher Development Center and Demonstration School in Rockford, Illinois, we are individualizing instruction for youngsters ages 5 through 12. But our individualized program does not just include children. As each teacher comes to us for training, she is asked to develop a personalized program under the Center's supervision that will work best for her; choosing from the many known educational methods that research shows will work well for students.

In our first grade reading programs, for instance, one teacher uses the Scott-Foresman Dick and Jane primer, another used the Educational Development Laboratories' Reading Machines, another teacher groups children 5 through 7, who are ready to read, together. Still another teaches reading by the language experience method.

Each of these programs is producing good readers because each teacher is working with the program that works best for her. Often, however, as visitors tour our school, it is the language experience room where Clare Almquist teaches that produces most of the questions. Here is a reading program exactly reversed from the reading programs that most visitors experienced during their own school days. Here the beginning reader is not learning to decipher strange markings on cards or books that stand for words chosen by someone else. Instead the child indicates to the teacher through his own spoken words or language, the words he would like to read. He finds out that thoughts and stories created by him can be put down in marks (called words) on paper to become his very own book. The motivation understandably runs high for that child to want to read what he has just seen written.

From the very beginning he is working with familiar words and ideas. He finds that what he can think and talk about can be written down, that what he can write, he can read, and then, wonder of wonders, he can even read what others in his own reading group are telling the teacher or writing down on their papers.

Simple as this concept may sound and rewarding as the method can be, teachers of language experience caution that it is really a very complex way to teach children to read.

Much planning must go on before a teacher goes into language experience teaching. She must ask herself if she will be willing to allow the children to be more responsible for their use of time, as they must be when she works with an individual child. Is she willing to continually assess if they are behaving in a responsible manner before she allows more freedom? If so, from that very first day of school, she must provide many opportunities for the children to grow in self-discipline.

One of our country's most ardent supporters of language experience, Mrs. Evawynne Spriggs of Eugene, Oregon, thinks that even first graders can use materials and equipment independently, and should be shown how to use it on the day the equipment is first introduced. Preceding the introduction of materials would be a class discussion on how they got their room (Mother and Dad pay for it with taxes), whose room is it, and who is to take care of it if it belongs to all of us? Beginning on that first day, emphasis is placed on caring for the room and the materials in it. Each child can decide what he can do to help care for the room and accept that job as his responsibility.

The custodian can be invited in early in the year to describe things children can do to help. When listed on the board or chart, these things produce a reading lesson with real meaning, as well as a social studies lesson on our interdependence with those who work around us. Once room responsibility has been established, the children are ready to be stimulated with materials and ideas. That is the beginning of wanting to read.

For the child to have words to communicate to his teacher the room he enters each morning should be full of interesting things that whet his curiosity and encourage him to explore. The teacher may set up interest centers in corners, on tables, in cupboards, or even in bags, which he can go to when he arrives in the morning. The library corner should be an inviting place, full of picture books of all kinds, nature books, or National Geographics. In the corner could be a rug or a child-size rocking chair for him to sit in while he explores the pages of the books.

In a spot where the children can help themselves to large pieces of paper, an easel should always be ready along with a large choice of colors.

Pictures are really the child's way of communicating before he can express himself in writing. From these pictures will come the first stories. The teacher asks the child to tell her about the picture. She may jot it down to be written in manuscript later, or put it on chart paper at that moment. After stapling the story under his picture, she tells him, "This is what you said," as she runs her hand under the words of his story. Then she asks him to read it back to her. Because they are *his* words, he usually can remember what the sentence says, and feels genuine success as he reads his first story. She encourages the child to write, "By John," or "By Jimmy," at the bottom of his paper. This becomes a very important part of a story for the child.

Writing is begun before reading—with teacher help, of course. From dictating a whole story, the child progresses to writing an occasional word when he thinks he knows it, or when he can see it in the story already and can copy it. For group writing, when all the children are following a common theme, such as a recent field trip, words which they think they will need are written on the board beforehand by either the teacher or one of the children who knows the word. During the writing of the stories at first the teacher must be available for help with words, or have an older child who can help. The profits of dictionary work is evident when the children learn to look up words on their own. Our teachers find one of the best dictionaries for first graders to be WORDS I LIKE TO READ AND WRITE. If at all possible, each child needs his own copy of this or some other dictionary. The stories the children write will cover a broad range,

312

from something they have seen or done, to supplying an ending for a story, or telling about their pictures.

As the children are learning to express themselves, charts from group stories are written by the teacher, read to the children, and then read by the children. There is no controlled vocabulary, the emphasis is on ideas. Early in the year as they begin to wonder about something that has been brought in, or that they have seen, there is discussion about ways they can find answers to their wonderings. They can ask parents or older brothers and sisters, look in books, find pictures, and sometimes just look around and observe carefully. They learn to share what they learn with one another, or the teacher often reads from a book someone brings. This is the beginning of research, and we call it by its name.

The stories they write after this searching become the basis for many skill lessons to follow. For the children who tend to memorize chart stories, the story must be broken up into sentences and words. The children work in a small group on the words, and then write them on cards which become their own "word bank." It is not necessary for every child to know every word in every story; he will meet most of the words again and again. However, the teacher may help him see that each word looks a particular way. He learns that there are phonetic and context clues to help him remember each one. In the small group he gains confidence as he often hears the words that will become part of his reading vocabulary.

Reading in the beginning should be so easy and so exciting that the child feels immediate success. First of all, he must be able to speak in complete sentences. He needs to hear good patterns which he may through listening to records and the tape recorder, or to stories and poems being read aloud. This reading to the children should be carried on all through the year, at school and at home. One suggestion is to ask on the report card sent to parents, "What have you read to your child this month?"

313

As the teacher reads aloud to the children in the early weeks of school, she should choose some really good literature, and some stories that are easy enough for the children to read. She "sells" every book so that reading becomes something the child wants to do. The children, when encouraged by the teacher, notice that many of the words are those they have seen in their chart stories and in stories they have dictated.

Before long one child after another will announce to the teacher that he knows how to read a book or story. Perhaps it is one of the books which he has been reading along with the tape recorder. The tape-recorded stories are from easy books with several copies available, especially folk tales or make-believe stories, recorded by the teacher. The children learn phrasing and have a good model for expression. At first they read along with the tape recorder, the teacher, or an aide. Then they work on the story independently, one page at a time, until they are ready to read the whole story to someone else.

One period should be set aside for "reading time" every day from the very beginning of the school year. During this time, there is no drill on words, no taking apart of sentences; only reading for the enjoyment of reading. For first graders, early in the year the teacher may read part of the time, then allow the children to look at books as she moves among them, stopping to read to this one or that one, encouraging them to "read" the pictures. As more children are ready to read, a larger portion of the time will be devoted to "reading conferences" with the teacher or an aide listening to the individual children reading from the books they have chosen. She talks with each child, asking why he chose that book, and what he liked about it. She makes notes on his card about his reactions. If he is unable to read the book he brings to her, she might ask, "Was it too hard?" "I'll read it to you." Then she will take time to help him find one that is not too difficult.

During conference time, the rest of the children are reading or looking at books, or perhaps making a picture about a story they have read. They read individually or with partners. Sometimes a pupil chooses someone who is reading the same book; perhaps the teacher suggests another child who could read with him or listen to him. This should be an informal, pleasant time, with children choosing where they want to read as long as they don't disturb others. In the beginning there will need to be constant evaluation with the children as a group about how well they have handled themselves during the reading period. There may be times when the group decides that they should read at their desks for a few days until they are ready to accept the responsibility for themselves in other parts of the room.

It would be naive to expect that just *wanting* to express themselves enables children to do it. They must first be taught the skills necessary to free them to express themselves. In my opinion, this is the point where the language experience method may be misused, and gain for itself a bad name. The real language experience teacher uses phonics skills all the time, realizing the need for good phonics background. From the first day of school, during periods separate from reading time, emphasis is placed on the fact that the words are made up of letters, what those letters say, and what their names are. Phonics works into the writing period well because words are separated from each other more naturally there.

In the early part of the year, there should be a writing lesson every day until the children know their letters well. To help children have a positive feeling about writing, comments should be made about letters that are well-formed and the poorly formed letters ignored. Imagine the discouragement of a 6-year-old who has done his best and has to take home a paper full of teacher's red marks!

In addition to the regular phonics lessons, sounds are emphasized as other kinds of work are going on. As chart stories are made, the letters may be named and the children urged to listen to the sound the letters make. Comparisons among the words are made, as the children look and listen for those words that begin alike in the story. Later they look for endings that are alike, or for sounds that are in the middle of words.

Alphabet cards should be available for the children to work with together with an aide, an older child, or a volunteer mother. There seems to be a strong correlation between knowing the letters of the alphabet and learning to read and spell. Parents who want to help the child at home can be encouraged to work in this area.

Listening during music class can be training for phonics—listening for particular sounds, high and low, note phrases that are alike or different. As they learn singing games, they listen for the rhyming words. Becoming conscious of the make-up of words should permeate the classroom, without stifling the child's enthusiasm for reading and writing. This enables him to use words he chooses by himself early in his school life.

While the teacher is working with small groups of children, the remaining children must know what to do. Because they are not using workbooks, and little work is on the blackboard, many activities must be available from which to choose. As with the reading period at the beginning of the year, there is an evaluation of the way they have handled their activity time each day. Emphasis is on the positive. Good models are pointed out, rather than negative behavior. To help the children learn to make good choices and to be persistent, they are required to stick to whatever activity they have signed up for at the beginning of the day. Discussions at the end of each day about the various centers gives the children ideas for tomorrow's choices. Older children, volunteer mothers, or a teacher's aide can help the activity period run more smoothly, but children can learn to work by themselves without disturbing others. This frees the teacher to work with small reading groups.

During the activity time some children may choose the math corner, in which games and manipulative materials are found. The easel may be the choice of some, or the language master, or listening station. Chart stories that are made into books provide free-time reading, and are read and read again with great interest. The library corner, science table, writing center, or writing on the blackboard may be the choice of others. Some may want to copy words from writing books. Following notes on the zither is most rewarding, and does not disturb others. As the children become more independent, many choose to write stories about pictures found in magazines. One of the most popular activities is playing with puppets or dolls creating puppet shows to present to the group later. A box with a hole cut in the front and back can become a stage. Children find it easy to improvise from simple things.

During group reading time, children of varying abilities work together. This is especially important for the child whose language is characterized by many errors. He has the opportunity to listen to others with correct language usage, and no one is pointing out his deficiencies. When it is his turn to tell a story, or to add a part to a group story, the teacher listens to his whole story. She can then select one or two things to record on paper to read back to him. She can edit the sentences without dealing directly with his errors.

There will be some children who are unable to speak in complete sentences, who respond with only one word. Such a child needs a warm, accepting atmosphere that provides many opportunities for success. He needs to feel that his one word can describe a picture; that there is no need for him to tell a long story just because the very fluent child is already able to do that. This type of child will probably be much slower all year in creating original stories. He must feel accepted for what he can do. One such child

317

wrote this story, after the hatching of baby chicks in the spring. "The baby chicks hatched. First one. Then two and three." For this little boy, simple though the story may be, it was a great experience and the feeling that he had as he waited for each chick to come out comes through in his story.

The words *language experience* have special meaning—the children must have many experiences on which to base their language of talking and writing. Field trips, walks around the school, film displays assembled by the teacher and children, interviews of guests, caring for a classroom pet, or their own songs and records may provide material for either a story or chart using the words of the songs. Singing games with much repetition of words make good reading material.

With language experience the science and social studies units form the basis for much of the story material. Trips and units are planned by the children on large group charts. After an experience the children write individual stories and work on individual or group projects. Murals, movies, puppet shows, dioramas, are some of the activities large and small groups can do cooperatively. Stories in basal readers and library books that go along with the unit are read during reading time, some to be just enjoyed, others to be reported on to the entire group.

Discussing current events makes the children feel they are a part of the grown-up world and provides rich material for pictures and stories. Often they continue on their own after a story has been written by the whole class, perhaps because the material is more familiar to them, or because they have thought of something the group left out.

Exploring with all the senses provides rich experiences about which the children can talk and write with first-hand authority—how things feel, how they smell, how they taste, and how they look.

These are good for all children, but especially so for the children with language disabilities. Discussing ahead of time the steps they will follow will help the children derive the most out of an experience, such as working outside for 5 minutes. On their return they will talk about what they experienced, then make a picture or write a story and be better able to describe through their senses what has just happened to them. These stories and pictures may be made into a book to be shared by the whole class.

An on-going activity covering several weeks, such as hatching eggs in an incubator, is most rewarding for teacher and children. To watch the struggle of the chicks as they try to emerge from the shell, then observe the change in an hour from a limp, wet mass, to a fluffy ball is an experience they will never forget. Each small group of children sees the happening in a different way. One group may tell the story in sequence. Some will hold the chicks and tell how the chicks feel to them, and imagine how the baby chicks are feeling. With eagerness they come to school each morning, anxious to see how their chicks are and to watch them change from day to day. It is always great fun to have little animals as friends and to keep track of their progress with that marvelous language they are learning to write down.

Throughout the year in every way possible the child is given a chance to express his thoughts, to say what he thinks about things going on around him, and to talk about things he hopes to do. He is given many opportunities to speak—responding to stories and poems, answering questions, telling about his own experiences. He is encouraged to value not only his own ideas, but those of the other children as well. In the beginning he may only express his thoughts on paper by painting, drawing, and using other art media. But before long he will learn that his thoughts have become visible as he watches someone write them down, and then learns that he can read them. Gradually he learns that there are patterns in the speech sounds and in the letters that represent those sounds, and by reading those patterns he can unlock the mystery of new words.

319

There is no set pattern for the teacher of language experience to follow, yet she must keep in mind at all times where she and the children are going. The children in her groups will vary from day to day, from hour to hour. There are some kinds of instructions that lend themselves to total class work: reading aloud to the children, class meetings, giving instructions on letter formation, introducing games, learning songs. The whole class may, on occasion, listen while a child tells about his picture, and watch as the teacher writes the story. Plans for the day will be made with the entire class, as will plans for some particular experience.

In some cases small groups are more efficient—for skill instruction, role playing, working on projects, sharing stories, working with interest groups on some area of study and letting children read from books made up of their own stories. And very important to a feeling of success, there are no fast or slow groups—as soon as the purpose for a group is accomplished, the group is disbanded.

In still other ways the teacher works with the individual child— taking dictation from his pictures, furnishing words for stories, the reading conference, helping him decide on an activity for his free time. She will be available for listening when he comes in the morning, when he is ready to bubble and share his thoughts. The wise teacher has been observing the children at work and play for social and emotional problems, and will find these little morning chats to be the best time to gain insight into ways she can help. Always the teacher must keep in mind that the child is more important than the program. He cannot learn when his whole being is concerned with his other problems.

Teaching the language arts through language experience is not for the "dabbler." It needs to be a well-planned program, yet flexible enough to take into account the interests of all the children in any one class.

320

The goal of the language experience teacher becomes that of teaching every child what he needs to know, when he needs to know it, while at the same time helping him to maintain his sense of worth.

This was never more obvious than when at the end of the year the more advanced readers were easily moved into a selection of reading books and primers. When it was attempted, however, to place a few of the less mature readers in a beginning primer, they replied, "Oh, Mrs. Almquist, please let's go back to our real reading."

Perhaps what is "real reading" for each child is what language experience is all about.

BUILDING HABITUAL READERS IN THE THIRD AND FOURTH GRADES
Betty Piotrowski and Nancy Sandberg

The key to the building of habitual readers lies in the appropriate blending of a strong basic skills program with a classroom climate in which interest, enthusiasm and desire for reading are encouraged.

Effective instruction in reading at any level must be based on accurate information relative to each child's strengths and weaknesses. It is vitally important that the teacher adjust the learning situations to meet the needs of each youngster in his classroom.

Paramount to implementing a reading program at any level is the teacher's knowledge of previously taught or learned skills plus the review and refinement of these before the introduction of new skills.

The Basic Skills Program

Our goal in the Basic Skills Program is to develop competence in the following areas:

Word attack skills

Vocabulary development skills

Comprehension skills

Oral reading skills

Dictionary skills

Specialized skills for the content subjects

Common study skills (skills used when there is intention to do something with the content read) such as: selection and evaluation, organization, recall, location of information, following directions.

A further "spelling out" of content embodied in the above major areas and relative to the instructional level can be derived from the following sources: PERSONALIZED READING INSTRUCTION by Walter B. Barbe, THE NONGRADED PRIMARY SCHOOL by Lillian Glogau and Murray Fessel, IMPROVING THE TEACHING OF READING by Emerald V. Dechant, CREATIVE TEACHING OF READING AND LITERATURE IN THE ELEMENTARY SCHOOL by James A. Smith, READING INSTRUCTION FOR TODAY'S CHILDREN by Nila Banton Smith, plus the skills outlined in the basal readers.

Following the need for knowledge of the basic skills is the opportunity for further exploration and discovery which hopefully results in greater satisfaction. Specifically, the reader will be exposed to some higher-level reading skills which will help him judge, see differences between the good and the mediocre, between the good and the superior. He will grow in ability to recognize and respond emotionally and intellectually to literature.

The Classroom Climate

The Teacher. Especially essential to the creation of an atmosphere that would encourage the reading act are the following teacher behaviors.

The teacher is more of a listener than a "teller."

The teacher encourages children to express opinions and uses clarifying responses to help them develop their own value system.

The teacher shares his own childhood experiences involving both positive and negative feelings thereby giving the children sanction to express their feeling without guilt.

The teacher makes a positive effort to become acquainted with each child's strengths, weaknesses, special interests, and such to better provide meaningful learning experiences.

The teacher involves children in planning, setting goals, and evaluating self and many classroom activities.

The teacher accepts many answers to questions helping children to see there is not always one "right" answer.

The teacher is consistent in his own behavior; he is someone to be depended upon.

The teacher encourages differences of opinion: challenges, stimulates discussion of divergent opinions.

The teacher is a creator of excitement. He makes an effort to expose children to varied learning experiences in a way which suggests the excitement in learning.

The teacher is an authentic person who can "show her clay feet" with no defensiveness.

The teacher lets children experience the consequences of poor choices, errors in judgment, and so on as part of the learning process.

The teacher provides sufficient structure to the environment, schedule and learning situations in order to give the necessary security without taking away the freedom of each youngster to work toward his maximum potential.

The teacher seeks a cooperative relationship with parents which results in a mutually helpful experience for parent, teacher, and child.

Hopefully, every teacher is in the classroom because he finds involvement with children personally gratifying. Most children reflect the teacher's enthusiasm and joy in teaching.

The teacher's personal proficiency is not threatened when working cooperatively with supervisors, consultants and other resource personnel.

Materials. If the teacher is to strive toward the goal of developing habitual readers, he must provide a wide variety of printed materials such as:

hard cover books (basal readers, trade books, supplementary and complementary readers)

magazines

newspapers

324

pamphlets

books made by children

experience charts

general reference materials such as encyclopedias and dictionaries.

In addition to printed material many of the following should be
available:

slides, film strips, films, television—proper use of audio-visual
equipment can enrich learning at all grade levels.

tapes—child might make comments about book read, and so
forth.

shelves with variety of reading materials.

"reading corner"—desirable to have rugs, cushions, rocker, or
such in a spot to retreat to for independent reading experiences.

easels—children could make chalk or crayon, or other illustrations of favorite books.

art materials—mural paper, chalk, tempera, treasure box, and
other materials for children to use for posters, and so forth
related to books or reading material.

puppets, shadow boxes, clay, felt boards, bulletin boards,
games and commercial devices such as flash cards, word bingo,
and so on.

The physical setting of the classroom should be such that exploration and discovery of the excitement of reading and optimum use of materials are encouraged.

While materials continue to be refined and sophisticated and to play an important role in effective teaching, they are not to be regarded as panaceas. Wise use of materials combined with creative teaching are paramount to a sound instructional program.

Based on a blending of a strong basic skills program with an intellectually stimulating classroom climate, the student will hopefully develop all or some of the following attitudes toward himself in relation to reading.

> The child regards a book much as he does his best friend. He contrives, manipulates to find time for choice reading.

> The child views books as written conversation. He sees himself as an author.

> The child views reading as an extension of self. He relates literature to his own life, his peer group, his own times. He sees reading as inter-related to activities inside and outside of school. He identifies with story characters in feelings, experiences, and so on.

> The child often chooses to read in preference to other choice activities and can become completely absorbed, if only briefly, in his reading.

> The child seeks opportunities to share favorite passages from materials being read and seeks out a teacher, parent or peer to "tell" about the current book.

The child begins to develop a taste for a particular author, kind of story, and such and makes inquiries from peers, teacher, or other adults about where more books of this kind may be found.

The child becomes a "consumer" of books. He frequents the library, trades with friends and desires to own his own books.

The child sees reading as a source of information about his world. (Newspapers and magazines)

The child discovers "what *he* is like as a reader" (develops own style concerning way he likes to handle a book front-to-back; back-to-front; middle-to-end; his speed of reading, the way he sounds when he reads, and so on.

(Final step) The child recognizes his own attitudes toward reading. It achieves meaningfulness for him. He asks where reading fits into life.

Reduced to its lowest terms: Power + Pleasure = The Habitual Reader

A SYSTEMS APPROACH TO MATHEMATICS
Grace Donewald and Joyce Holmberg

A systems approach to mathematics has been developed at the Teacher Development Center in Rockford, Illinois. It is one of the many programs at the Center designed to enable teachers to more easily plan a continuous progress program for students. Rockford teachers have, in the past, been using the Laidlaw math textbooks in the teaching of mathematics. However, as they moved toward more individualized instruction in math they needed, first of all, individualized material that would coordinate with their textbooks, and second,

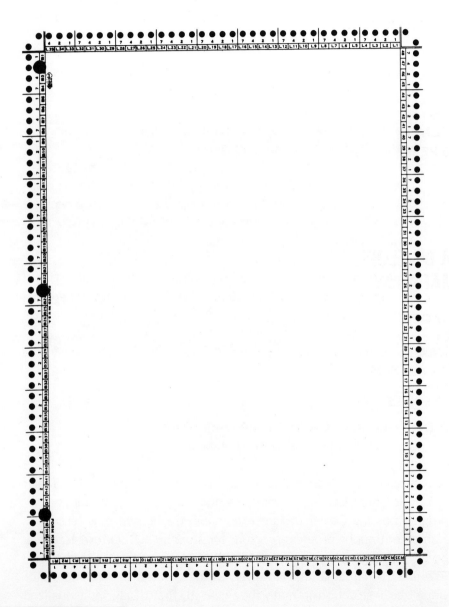

TEMS
D HERE

R DEVELOPMENT
MATICS SYSTEM

S OF:
ET
H CARD
DEX, MATHEMATICS
RIALS
MATERIALS

NUMERATION

- SETS, SUBSETS
- 1 TO 1 CORRESPONDENCE
- =, ≠ SETS
- NUMBERS, PLACE VALUE 1-10
- ORDINAL NUMBER CONCEPT
- EMPTY SET
- MONEY THROUGH 25¢
- NUMERALS, PLACE VALUE 10-999
- RENAMING NUMBERS, 2 PLACE
- RENAMING NUMBERS, 3 PLACE
- MONEY 50¢, $1.00, SYMBOLS
- PLACE VALUE, THOUSANDS
- ROUNDING OFF NUMERALS
- ZERO CONCEPT
- ADDRESSES, DATES, TELEPHONE NUMBERS
- NUMERALS, PLACE VALUE, THROUGH BILLIONS
- READING, WRITING WORDS THROUGH BILLIONS
- ROMAN NUMERALS
- EGYPTIAN NUMERALS
- READING, WRITING, PLACE VALUE, 12 DIGIT
- OPERATIONS SYMBOLS
- NUMBER PATTERNS, SKIP COUNTING

ADDITION

- BASIC 100 ADDITION FACTS
- 2, 1 DIGIT NUMERALS
- COMMUTATIVE CONCEPT
- ASSOCIATIVE CONCEPT
- EXPANDED NOTATION
- NUMBER LINE CONCEPT
- 2 DIGIT ADDENDS WITH GROUPING
- 3 ADDENDS, 2 DIGITS
- 3 DIGIT ADDENDS
- 4 ADDENDS, 5 DIGITS
- VOCABULARY
- IDENTITY NUMBER
- 5 ADDENDS
- CLOSURE

SUBTRACTION

- BASIC 100 SUBTRACTION FACTS
- 2 DIGIT MINUS 1 DIGIT
- 2 DIGIT, REGROUPING
- 3 DIGIT, NO REGROUPING
- 3 DIGIT MINUS 2 DIGIT, REGROUPING
- 3 DIGIT MINUS 3 DIGIT, REGROUPING
- 4 DIGIT MINUENDS, 3, 4 DIGIT SUBTRAHENDS
- WITHOUT REMAINDER NUMERALS
- VOCABULARY
- 8 DIGIT MINUENDS

- CHECKING ADDITION
- CHECKING SUBTRACTION
- CHECKING MULTIPLICATION
- CHECKING DIVISION

329

they needed a systematized approach for the use of these materials. Many Rockford teachers who were interested in this individualized instruction joined with the Teacher Development Center staff in developing a systems approach to mathematics. The idea for recording student progress in the math program was created by Mrs. Grace Donewald, a teacher at the Center. Although record keeping may seem like a final step in any math lesson, it is such an integral part of the whole system that it should be looked at first.

The halo sheet represents the expectations of the school for the student during his 6 years of elementary education. He can measure what he is able to do and we can talk with him and his parents about his ability as he progresses through the elementary school. The teacher introduces the halo sheet to the youngster after she has identified through diagnostic testing and observation the subject matter labels on the sheet which she feels the student can handle with competence. The yellow key sort card is the individual child's record punch card. The holes on this card are matched to the dots on the halo sheet when a child has mastered a particular skill. The hole will be marked where it corresponds to the skill just learned and later punched out with a U shaped notch made with a key sort punch. A sorting needle is run through a hole representing a subject matter area such as "Basic 100 multiplication facts." The cards that have been notched will fall off the needle. The cards remaining on the needle are those of students who still need to learn that particular skill.

The time-saving asset of the cards now becomes evident as the composition of any one skill group is determined in minutes instead of hours as it was previously. At the time of the notch a notation is made next to the notched hole, telling the month and year that particular skill was learned. In the event that the student later feels that he has forgotten that subject matter, the card can be mended or taped with special card savers so that the student's card will stay on the needle for grouping. The teacher can also quickly set the cards back into alphabetical order using this sorting technique.

In summary, the halo sheet serves three purposes: the first is for the discussion with the student to show him what he can do. Then the teacher and student together can set the immediate goals for what work the student will do next. The second purpose is for discussion with parents. A conference can then include specific information about a student's performance. As the teacher refers the parent to the record punch card and halo sheet, the discussion can center around what the student is learning.

At the beginning of the year the teacher spends a considerable amount of time introducing the children to materials pictured on the sheet entitled "Overall flow of the systems functions." They are shown the pretests, textbooks and reference materials available to them to use in learning. The children are then exposed to the practice materials and, finally, the mastery tests. After the teacher is satisfied that every child in the room knows how to use the materials, she gives them a placement and diagnostic test to determine the proper place for them to begin their work. The overall flow sheet shows a picture of the class in the upper left hand corner. All of them have been previously oriented to the materials.

The student then takes the pretest for the unit in which he is placed. The pretest is taken without specific preparation by the students and is done without consulting reference books. If the student passes the pretest the teacher will then record it. If he meets the teacher's criteria for passing that test he may by-pass all the rest of the sheets for that unit. Then the teacher and student decide mutually on the next place for him to begin work. If the student does not pass the pretest, he begins working with the textbook or the skill sheets to cover the materials the pretest indicated.

The skill sheets supplement the textbook and provide an opportunity for the student to test his knowledge and check his own work. He can decide for himself whether he is ready for the mastery test or wants to receive additional help. At this point there is a

OVERALL FLOW OF SYSTEM'S FUNCTION

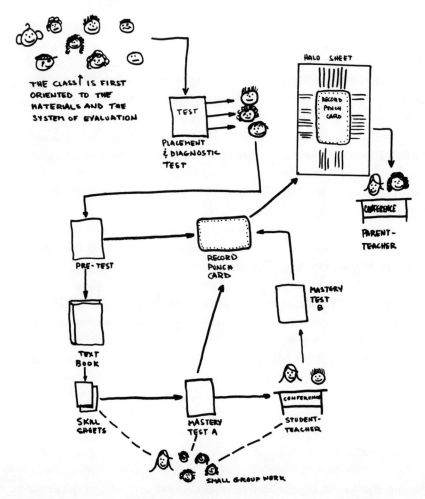

THE CLASS IS FIRST ORIENTED TO THE MATERIALS AND THE SYSTEM OF EVALUATION

TEST

PLACEMENT & DIAGNOSTIC TEST

HALO SHEET

RECORD PUNCH CARD

CONFERENCE

PARENT-TEACHER

PRE-TEST

RECORD PUNCH CARD

MASTERY TEST B

TEXT BOOK

SKILL SHEETS

MASTERY TEST A

CONFERENCE

STUDENT-TEACHER

SMALL GROUP WORK

conference with the teacher which may be followed by the mastery test. He takes this test alone and without the use of reference materials. The teacher may also assign the student to work with her in a small group before taking this mastery test. If the mastery test results are negative he will also participate in small group work. These small groups are composed of students with the need for exposure to direct teaching of specific materials. The recognition of the need for small group attendance may be initiated by either the teacher or the students. The student and teacher conference may occur at any time. It should definitely take place when a student does not show competence on mastery test **A**. At this time the student and teacher agree on the preparation necessary for the student to meet the criteria established for performance on mastery test **B**. The **B** mastery test is then taken. If teacher and student have planned and done their work well, the student will meet the criteria established by the teacher. The record card can be notched after the pretest or after mastery test **A** or **B**.

Grace Donewald emphasizes how the halo sheet and record punch card have helped her as a teacher as well as helping her students. The time it takes her to decide tomorrow's lesson has been reduced from about 3 hours a night to approximately 10 minutes. This gives her time to plan other parts of the students' day. The students have benefited because the experiences in goalsetting let them know clearly what is expected of them. The halo sheets and record cards show this progress clearly and list alternatives for further work.

OPERATION THRESHOLD
Joyce Holmberg

Opening the Doors of the World of Work

Executives in Rockford industries have from time to time expressed a concern that certain jobs are not desired by applicants. Upon further questioning, it was revealed that most of the unselected jobs were ones for which the applicant had no previous knowledge or had never seen in operation.

Vocational choice is a process which begins early in life, even though final occupational choices are often delayed until the age of 16 and sometimes beyond because of expanded educational opportunities. When a young child is asked what he wants to be when he grows up, he answers: doctor, fireman, truck driver or something else he has seen in his individual world. Such occupations as engineer, machine operator, office manager, or "What my Daddy does," are seldom mentioned. These are the vocations that take place behind doors closed to children; not visible to them in their day-to-day existence.

We talked to the superintendent of schools about a joint project with Rockford business and industry to bring the elementary child and job together. We wanted, in the process, to give the child a respect for what his own father and other fathers were contributing to the community. It is obvious to the child what mother contributes to the home and community; father's role is often very nebulous. We presented our ideas to the industrial relations committee of the Rockford Chamber of Commerce and received their suggestions. A parent meeting to explain the project was also held.

We began a pilot project on November 1, 1968, opening the doors of the world of work to our forty sixth-grade boys. Each boy was given an opportunity to visit his father at work enabling him to know firsthand "what my daddy does." Through his subsequent report to the class, all children were able to explore the worth of each father's job and how it contributes to the economics of the community as a whole.

Each boy visited his father whenever possible on his birthdate. Those whose birthdays fell in the summer chose another day.

Boys without a father in the home visited mother at work or accompanied a classmate on his visit. The day of the visit, each boy left in the morning with father, carried out a planned schedule for a half day on the job, had lunch and returned to school that afternoon with a report of his visit.

Transportation back to school was the responsibility of the parents and when this was not possible, the teacher. The school insurance covered the visit at a small cost of 7 cents a day. We received publicity in the local newspaper and local industrial organs.

The project was well received by students, teachers, parents and business people.

Below is a planning sheet showing suggested business visit projects from which the child and the teacher worked out an appropriate format for each visit.

Suggested Business Visit Projects

Thirty minutes of actually working with father: selling groceries, filing papers, and so on. Write a paragraph of this experience.

Observe father: Do an every 10 minute check on what type of work is in process: language skills in writing, listening, speaking, reading, math, mechanical skills, physical skills.

Tour business.

Interview three or four other people at place of business.

Do a layout of building or work area.

Sketch machine, truck, tools used.

Answer:
What does Dad see around him all day?

What does he hear?

What does he feel and touch?

Is he part of a work group?

Does he work alone?

Does he work all year?

What hours does he work?

Is this the first job he had?

What kind of education is necessary?
      _____apprenticeship
      _____college
      _____special talents (examples)
      _____trade school
      _____special personal qualities (examples)

Where is the business located?

What kind of neighborhood?

How far from home?

What does Dad see out the window?

What are the products? Where are they shipped?

What category does Dad's job fall into? (outdoor, mechanical, computational, scientific, persuasive, artistic, literary, musical, social service, clerical)

Explain what would happen to the business or the community if your father's line of work suddenly was removed.

A CALL FOR COMMUNITY SUPPORT
JoAnn Anderson

To: Thirty-two community leaders representing business, government, the arts and professions in Rockford, Illinois.

Subject: Request for help in development of instructional materials to assist elementary school children in learning arithmetic problem-solving.

Dear Volunteers (Hopefully),
This summer we at the Welsh TDC will be designing and/or polishing instructional materials to aid Rockford's teachers in helping children to learn skills and to develop concepts in social studies.

One of the most important areas of the curriculum for the elementary school child is arithmetic problem-solving, and yet, in my opinion and the opinion of many teachers, commercial materials are often dull and irrelevant to today's children. At the same time, commercial materials are often extremely expensive because they are often packaged as programmed materials or as individual workbooks.

It is our purpose to design materials which will be relevant to the child by involving him in solving arithmetic problems based upon real current information. Our major goal will be to increase the competence of each child in solving arithmetic problems through reading or listening. Secondary goals are to encourage the child at higher levels of thinking and to help him to begin to understand the opportunities and complexities of his community.

The final product will be a teacher's guide to arithmetic problem-solving which may be used by the teacher in a variety of ways: arithmetic problem-solving, blackboard work, transparencies for group reading, individually prepared dittoed worksheets for children to read, etc. Also, audio tapes will be made available to each school who elects to use them for use in learning centers or classrooms.

HOW CAN YOU HELP?

1. Assess the materials you have at hand or that you can get which describe your work, industry, or institution.

2. Call upon your colleagues and ask them to do the same.

3. Collect one copy of anything which you are willing to share with us and send it to the Welsh TDC, or call Millie Carus, 399-5931, and we'll make arrangements to pick up materials. The due date for these materials is June 26, 1970, so that we will have time to work on these.

4. Assess the community groups with whom you are involved and ask them for materials which describe membership, organizational patterns, purposes, and amount and source of funding. Groups like: scouting, hospital volunteers, church groups, men's and women's service groups, etc.

That's it! We'll take it from there. At the end of the summer we'll be happy to share our products with you. If you would like approval of the problems designed about your organization, please so indicate and, at the same time, indicate the person whom we would contact.

If we are to complete this kind of curriculum development with limited resources, we'll have to have this kind of help. Without it, the time involved simply becomes overwhelming.

Thank you so much,
JoAnn Anderson

Examples of how finished products might look:

1. In Rockford there are _____dentists. If everybody in Rockford needs a dentist, and the population of Rockford is _____, how many people does each dentist need to service?
Thinking questions following problem-solving (oral or written):
Will everybody in Rockford go to a dentist? Why or why not? How do we know if they do? Could we find out? How? Design a study which might give us this factual information. If the answer is "Yes," why would everybody spend money on a dentist? If the answer is "No," why not?

2. _____Company makes machine tools. This company sells to the following countries: (list) How many countries buy machine tools from _____Company?
Locate countries on a map. What might be the reasons why these countries buy machine tools from Rockford, Illinois, U.S.A.?

3. A foreman in one of our factories earns _____each week. $_____is taken out of his check for U.S. income tax, $_____ for state income tax, $_____for a saving plan he chose, $_____ for health insurance, $_____for union dues. How much money does this foreman take home every week? What percentage of his check does he take home?

4. Rockford Hospital has _____paid employees. There are _____ nurses, _____kitchen help, _____custodians. What percentage of the hospital's staff are nurses?

5. The Rockford Art Association has _____members. _____
of these are adults (over 21) and the remainder are students. How
many student memberships are there?

6. Each summer the Rockford Art Association conducts art classes
for children. These classes meet 5 days a week for a period of 2
weeks. The cost of a class per child is $_____. How much
money does each hour of class attendance cost?

7. There are _____Americans from ages 25-65. Of these, _____
have been diagnosed as having lung cancer. Of those people having
lung cancer, _____smoke cigarettes. The remaining people who
have lung cancer do not smoke. How many people who have lung
cancer are not smokers? What is the ratio of smokers to nonsmokers
in lung cancer incidence?

8. The City of Rockford has a budget of $_____. This is the
way it is spent. (list major budget items) Make a graph showing
how money is spent. Problems would have to do with proportions,
rations, sums, differences, etc.

P.S. If you would like to design your own problems, great! We'll
rework to a suggested grade level and appropriate reading levels.

THE ASSESSMENT OF OUR YEAR IN
COLLEGIAL TEACHING 1969-1970
Greg Houston and Randall Larson

Our Rationale for the TDC

It is our opinion that a school like the TDC must exist in any
school district with the magnitude of the Rockford District #205.
We believe, in accordance with our involvement, that the assets and
liabilities of this program are truly essential to the field of education
in the seventies.

340

It is commendable that many individual teaching staffs at various schools attempt to design innovative programs. However, we feel this is very costly from a financial view, as well as from a lack of cooperation on the part of the administration and fellow colleagues. Hence, a school with the designed philosophy of experimental change and the teacher desire to learn must exist.

The TDC (Teacher Development Center) is more than a Title III grade school designed for teacher training. It is a unique institution whereby teachers and students have the inherited right to search, to speak, and to blunder. It is a place where learning of trivial things has been replaced with meaningful experiences of life. It is an institution that values students' opinions.

It appears from our experiences that if change of any type is to take place in the Rockford Education System, it will be initiated when teachers trust the administration and when the administration trusts the teachers. The level of efficiency of a democratic system in contrast to an authoritarian system maximizes decision-making at all levels. Teachers must have the stamina or "guts" to say, "This I believe!"

The apparent hang-up in education is not innovative programs. Instead of the voluminous number of innovative programs, the real problem seems to be the implementation of *any* program that is truly child oriented. If we believe in the educational theory that children learn first and best from meaningful experiences, why have we divorced ourselves from them? It is our opinion that any change must first start as it did at Welsh School, with a change in the perception of the teacher role. We cannot continue with the role of "near God" or of "fountain of knowledge." Instead, we must give ourselves with all our strengths and weaknesses to the development of student attitudes, skills, and knowledge.

To us, a teacher must be seen as an individual with a distinct value system. We are convinced that all teachers have values but are afraid to take a stand on what they believe. At Welsh School the teaching staff has the unique opportunity of sorting through much education theory and has the additional experience of personal and meaningful interactions with colleagues. These experiences often serve as a catalyst for what we truly believe.

There is a permeating and contagious enthusiasm of caring for each other. This is apparent at the teaching level as well as the most important level of class peer relationships.

This care is a genuine concern for you. It is our opinion that care can be sincere only when you are accepted as a total being. At the TDC we all care because we have found the true joy of sharing, or searching, and of being ourselves.

Our Role—Collegial Teaching

Our Definition. Two or more adults who are willing to share skills, talents, ideas, feelings, and the total self for the development of student attitudes, skills, and knowledge.

Why Collegial Teach? We feel the real value of collegial teaching is the opportunity afforded each child to interact with each member of the team and by so doing benefit from the contribution of each individual. Through this opportunity many student-teacher hang-ups are resolved so that meaningful learning can take place. Individual differences among our students today require individual differences in methodology and approach on the part of the teacher to meet their divergent needs. Collegial teaching does just this. It provides divergencies in methodology and approach to individual problems and a much needed flexibility in order that each child's learning experience be a meaningful one.

Who Can Collegial Teach? It is our belief that in order for two or more people to be successfully involved in a program of collegial teaching, they must be just what the term implies: colleagues. Each must exhibit a great deal of compatibility in regard to similar values, a genuine willingness to give and take, and extreme honesty in dealing with each other.

Another necessary prerequisite for collegial teaching is the ability to establish meaningful communications with each other. This can be accomplished through listening nonjudgmentally to what the other person is thinking and feeling—owning his own position after listening—and finally, solving differences to the mutual satisfaction of both parties.

Monday—Planning the Week. Educators have talked for years about involving students and teachers in the learning process. In our collegial experiences which include math and the total language block, we have discovered many ways of involving these two parties for one common purpose. However, we feel that the most effective technique has been goal-setting.

Goal-setting is not new but we think the approach used in our experience is truly unique. It is our belief that when there is mutual trust and understanding one can truly establish appropriate learning focus goals.

We, students and teachers, take the entire morning of every Monday to establish together our long range weekly goals and our short term daily goals. It is our opinion that goal setting is so essential that we justify the use of so-called "precious time." Our precious time absorbed in goal-setting pays the fantastic dividends of sincere involvement and genuine wholesome, positive success.

The "precious time" includes the sharing of student and teacher expectations. Most students are realistic in their academic expectations.

343

However, we feel that a few students need to be told of our expectations for their academic program. This may include the request to be included in a direct teaching group based upon our appraisal of their needs.

When this has been done, including the student's request for additional direct teaching groups, he will write his personal goal commitment.

In order to further discuss our goal setting process, we have subdivided our detailed explanation into specific questions.

Goal-Setting

Student goals? Are they important? We believe they are not only necessary but essential if we are going to improve or change an attitude of a student. Student goals can vary from positive behavior to academic success. An example of each would be: a desire to improve the communication skill of listening by always paraphrasing what has been said, or the mastery of nouns by a set date. The joy of accomplishment truly pays dividends for anyone who cares!

Can specific daily goals be made on Monday for the entire week? We don't believe this can always be done because of the encouragement of spontaneity in the formation of direct teaching groups. These groups are based upon student request or our observation. In the development of the total family concept each student believes in the respect and admiration for each other. This includes the recognition that everyone has strengths and weaknesses. Hence, students do ask for help!

Do the majority of students reach their goals as scheduled per Monday? If the accent is only on positive behavior there is a real encouragement to meaningful accomplishment. We have found it very gratifying to announce on Friday the students who have met their goals. If one attempts to divorce student trust from such a program, the experience will probably be most ineffective.

Initially, are all students able to write behavioral goals? No, many students, as well as teachers, are unable to write goals without patience in instruction. We believe that children must be included in the process of their education. Frankly, our children are different. They are extremely honest yet sensitive and truly feel all people are basically good.

What happens if a student does not make his goal? If a student does not complete his goals on Friday, there is absolutely no punishment. Although we value meaningful accomplishment and accent only positive behavior, we will further assess with the student various causes or reasons for the lack of success. Very seldom does the same student fail to complete his goals in the same academic area for two successive weeks.

The Remainder of the Week

Unlike Monday, the remainder of the week finds a high degree of self-directed learning based on long term expectations established by the teacher and short term or day to day goals set by the students in light of those expectations. With this high degree of self-directedness, the need for planning the remainder of the week, on a day to day basis, has been virtually eliminated.

We feel that with personal goal-setting and self-directed learning, we as teachers have been able to assume our true roles as preceptors of learning. We are able to assume a much more professional role as guides to learning, giving support, encouragement, and aid in evaluation to our students.

Our typical day begins with math, during which one of us is involved in a small group direct teaching experience based on individual student need. While this is going on the other team member circulates through the remainder of the class answering questions, evaluating progress and providing much needed encouragement which so many times is the key to success or failure. These roles are interchangeable thus providing the best of both to the class, not only in the direct teaching experience but also in the supportive role.

Upon conclusion of the math segment of our program we move into the area of language arts, which consists of language, reading, and spelling. During language the stress is on communication, both oral and written, with emphasis on making the student's written and oral communications as relevant to his own personal experience as possible. It is this relevancy which provides the springboard for real accomplishment in the language area.

The primary goal of our reading program is to develop or instill within each child the love of reading. We have used a multitext approach to reading much to our own satisfaction and the satisfaction of the children. Their enthusiasm is mirrored by their remarks in personal reading conferences. Bonnie, a bright enthusiastic sixth grader, stated it well, "I've read more this year than I ever have in the past. For the first time in my life I look forward to reading time. I even read some during Circle R time." Circle R is a time of responsibility during which the children select their own activities.

Spelling is done continuously; however, the direct teaching in spelling is done 3 days a week. On those days the words are administered by student assistants who present the words in conjunction with a special student-chosen theme for the week. Such a theme was centered around the successful flight of Apollo 12 when our student assistant chose such words as "lunar," "galaxy," "capsule," "orbit," and "astronaut" as some of our words for the week. The words are corrected as a large group with the student assistant providing the correct spellings from his preplanned list of words. We approach spelling in this way hoping to make it as relevant as possible to each child's experiences.

Our General Philosophy

We think that educators must adapt their methods of instruction to the needs of the individual. The vast array of individual differences found in our classroom today emphasizes the necessity of providing an individualized plan of action to meet these divergent student needs. Many teachers are convinced of the need for such a program but see its implementation as an impossible task for them to undertake. It is for this reason that many schools that cry out for just such a program are forced to continue using the traditional approach.

We feel that the major source of difficulty is the misconception regarding the term "individualized instruction." Like so many labels being given to educational methods, it means different things to different people. One thing it does not mean is individual tutoring. Individualized instruction never implies that the teacher take on the role of a tutor. Individual tutoring with the number of students in our classes is a totally unrealistic goal, if not an impossible one.

The issue of one's philosophy of collegial teaching is really most difficult to examine. However, we feel there are some similar elements or feelings that are universal if one believes in individualization. We have attempted to identify these universal truths that we believe are vital and have discussed them as separate but related items. We therefore have posed questions we feel to be relevant to a better understanding of our program.

What is individualized instruction? Madeline Hunter, principal of University Elementary School in Los Angeles, states that "Individualized instruction means something appropriate, but not necessarily different, for each child." Individualization places great emphasis on the use of diagnostic techniques in finding out what children know, how they learn best, and how they think and feel. It provides flexible grouping patterns in the classroom, which are designed to meet a specific, immediate purpose. This small group instruction

347

geared to specific and similar needs increases the economy and efficiency of group instruction and is the essence of individualization.

Dr. Glen Heathers of New York University says that, "Individualized instruction consists of designing and conducting with each student a program of studies that is tailored to his learning needs and his characteristics as a learner. This calls for guiding each student's progress week-by-week and day-by-day, in terms of learning prescriptions made especially for him." The emphasis is on the student as a person and the teacher as a person, thus establishing an equality base for student-teacher communication.

What does our program include? Our program of individualization includes the following points: Teaching is characterized by attempts to diagnose where the student is at the beginning of instruction in order to base subsequent instruction on the results of this diagnosis. Learning is directed toward "learning how to learn," toward the concept approach to learning, rather than toward the memorization and feedback of facts. Our classroom has available numerous learning materials—tapes, records, film strips, language masters, television programmed materials—and is no longer a slave to the textbook. Attention to individual difference shows up in relevant assignments, class discussions, student groupings and evaluation.

Is evaluation important in our program? We have found evaluation both by teachers and students essential and paramount to our program of individualization. Our program encourages self-evaluation by pupils, and allows us to use varied evaluative measures in order to determine the individual's growth and progress.

We feel continuous evaluation is the backbone of a program of individualization. Under our program, evaluation becomes a learning process involving both teachers and students rather than a unilateral judgment.

Our program provides an opportunity for our students to develop responsibility, self-direction, skills and learning, a realistic self-concept, decision-making powers and evaluation skills. In our opinion, providing self-direction and a realistic self-concept are two points that offer what no traditional approach offers—a feeling of self-worth. It is this that makes our program a truly exemplary one.

What is the role of the teacher? Our program also provides an opportunity for us to develop a new and more professional role. Under this program we act as preceptors of learning rather than fountains of knowledge. We perceive ourselves as a consultant, resource person, manager of learning resources and an assistant in student self-evaluation. This role requires us to acquire certain basic skills. First, we must be able to establish an equality base for student-teacher communication. This can be accomplished by being trusted by students, being a good listener, and having patience. Second, we must be able to recognize and cope with emotions instead of declaring our own bankruptcy by labeling students as emotionally unstable. Third, we must learn to be experts in a supportive role.

Perhaps John I. Goodlad summed it up best when he said, "Individualization is knowing children like they have never been known before." Being sensitive to their individual goals, concerns, and aspirations, as well as common goals and needs, is necessary to any successful teaching endeavor.

Unquestionably, increased individual responsibility and commitment are needed in our society today. In order that learners may become increasingly responsible and committed, their potential as individuals must be discovered, developed and released. The times demand that the individual's potential be discovered, developed, and released because of the multiple benefits which the realization of this full potential can eventually offer the individual person and the society in which he lives.

A MODEL FOR TEACHER TRAINING

Merrill Harmin, Ph.D.
Director, NEXTEP Program
Southern Illinois University
Edwardsville, Illinois

Merrill Harmin describes in this article a training program designed
to help prospective teachers direct their own learning responsibly
and interdependently, and be able to use their knowledge skillfully
and comfortably. After setting out the postulates upon which the
program was planned, Dr. Harmin details the instructional, field,
community, and recorded elements that are used to implement it.
He also discusses the responsibilities of students and faculty in actualizing the program, and concludes with a brief statement describing the response to the program to date.

I am heartened by the existence of programs such as the one discussed in this article, because it incorporates trust in the student's
ability to make responsible choices and flexibility to permit him to
exercise those choices. It does allow for individual differences and
independent learning; at the same time, it encourages interdependent
learning and provides opportunity for interpersonal support. The
willingness of those involved to experiment and explore alternatives
and to risk departure from traditional approaches gives me hope
that those trained in this program will carry the same adventurous
attitude into their classrooms and will give their own students opportunity for the freedom and responsibility that can make learning
an exciting and fulfilling process.

M.B.R.

A MODEL FOR TEACHER TRAINING

If there is anything a program for training teachers should do, it is practice what it preaches. This is a simple proposition, but extremely difficult to carry out in practice, partly because some of our exhortations to others go well beyond what we are capable of doing ourselves. (Should we stop preaching good practices just because we are unable to act that way?)

Yet a small group on the Edwardsville Campus of Southern Illinois University, protected from many political pressures by money from the U.S. Office of Education, came together and tried to do just that: practice what it preached—while training a group of graduate students to be supervisors in the schools. Our first problem was to know what we wanted to preach, and in answer to that question we developed the following list of twelve teacher education postulates that guided our work.

Knowledge. A teacher must know many things, especially the subject matter he will teach and basic principles in the social sciences and humanities. We have to become clearer about what knowledge is useful, however; and we have to find more diverse ways of permitting learners to acquire this knowledge, so that each may learn in the style that is most efficient for him.

Personal Qualities. A teacher education program should be aware of those personality factors which tend to limit professional competency, and should help persons to change them when they wish to do so and when it is possible to help them. For example, a person who is not open to experience, who defends strongly against change, might be helped to recognize his defensiveness and deal directly with it. Or a person who feels insufficiently adequate might be helped to bolster his self-concept.

Skills. It is not enough for a teacher to be knowledgeable and have suitable personal qualities. There are skills to be mastered, skills which do not always come with knowledge and maturity. Many teachers can profitably use training in such skills as, for example, handling disruptive behavior problems, organizing groups for self-directed study, writing programmed lessons, and helping children with emotional needs. Skills training is especially useful for those practices which go beyond the traditional; such training helps a teacher to teach in ways *other* than the way he was taught.

Integration of Knowledge, Personal Qualities, and Skills. A teacher education program should help a teacher integrate what he knows, is, and can do. These three components of a program should not exist separately. It is of little use to have a knowledgeable teacher who cannot perform adequately, or a skillful teacher who feels unhappy when he uses these skills, or one skillful but unaware of which skills to use in which situation. A competent teacher knows what to do, can do it well, and feels good about doing it. Some place in a teacher education program each learner has to see to what extent the three elements blend for him. Frequent practice opportunities help with this task.

Individualization. The teacher education program should respect individual differences in learning styles, learning speed, learning order, and, within limits of acceptable practices, learning outcomes. This requires providing individuals with opportunities for learning experiences on an individual basis. Educational technology can help here.

Becoming Self-Directing. The program should help teachers in training move toward increased independence in learning, toward responsibility for personal growth, and toward increased ability to manage that growth. We want teachers to continue to improve after they have left our program. Accordingly, using grades and curriculum requirements for learner motivation is not as useful as using the learner's interest in becoming a competent professional.

Ends and Means. The program should help persons learn professional skills in a context which associates them with professional goals and which permits their revision. Rote learning is ineffective for this. A professional person should be aware of reasons for his job and should be ready to re-evaluate his procedures in terms of his and society's goals.

Complementing Strengths. Not all teachers must be expert in all phases of teaching, but each should know his strengths and be ready and able to cooperate with others in using their strengths. The program should help teachers acquire sufficient self-knowledge and co-operative skills to do this.

The Teaching Process. The teaching process is profitably seen as a series of choices made with predictions in mind about their impact on learners. The teacher, in this view, observes a situation, decides what he might do, and then does it. Crucial is his ability to understand typical situations with which he must deal, the ability to make accurate predictions about what various actions of his might accomplish, the ability to perform in enough different ways so that he has a range of action choices, the ability to obtain feedback on whether or not the predicted outcomes come about, and the ability to revise his understandings and his behavior on the basis of this feedback. Teaching is a process of making choices and constantly evaluating those choices. Being aware of how others perceive situations is a basic element to this process.

Open to Change. A teacher education program should be flexible, with revision based on regularly re-examined goals and evaluation of alternative procedures. The program should guard against becoming static and defensive.

Growth Climate. A teacher education program should strive for a climate that maximizes individual and collective growth. It is important to limit the levels of anxiety and competitiveness to maximize the nonpossessive warmth felt among program members and the patience and understanding shown between members, and to maintain an open communication system that leads to shared efforts and responsibility.

Model of Effective Teaching. Finally, a teacher education program should be consistent with an effective elementary or secondary school program. It is wise to teach teachers in the style that we wish them to use.

Accepting the above postulates, the question we faced was how we could organize time, staff, students, rooms, books, and ideas to best actualize these principles.

Much creative activity and trial and error went into several program models, but the one we are currently working with seems to satisfy most of our demanding criteria. One way to present that model is to list the elements that are in our program and the responsibilities that we define both for the students being trained to become effective teachers and for the faculty trying to help them. It is noteworthy that we believe that this outline not only delineates an ideal college program for teachers but also, with modifications, an ideal elementary school curriculum, an ideal curriculum for preparing lawyers, and an ideal in-service program for teachers.

Instructional Elements

Learning Units. Units are the basic instructional element in our program, our replacement for what are ordinarily called courses. Units are variable in terms of length and method; they are meant to be designed to suit the unit objectives and the personnel involved. In general, however, we try to divide our teacher education experiences into many brief units rather than a few large ones, so that a student can sample an area without making a huge commitment to it and so that he can shift directions when such a shift serves his purposes. Units are of several types:

356

Objectives Specified. These are units with clear goals. Ideally such units contain alternative learning routes to those goals. Goals may include teacher education knowledge or measurable professional skills, or both. Many students will be certified as competent in such units merely by being tested as competent, without having studied with unit personnel or materials.

Methods Specified. These are units with clear methods, with different students taking different things from them. Sensitivity training is an example of a unit with only methods specified. Other units in this category are designed to help the teacher become his natural self in a professional context; the method of such units is generally to have the student perform and then learn how to critique his performance in terms of effectiveness and self-satisfaction.

Nonspecified Units. These are units that cannot clearly specify either goals or methods. Examples would be groups that gather around the charisma of an instructor and groups that wish to remain free to explore an area without constraints either of goals or methods.

A student is free to select from the available units according to his best judgment and, as long as he seems to be using his time in the program productively (as evidenced by his periodic progress reports), no "guidance" is offered him. (He may, of course, *ask* faculty and other students for guidance.)

Some students, however, are constrained in unit selection by state re- quirements that say what competencies the faculty must confirm for them if they are to be certified. And most students are constrained by the need for a meaningful Professional Competency Statement, the form the program provides each student to take to prospective employers. This form outlines the competencies of the student, as best the student and the program can identify them.

Some Learning Units might be relatively narrow (how to ask thinking questions, ideas of John Dewey) while other units integrate competencies studied in the more narrow units (using a problems approach in the classroom, developing a philosophy of teaching).

Units usually include integrated attention to skills, understanding, *and* feelings. There is an attempt to avoid students having knowledge while lacking the skills to use the knowledge, or having skills that they feel too uncomfortable to use.

Teaching aides (advanced students) help with instruction in units; faculty may teach advance students and do research. Programmed materials may be used when appropriate and available.

Independent Study. Students always have the option of designing (with help from others if they wish) programs of individual or small group study. A contract system is used to guide such studies.

Assemblies. These are occasional large group meetings and all students are expected to attend. Assemblies provide input to the system. They might introduce a new unit, introduce a new faculty member, or present a new idea. Assemblies are conducted by a leader, who may be a student or a faculty member, and are scheduled by a joint faculty-student assembly committee.

Field Elements

Laboratory Practice. These are "manufactured" field experiences and include writing or saying aloud what one would do when faced with a hypothetical situation; role playing; responding to a problem simulated by slide, tape, or film; and microteaching. Laboratory experience can be used for practicing skills being studied in learning units or for diagnosing weaknesses and building strengths.

Observation. Observing students or faculty members in nearby schools.

Practice Teaching. This could be of three general types: (a) Focused Teaching (a short-term experience to practice a competency in a real situation; often a one-shot visit); (b) Teacher Assisting (helping a teacher with specific tasks, such as grading papers, tutoring, acting as a team teacher); and (c) Student Teaching (internship and extended practice with large responsibilities).

Service Experiences. Providing professional services gratis, primarily in needy situations (such as in overburdened schools), but with supervision close enough to help the practitioner develop his competencies.

Employment. Professional employment without responsibilities to the training institution, although with the possibilities of a collaborative association with it.

Community Elements

Community Meetings. These are meetings open to all faculty and students. Community meetings monitor the institutional climate, act as a forum for process evaluation, and develop suggestions to the faculty for program improvement. Thus a community meeting is called regularly to consider such questions as these: Is there some way we can better help one another here? Is there some change needed in the current program? Are there any problems or conflicts that the large group can help resolve?

There is no leader at the meeting, although the community may choose someone to convene the group and post an agenda, and status differences are ignored. Decisions are made by consensus whenever possible.

A large institution may divide its population into smaller communities, give each community substantial autonomy, and use a representative council for institution-wide process evaluation.

Core Groups. These are small groups, four or five students in each, grouped on the basis of compatibility. These groups have long-term stability and provide a home base for each student. Groups are in control of their own time and agenda, although once-a-week meetings are expected initially. Core groups serve these purposes:

> To provide a secure and intimate group in which each student may talk about his learning progress and problems.

> To help meet the social and emotional needs of students, needs that otherwise might be overlooked in the complex program here outlined.

> To provide a group to which the student may turn for opinions about his periodic reports, learning contracts, and other work.

> To provide a forum for initial discussions about program changes, or other issues that a student is considering for the community meeting agenda.

Early assemblies teach students how to make use of core groups. The unit on small group interaction is recommended for study by core groups wishing to maximize effectiveness.

Cross Groups. These are temporary small groups formed by having members of each core group split into new groups. These groups typically share problems and ideas. Such cross fertilization is important to ameliorate core group bias, to help in problem solving with community-wide issues, to broaden student contacts, and to facilitate institutional communication. Core groups or cross groups often convene immediately before community meetings and serve to clarify issues that might be on the agenda of that meeting.

Informal Interaction. This is considered important to student growth and community health, and facilities and time are arranged to facilitate such interaction.

Advisors. Students are informed that they may choose as an advisor any faculty member from a posted list who has time available. (Only some faculty are interested in this role.) Students may choose to use core groups and other students to get advice and counsel, but since some administrative functions are handled through an advisor, each student must have one. Advisors, in any case, are to help and to support, and are not to dictate or control. Responsibility for learning programs and progress rests with the student.

Record Elements

Contracts. Students decide what they agree to do. Faculty do the same (faculty say in what ways they are prepared to help students). Contracts explicate the terms of those agreements. When contracts are in written form, as opposed to simple oral agreement they help remind one of obligations and purposes and are, in that way, self-enforcing.

Contracts are especially useful for individual study. A student may negotiate one with a faculty member, another student, a unit teaching team, or with himself.

Periodic Reports. Periodically, each student is asked to write a report of what he has been doing and what he plans to do. This review of recent experiences helps a student to recall and solidify learnings from his experiences that he wants to keep. It also gives him an occasion to reflect upon whether or not there were learnings in those experiences that might have been overlooked in the heat of the experiencing. Without something like periodic reports, life can be too busy for review and reflection.

These reports are typically shared with one or more students, often those in one's core groups, and then turned in to an advisor. The advisor gives feedback only when asked for it, or when the student's participation in the program seems so unproductive that it might be appropriate to deny him permission to continue.

These reports may be required biweekly at the outset and then monthly thereafter, or according to some other schedule. Occasionally a student will want to complete these reports more frequently than is minimally required, finding such reporting an important help in motivating and reinforcing study.

Competency Cards. These are cards that simply record what competencies a student has. Each unit that has specified goals offers them. Many field experiences provide them. Competency cards are filed for a student whenever a measurable professional skill, understanding or other attribute is identified. A student may acquire a high-level set of competency cards, and thus be given a high-level institutional professional recommendation, even without having had any training at the institution.

Professional Competency Statement. Students do not earn grades, although the institution may use grades temporarily until it has authority to discontinue them. Transcripts are not issued. Instead, students obtain a statement of their professional competencies. This outlines the competencies each student has demonstrated and the kinds of professional roles he seems ready for.

Students draft their own Professional Competency Statement, using periodic reports and competency cards as central source data. Often that statement is shared first with other students, such as one's core group. Then it is approved or modified in conjunction with the faculty, represented by one's advisor.

The Professional Competency Statement is what a student presents to a potential employer and to other training institutions, such as graduate schools. It is meant to provide a professional profile that is more valid and informative than is a typical college transcript.

In addition to the foregoing elements, our current program model specifies the following sets of responsibilities:

Faculty Responsibilities

To Instruct About the Program. A key function of the faculty is to teach the students the program's goals, procedures, and change mechanisms. The more the program departs from the traditional, the more insecure students will be until this function is fulfilled. Of course, this teaching need not be done abstractly; students might be helped to live in the program and thus understand its workings experientially.

To Instruct in Units. Faculty members also teach in the learning units. It is important to note that each faculty member makes public to the system (students and other faculty) those areas he can teach effectively, so that those students who want them can choose them. (Incidentally, this requirement serves to pull up short those professors who, when they look hard, find that they have nothing that they can teach effectively that anyone wants.)

To Revise the Program. Some faculty members specialize in revising units or other elements of the program, while others work at revising the program in its more wholistic sense; but our model requires attention to revision, to growth, to improvement. It is an explicit task of faculty members to work at making things better.

To Advise Students. Not dictator style, but counselor style: helping students understand alternatives and consequences so they may make wiser choices.

To Participate as a Community Member. The program is essentially a collection of people rubbing together for mutual satisfaction. Each faculty member is expected to collaborate with students, secretaries, and others in a nonstatus search for the best human conditions for all. The community meeting is the official forum for this, but faculty participation in core groups, informal interaction, student advisement, and faculty meetings also can contribute to this goal.

Student Responsibilities

To Improve Professional Competency. Each student is responsible for his own growth. He must search out, with help from advisors and other program elements, those experiences that he thinks might help him, and he must integrate whatever he learns from those experiences into his self. This is an active process and he is expected to work hard at it. We might call this a "responsible choice program"; each student is expected to guide his own work in a manner that is responsible to himself, to the training program, and to the profession.

To Instruct in Units. Students are expected to help teach other students and, when they possess special skills, faculty members. This is both to increase the number of instructors available in units and to strengthen the learnings of the instructing students.

To Advise Students. Students are also expected to help one another with program planning and with general learning problems. A unit on the helping relationship teaches students how best to do this.

To Participate as a Community Member. Students have the same privileges and responsibilities as faculty members in this regard.

These, then, are the elements and responsibilities we currently see as important for our teacher education program. See the accompanying outline for an overview of the program model. Exactly how the elements and responsibilities interrelate (in shifting, complex ways) and how they are introduced to students (gradually and patiently), is too large an issue to consider here. Let it just be noted that the program outlined above is more a target than a reality and that we move toward it with a mind deliberately open to revisions and alternatives.

OUTLINE OF CURRENT PROGRAM MODEL

Instructional Elements

Learning Units
    Objectives specified
    Methods specified
    Non-specified
Independent Study
Assemblies

Record Elements

Contracts
Periodic Reports
Competency Cards
Professional Competency
    Statement

Field Elements

Laboratory Experience
Observation in Schools
Practice Teaching
Service Experiences
Employment

Faculty Responsibilities

To Instruct about the Program
To Instruct in the Units
To Revise the Program
To Advise Students
To Participate as a Community
    Member

Community Elements

Community Meetings
Core Groups
Cross Groups
Informal Interaction
Advisors

Student Responsibilities

To Improve Professional
    Competency
To Instruct in the Units
To Advise Other Students
To Participate as a Community
    Member

NEW DIRECTIONS IN IN-SERVICE
EDUCATION FOR TEACHERS

Marshall B. Rosenberg, Ph.D.
Director, Community Psychological Consultants, Inc.
St. Louis, Missouri

Marshall Rosenberg discusses in this chapter the rationale for and content of in-service workshops for teachers which he conducts. Specifically, the article considers some of the personal problems (teacher attitudes) and impersonal problems (limitations of time and resources) in bringing about educational changes intended to vitalize teaching and avoid dehumanizing students. The article begins with a statement of the values on which the author bases his approach to education. He then discusses the process used in his workshops to help teachers clarify their own values and relate those values to concrete behavior. The next section is a description of ways of resolving attitudinal problems which interfere with consistency of values and behavior (fear of change, fear associated with making errors, distrust of student ability to assume responsibility for their own thoughts, feelings, and behavior). There follows a discussion of ways to deal with "impersonal" problems associated with in-service training: how to reach maximum numbers in minimum time and how to prepare teachers to meet resistance to change in the community. The chapter closes with comment about evaluative procedures which have been used to measure results of the workshops.

M. B. R.

NEW DIRECTIONS IN IN-SERVICE
EDUCATION FOR TEACHERS

I am concerned about the quality of education that teachers receive
in universities and colleges. I observe them being taught in a way
that limits their growth and in turn limits the growth of students
they teach. I see them being taught methods that imply that thirty
children can learn the same thing at the same time in the same way.
I not only believe that this is an ineffective concept with which to
approach teachers but I also see it as a way of unwittingly dehumanizing the students. I believe that it is possible to teach thirty children as individuals, that it is possible to have each student working
toward objectives that are within his realm of capability, to have
each student working toward his objective according to a time
schedule that fits his personal orientation (style, preference), and
working toward his goal in a manner that fits his unique skills and
approach to learning.

I started my present in-service work with teachers several years ago.
Until that time I was a clinical psychologist in private practice. The
majority of my referrals consisted of children with learning problems. On the basis of my training, I started my work with these
youngsters by evaluating their intrapersonal characteristics, as these
would underlie their learning difficulties. I was reinforced in this
approach by the general attitudes I found among school personnel
(teachers, principals, social workers, and others); they, too, believed
that the youngsters whom they had referred to me were having their
difficulties with learning because of some intrapersonal, "psychological," dysfunction. However, my accumulating experiences gradually
led me to realize that the "learning difficulties" of the children were
often as much a function of the teaching approaches taken with
these children as with the intrapersonal processes of the children
considered alone. Furthermore, many of the apparently dysfunctional processes occurring within the children could not be considered significantly dysfunctional from the standpoint of growing

developmental norms of children's behavior. These experiences led me to the conclusion that I would be accomplishing more by attempting to alter the aspects of the system that fostered problems for children than I could accomplish by putting "psychological band-aids" on the products of the system. Based on these viewpoints and my conclusion, I developed an approach to the teaching-learning process that I considered to be more effective in light of the increasing findings about learning disorders. The majority of my work, designed to implement this approach, has been done on an in-service basis with public school teachers. Recently I have been spending more time doing workshops for the faculties of teacher-education institutions.

The essence of the problems I now face involves trying to share new approaches to teaching that not only avoid dehumanizing students but make teaching a more vital and exciting profession. The specific content of my views of teaching are shared elsewhere (Rosenberg, 1972) and hence will not be the major focus of this article. Rather, in this article I hope to outline some of the problems I have encountered in my in-service work with teachers and some of my attempts to resolve these problems. I would like, however, to describe briefly the approach to education that I offer to teachers in our workshops.

To begin with, I value a teacher-pupil relationship characterized by mutuality, a relationship in which the teacher relates as a colleague rather than as a master to a slave. More specifically, I see such a relationship as one in which the teacher 1) openly presents his thoughts and feelings to students without making demands and without making absolutistic judgments, 2) shows empathy and respect for students' feelings and thoughts and thereby avoids ignoring the students, passing judgment, or giving advice, and 3) resolves conflicts with students through rational problem-solving techniques rather than by means of coercive techniques such as punishment and reward.

Second, I value an approach to teaching which requires that both the teacher and the student 1) know what the objectives are for a unit of instruction prior to beginning the work on the unit and 2) are committed to these objectives, preferably because the objectives have been reached by mutual consent. I have come to value this approach because I believe that, to the extent that the students are knowledgeable about objectives and committed to them, their motivation for learning is enhanced. To the extent that teachers recognize the importance of student commitment to objectives, I believe that teachers are in a better position to avoid the imposition of irrelevant information upon students.

Third, I value the teacher making adjustments in teaching methods on the basis of the students' individual styles of learning, that is, fitting the curriculum to the child and not the child to the curriculum. This involves the teacher learning to diagnose operationally the individual differences that influence learning and to make adjustments on the basis of this diagnosis (Rosenberg, 1968).

Fourth, I value the teacher functioning as a facilitator of learning experiences, rather than as a conductor of learning experiences. This requires the teacher to know techniques which enable students to learn on their own without direct teacher involvement. In part, this requires the teacher to supplement lecture and reading assignments with student-centered learning experiences, learning through games, learning through programmed materials, and so on.

These four areas comprise the content of what I try to share with teachers. It has been my experience that each of these areas represents a significant departure from procedures *and attitudes* followed by many teachers. As a consequence of these innovations, I have become aware of many problems in my attempts to share my views with teachers. I would like to describe these problems, as well as my attempts to resolve them, as a result of my work with teachers and school systems.

Attitudinal Problems

Marshall McCluhan has made reference to the fact that if one's status rests on a single way of doing things, change becomes annihilation. Keeping this in mind helps me understand the fear I see on the faces of teachers when I outline my beliefs about education. Often, the teachers have been educated in institutions that have taught them a single way of presenting their subject matter. They certainly have not been educated to deal with change. The sweeping changes in procedure that I recommend, therefore, can easily be overwhelming to teachers unless presented cautiously and with a great deal of appreciation for their concerns and hesitancies.

I try to cope with this fear of change by gaining the teachers' commitment to the values inherent in the approach I present. I find that the teachers with whom I work teach as they do, not because it makes intrinsic sense to them, but because it is how they were taught, and it is how their colleagues teach. In fact, with little provocation the teachers readily pour forth their concern with what happens in their own classrooms, their dismay with the apathy that exists on the part of many students, their sympathy for the slow learners, their guilt at the consequences of the grading system and their involvement in it, and so on. I begin by helping teachers to evaluate whether or not their approach to teaching is consistent with their personal values. This is accomplished by engaging the teacher in simulated classroom activities, for example, by way of role playing, videotaping the activity and then reviewing the videotape. This procedure provides the opportunity to look at specific teacher behaviors and relate these specific behaviors to values. For example, the sequence might involve a teacher who responds to a child who is interrupting in class by stating, "Wait your turn, Johnny." When asked what value such behavior supports, the teacher is likely to state, "It tells the child what he should do." At this point, I share my own values, mainly that except in rare circumstances, I value sharing my feelings and thoughts with others and allowing them to choose for themselves what they want to do more than I value telling others what they should do. I then show how I would put this value into action in a given situation. (In the example given, this would probably take the form, "I get annoyed, Johnny, when you speak before I get a chance to finish what I wanted to say.") I then allow time for dialogue between the teacher and myself in which we can compare the relative merits of our different approaches. Then if a teacher sees merit in my approach I provide opportunity for the teacher to practice behaving in a way consistent with the new approach.

To summarize this process, it begins with an assessment phase during which the teacher is given the opportunity to clarify his values as these are expressed in his concrete behavior. I want to stress the importance of continually relating values to concrete behavior. This protects the discussion from becoming overly abstract and intellectual. It also glaringly reveals to many people the conflict that exists between what they profess and how they behave.

The process continues with my sharing alternative values, taking care again to relate these values to concrete experience. I feel vulnerable at this stage because I am openly presenting what I believe, and hence I am subject to criticism and evaluation. My prior training as a psychotherapist provided me with more skills for conducting the first phase (helping the teacher to analyze his present adjustment) than for conducting the second phase (providing constructive alternatives for teachers). It seems obvious to me that if I want people to make major changes in their approach to teaching, I want to be as explicit as possible about what alternatives exist.

The process ends with providing the teacher with the opportunity to practice behaving in ways consistent with newly clarified or developed values. Again this is consistent with my desire to concretize the learning experience. I am not content to leave a workshop with a teacher intellectually understanding my approach to education and committed to using it when he returns to the classroom. I am too aware of the difficulty involved in translating intellectual learning into behavioral changes, particularly when these changes require changes in value that have been held for several years. After I have seen a teacher behave differently, even if only in a simulated situation, I have much greater confidence that new views have been learned.

A second attitudinal problem that I face in my work with teachers involves the fear many teachers experience in regard to making errors. The majority of teachers with whom I interact appear to believe that it is shameful to make an error. I am not surprised by this. Indeed, I find it difficult to understand how anyone could go through most schools in the United States' educational system and be comfortable in making errors. As Holt (1964) has stressed, our educational system, and particularly our grading system, lends itself to one of two strategies in regard to error: either to try compulsively and perfectionistically to avoid errors at all costs or to avoid making errors by not trying.

This second problem, namely the teachers' fears associated with making errors, hinders significantly my efforts with them for a variety of reasons. Since my approach often requires that teachers make major changes in their life-long patterns of behavior, it seems natural to me that errors will be made in the process of learning. The intensity of fear on the part of teachers leads to initial resistance to trying out new skills and frequently results in the teacher becoming quickly fatigued, two consequences which increase the amount of time required for teachers to explore and experience my approach. As I will discuss below, time for in-service education of teachers is at a premium in the school systems with which I have consulted; so I am vitally interested in minimizing effectively and quickly the resistance and fatigue.

374

I have tried to minimize resistance and fatigue by attempting to cope with fear of error in two major ways. First, I have designed exercises which initially emphasize group responsibility for any errors made; further exercises are designed to move gradually toward individual responsibility for error-making. For example, I may first suggest a small group activity in which the group as a whole is responsible for structuring simulated situations that reflect the new approaches that the teachers are trying to learn. These structured, simulated situations are then presented to the total group and are critiqued. If errors are made, the group shares the responsibility. At the other extreme are exercises in which the individual himself is responsible for behaving in a way consistent with the approach he is attempting to learn. This initial "sharing the misery" of error-making seems to enable each teacher to manage better the stress he will feel later when his own individual responsibility for error is more apparent. Second, as another means of alleviating stress, I introduce humor into the error-making process whenever possible and appropriate. This is touchy business because of the danger of humor being misinterpreted as ridicule or derision by a teacher sensitive at having made an error, but genuinely funny things do happen in these exercises, and spontaneous laughter is usually appreciated by all.

A third attitudinal problem that I face involves the teachers' beliefs about the ability of children to assume responsibility for their own thoughts, feelings, and behavior. In my experience, many teachers seem to have little trust that children have such ability. These teachers seem to believe that unless they tightly control students, anarchy will prevail in the classroom. This attitude is not conducive to making the changes in teaching I recommend. Since I value an approach that encourages students to be responsible for their own thoughts, feelings, and behavior and requires that they take an active part in decisions about their learning, I need to help teachers develop such trust in students so that as teachers, they will be free to implement the changes I recommend.

One technique I use in promoting such trust in youngsters is to engage teachers in role playing situations wherein they play the roles of students and I take the role of a controlling teacher. These experiences and the subsequent discussions help teachers to see the ways in which rebellious behavior can be provoked by the approach of the teacher, an alternative to their always viewing such behavior as simply reflecting a trait which exists within children. I also describe in detail actual classes that I am familiar with in which teachers are using the approaches I recommend, and, if possible, I arrange to have teachers visit such classrooms or to view videotapes of them. The realization that classes exist in which children do behave responsibly even when they are not tightly controlled is a revelation to many teachers. Even after teachers have viewed such classrooms they often remain skeptical, believing that *their* students somehow cannot exhibit such responsibility. At this point, I can only urge them to test out some of the recommended approaches to see for themselves whether or not they are possible. I then try to make myself available to the teacher in order to review whether their attempts have been successful or not.

These three varieties of attitudinal problems represent the difficulties I have faced with regard to the more personal aspects of the work I have been doing with school personnel. To say it another way, *attitudes* are held by people, in this instance by people who are principals, teachers, and so on; their attitudes have been problems. to me in the sense that those attitudes often make it more difficult for them to *experience* the alternative attitudes, procedures, beliefs, that are requisite to my approach. At this point, I should like to shift from problems related to personal matters to problems I have faced which stem more from impersonal matters, namely, problems related to 1) the *number* of people that I can reach; 2) the limitations of *time* available for in-service education of school personnel; and 3) policies, procedures, and resistance to change found in school *systems.*

Number of Teachers

As a person whose original training involved one-to-one counseling techniques, I have found it a continual challenge to develop techniques that enable me to work with a large number of teachers at a time while still providing them with the intensive experience necessary to bring about the changes I desire. One solution to this problem that I have used is to train persons from within the school district so that they can conduct the types of workshops that I conduct. In this way I not only reach more individuals but also leave the school system with people to carry on the work that I have begun. Another solution to the problem of numbers involves the development of techniques that allow a large number of people to be actively involved at one time. An example of one such large group activity I developed is what I call "vicarious role playing." This involves my role playing with one person in front of a large group but allowing each member of the audience the opportunity to write down verbatim what he would say were he in the position of the person role playing. I then provide a framework from which each member of the large group can evaluate his own performance. I have also developed a wide variety of small group activities that require either minimal or no participation on my part. This requires my providing the teachers initially with clear standards by which they can gauge their performance. Once they have these standards they can then engage in an activity and critique one another. During such activities I can circulate and supervise to make sure that the groups are critiquing appropriately.

Time Problems

A problem closely related to the number of teachers with whom I deal involves the amount of time allotted me to work within the school system. The time may be limited by several factors; the institution may be limited financially, either with regard to the amount of my time it can purchase or to the amount of time available for

377

teachers to undergo in-service educational programs. Attempting to resolve the time problem is another difficult challenge. In my prior clinical work, my clients often allowed me the luxury of working with them for months, sometimes even years. In contrast, I am often asked to accomplish in 3 days what was accomplished previously in months.

One practice that I have found helpful in coping with the time problem is to start my consulting work with a group by providing the participants with reading materials prior to my arriving to work with them. For each phase of my work, I have accumulated prepared reading materials designed to introduce the participants to the work that I will do with them when I arrive.

A second procedure that I have found helpful with regard to time pressures involves beginning my work with a group by developing measurable objectives. As Mager (1964) has pointed out, once a learner is clear about what is expected of him, the entire process of instruction proceeds with greater efficiency than when these objectives are only in the mind of the instructor. For example, in working with teachers to develop their abilities to relate interpersonally, I begin by presenting as specifically as possible the interpersonal *skills* that I consider to be effective, and the *criteria* by which the teachers can evaluate for themselves their proficiencies with these skills.

A third practice I have found helpful in coping with the time problem is to supplement verbal activities with action or experiential techniques such as role playing, psychodrama, and other structured group activities. I find that action not only speaks louder than words but faster than words as well.

A fourth practice that has been effective in dealing with the time problem involves the use of television feedback exercises. I use television in providing clear feedback to teachers about their interpersonal behavior. When I can get a teacher to see and hear what he is doing, it seems to have greater impact than when I give him verbal feedback about his behavior.

My concern about reducing time requirements is a continual one, and as a consequence I am constantly on the lookout for approaches that might move in that direction.

System Problems

I am painfully aware that the systems in which teachers work do not always support the changes I advocate. I am thus in a position of wanting teachers to make changes that are likely to provoke the wrath of students, other teachers, school administrators, and parents. I am also painfully aware that I leave the community after a short time and do not have to bear directly the brunt of attack that educational innovation frequently entails. Before I leave a community, therefore, I try to do whatever I can to aid teachers in developing confrontation skills necessary to deal with resistance to change. I have designed role playing activities that have the goal of aiding teachers to anticipate the types of pressures they are likely to encounter. Also through role playing techniques I work with the teachers toward the goal of developing confrontation techniques that maximize communication and minimize antagonism. I also let teachers know that I try to be available at any time via phone to deal with specific problems when they arise.

Evaluation Procedures

Finally, I would like to briefly note the type of changes that have taken place in the workshops I have conducted.

Evaluations have often been conducted by the various school districts for which workshops have been conducted. One such evaluation (conducted by the public school system of University City,

379

Missouri) will be reported on here. In this workshop the primary concern of the evaluators was whether or not the participants changed their beliefs about relating to students during the course of the workshop. To measure this dimension they used an instrument based on the ideas of O. J. Harvey (1961). The instrument, a booklet titled, "This I Believe," was administered to the participants the first and last days of a 10-day workshop. A research specialist for the school system scored these instruments from each respondent in terms of the flexibility and openness reflected in the thinking of the respondents and statistically analyzed the data. The test instrument consisted of six topics, one printed on each page: each topic concerned one dimension of the respondent's beliefs concerning relating to children. The six were:

1. This I believe about disciplining a child

2. This I believe about communicating with a child

3. This I believe about setting goals (for example, setting goals about academic performance)

4. This I believe about children's mistakes

5. This I believe about a child's resisting my authority

6. This I believe about what is most important in child management

The respondents were requested to complete briefly (at least two sentences) each item. They were instructed, "Be sure to write what you genuinely believe . . . . Spend no longer than 2 minutes on each page. And once you have turned a page, do *not* turn back to it." Statistical analyses were interpreted as indicating changes in participants' beliefs about relating to children in a direction of increasing openness and flexibility of beliefs in all six of the categories measured. The data were *statistically* significant for four of the six categories: 1, 3, 5, and 6, as listed above.

I am convinced that the majority of teachers are eager to alter their approach in the classroom in a direction that permits increasing trust and autonomy to exist in the teacher-student relationship. I am convinced that these changes can be brought about in relatively short periods of time. I'm excited about the opportunity I have been given and continue to be given to do what I can to facilitate these changes being made.

References

Harvey, O. J., Hunt, D. E., and Schroder, H. J. **CONCEPTUAL SYSTEMS AND PERSONALITY ORGANIZATION.** New York: John Wiley and Sons, 1961.

Holt, J. **HOW CHILDREN FAIL.** New York: Pitman Publishing Corp., 1964.

Mager, R. **PREPARING INSTRUCTIONAL OBJECTIVES.** Palo Alto: Fearon Publishers, 1964.

Rosenberg, M. B. **DIAGNOSTIC TEACHING.** Seattle: Special Child Publications, 1968.

Rosenberg, M. B. **MUTUAL EDUCATION: TOWARD AUTONOMY AND INTERDEPENDENCE.** Seattle: Special Child Publications, Inc., 1972.

COMMUNITY, CURRICULUM AND CONTROVERSY

Glenys G. Unruh, M.A.
Assistant to the Superintendent
School District of University City
University City, Missouri

Glenys Unruh discusses here the procedure used in one public school system for introducing new and controversial curricula in ways that promote community understanding of the programs involved. She describes ways in which the school administration involved parents in preparing for the introduction of social studies units dealing with racial issues. Emphasis is placed on providing opportunities for parents to actually experience the teaching procedures planned for the students.

M. B. R.

COMMUNITY, CURRICULUM AND CONTROVERSY

Introducing new curriculum developments to the community of
University City used to be a fairly innocuous process. That was at
a time when this was not only a geographical community but also
a community of common purposes and attitudes. That was before
the days when articulate citizens all over the country suddenly became authorities on sex education, phonics, Black Studies, and
other school topics. That was before students in many communities got into the act and, under the banner of RELEVANCE,
mounted protest demonstrations and submitted lists of demands,
frequently at variance with the demands of adult citizens.

Small wonder, then, that the staff of this school system made
unusually careful preparations this year before introducing in the
sixth grade a series of controversial social studies units centering
on social issues. Former procedures for working with the community were reviewed, a few techniques were salvaged, others were
revised, and new ones were added.

In the Past

From time to time over the past several years, new curriculum developments have been successfully introduced into the University
City schools and accepted by the community. In each case, a
general pattern was followed. Felt needs, promotional publicity,
and children's achievement were all recognized as essential to the
process. Each new curriculum development was thought to be in
harmony with the beliefs and purposes of the school system and
was viewed as a way to improve previous practices as predicted
from analysis of data, study of research, and subjective observation
of the needs of people and society. In every case there was a prior
process from which evolved commitments on the part of the faculty.
Pilot studies were usually conducted to allow room for assessment
of the reactions of a few children before introducing an innovation
on a broad scale.

Parents and other citizens were involved as fully as possible. At no time were curriculum innovations disguised or kept quiet; every effort was made to inform the community about curriculum changes. Countless PTA meetings over the years were devoted to live demonstrations of new programs, panel discussions, and tours of buildings with displays of new materials and equipment. Parents of children who were going to camp or were to be introduced to the new math or i.t.a. were invited to visit classes, view educational films related to the subject, or discuss the new program with the teachers. Driver education, for example, was installed only after a citizens' committee had made a thorough study of the advantages and disadvantages of the program as related to costs and other factors.

Over the years frequent reports have been made to the Board of Education on all curriculum matters. The school's publications have constantly provided information on changes in the program, photographs of children at work, and testimonials from parents and teachers. An active and promotional public relations program has included a plan for guiding visitors on tours through the local schools to observe innovations firsthand. The best support for new curriculum programs has been the effects on children. The introduction of new math and i.t.a. posed no problem when children were found to be reading better and computing mathematics better. Standardized test scores have provided a means for continuous assessment and feedback on pupil achievement in the "basic" subjects. Students who have been "turned on" by discovery methods in science transmit this enthusiasm to their parents and neighbors.

Controversial Issues

In the past, these procedures for introducing new curriculum developments were successful. But what happens when the new curriculum development involves a social issue with political or ideological overtones? Mathematics is a comparatively neutral and noncontroversial subject area. People's views differ on how to teach or

386

whether to teach about social problems, promotional publicity may have a reverse effect in an emotionally charged atmosphere, and pupil achievement is difficult to measure in the attitudinal realm. New curriculum developments have provoked no quarrels when the school has developed new programs in line with the traditional purposes of education: work skills, citizenship, health, and intellectual excellence. As schools move harder into new purposes of alleviating society's complex problems, resistance and hostility may result unless considerable effort is put into new interpretations of the role of the school.

In preparing to make changes in the social studies curriculum of this school district, we recognized that in the past many schools have hesitated to introduce the slightest controversial dimension because of the likelihood that the school's various publics will disagree. We also recognized that school programs in general have become pallid and irrelevant as a consequence and that in most schools students have not been involved in problems, subject matter, and decisions that seem real and significant to them. Alienation of youth, increase of activism, and withdrawal from society are reported from all parts of the country. Generally speaking, citizens seem to have failed to grasp the full meaning of the technological age toward which we are racing or the significance of the responsibilities of citizens in an intercultural, interdependent civilization. Caught napping in a world that is changing too rapidly, many citizens have tended, when anxious and fearful, to look for a cure in the customs and traditions of the past and to call for a "return to the three R's," or similar panaceas of ultraconservatism.

Obviously, none of us can flee from the problems of society that surround us. With the aid of instantaneous communication via television, increasing complexity of urban living, and wider contacts with the outside world, young children are learning about society outside the school. And so we ask ourselves whether there is any recourse than to bring to bear the resources, the will, and the intelligence of the adults in both school and community on the problems of the changing role of education. Assuming that there is no other option than to teach children how to examine social problems, and assuming that some degree of conflict is probable between the school and the public, what preparation by the school staff would be most helpful to educational progress?

A Course of Action

Available to the University City schools are the resources of the St. Louis-St. Louis County Social Studies Project which is designed to aid schools in introducing the newer curriculum developments in social studies. Two or three teachers from each of several school districts and professors from Washington University meet regularly with the staff of the project to plan for dissemination of materials and ideas, arrange for field tryouts in several elementary and high schools, and develop inservice training plans.

One series for the intermediate grades includes a unit which presents the dilemma of farm workers forced by the effects of automation to move to the city. Another unit is built around the problems created when tenements are cleared and replaced with housing at rents too high for the former occupants who must then be dispersed to new locations and separated from their former friends and neighbors. Pupils not only examine social problems, but do so in very real and different ways. Role playing is introduced at strategic points and young children act out the roles of adults and put the thinking of adults into words. In the conventional social studies curriculum, safe topics, such as the geography of South America, were studied and if a role were played, the pupil might have play-acted little Pedro who was about his own age. No social issues were involved. The content was mainly concerned with understanding what it was like to harvest coffee beans and get them to market.

A third unit of the series involves the conflicts of black/white integration in formerly all-white suburbs. This was the unit we planned to introduce. It was timely in our community, perhaps too timely. Our geographical community was embroiled in a bitter dispute over de facto segregation and racial tensions were aroused. Sides had been drawn with one group advocating reorganization of the elementary schools into primary and intermediate centers to help relieve de facto segregation by busing children if necessary. Another faction supported the neighborhood school concept and denounced busing as evil. Moreover, the school in which the unit on "Changing Neighborhoods" was to be introduced was a sixth grade center made up of overflow classes from four neighborhood schools representing both sides of the community dispute. An educative process on the black/white dilemma would be most appropriate in this particular school, but also might set off new hostilities. With these possibilities confronting us, we made careful preparations. Several educators, both black and white, who were involved in the metropolitan project and who represented the university and nearby schools worked with several teachers of University City in planning an evening with the parents of the sixth grade pupils. By reaching beyond the borders of our own district for resources, we felt that parents might be helped to understand the unit in the context of a broad view.

The evening's presentation began with a general assembly. A professor from the university spoke about the thrusts and characteristics of contemporary social studies. He described the series of units on social issues and observed that each unit dealt with some element of conflict which has been generated by change in our society. Both sides of a dilemma are presented in the unit, he noted, so that the school could not be accused of leaning to one side. Children are led to identify with real people, not with shadow figures or abstract concepts such as the mountains of Switzerland. The professor stated that the purpose of the newer mode in social studies is to create citizens who can and will make rational public-policy decisions. When the student is faced by a dilemma and applies his thought processes to it, he learns how to make decisions by making them. The youngster is helped to look at differences between empirical arguments, fact arguments, and value arguments. The speaker continued with an explanation of the "Changing Neighborhoods" unit. He told the parents frankly that they would find analogies in this unit to University City, Teaneck, and dozens of other suburbs.

The unit opens with an introduction to a black middle-class family who live on the fringe of the black area of a large city. They are expressing a desire to live somewhere else where they can enjoy life more. They are also considering problems of finance, moving, and making new friends. Built into the unit are budget games in which children learn to figure costs of housing, moving expenses, and living expenses in different neighborhoods. Through the use of films and filmstrips, tape recordings, and role playing, a conflict develops within the family and between the family and other blacks. Should the Davis's move to an integrated suburb? They do decide to move.

Then the scene shifts to the white suburb and to various illustrations of the reactions of the white community. Negative attitudes and fears are brought out through neighborhood association meetings, and other types of role playing. Through a film presentation at one point, a white liberal father faces his dilemma in a dream. He finds that his belief in equality, justice, and freedom are in conflict with his fear of violence, his fear that property values will decline, and his subconscious bias in favor of whites.

During the evening, the parents viewed some of the films, and viewed video tapes made in a classroom in which a similar unit had been presented. It showed that as the children discussed the dilemma, the teacher did not inflict her ideas, but used the chalkboard to list ideas on both sides and to help children distinguish between fact and opinion. Parents were also involved in role playing to help them understand how such activities can be an aid to understanding a problem.

At the close of the evening, the tone of the parents' remarks were, "Why have we waited so long to teach this way in the schools? Let's get on with it!" The unit was successfully introduced in the classes of the sixth grade center to 300 pupils over the next 4 weeks without adverse criticism from parents and with the advantage of improved relationships between black and white children.

Relationships

"Changing Neighborhoods" is one illustration of an effort to bring the school and community into closer working relationship. Some other illustrations are briefly mentioned below. There is no limit to the opportunities that can be created to involve students, teachers, and other citizens in significant decisions concerning curriculum. It takes more time and effort but, in the long run, it will bring rewards. Unless community and school can work together in a process of mutual identification of and involvement in real and significant problems, where they examine evidence, search for rational solutions, discuss, and cooperate together in action, America's system of public education can only regress.

Some ideas for community-school cooperation that are presently being practiced in University City include the following:

Parents of 4-year-olds accompany the children to school and observe new teaching techniques for the young child, study modern theories of learning, and assist in making educational materials to be used at home.

Parents of a twelfth-grade social studies class come to school one night each week to study the same lessons their sons and daughters are studying to experience firsthand the changing nature of the social studies. In a course entitled "Humanities in Three Cities" a comparison is made of the politics, sociology, art, architecture, and government of ancient Athens and Florence, and modern New York City.

A curriculum for Black Studies is being planned by a committee of teachers, students, and lay citizens representing various viewpoints. The committee is not only suggesting outlines for Black Studies, but is locating resources and recruiting black teachers to join the faculty.

Countless community forums, coffees, and other opportunities for discussion of school problems are provided in this community. Some of these have a direct and others an indirect bearing on curriculum development, but generally provide opportunities for growth in knowledge and understanding of the tasks of the schools.

These are illustrative examples of ways the school and community are presently endeavoring to work together. Even greater efforts are going to be necessary. The need for continuing education for persons beyond school age has never been more evident than it is now.

CHANGES CHANGE AGENTS WANT

Ruth Bebermeyer, M.A. (ed.)
Peter Lippincott, B.S. (ed.)
Staff, Community Psychological Consultants
St. Louis, Missouri

This chapter reports some of the concerns expressed at a recent Conference of Educational Change Agents attended by people actively involved in effecting educational changes. They came together to pool resources and ideas, to explore alternatives and to clarify issues in the hope that they might thus help each other to work more productively. The participants agreed that education as it presently occurs in most schools does not provide students with the human resources to solve the problems they face, but the discussions reveal a diversity of thinking about the kinds of changes that are desirable and the ways of achieving change. Several thought that the public school system is now hopelessly inadequate and must be abolished if significant improvement in education is to occur, others held that fruitful change can occur within the present structure, some thought that the thrust for change must be aimed toward the community in which the school exists rather than toward the school itself.

The conferees did not attempt to arrive at solutions so much as to reveal problems and alternative approaches toward solutions. Therefore, this chapter does not follow the pattern of the others in this book in describing and evaluating an operational program. It is included to illuminate issues and to indicate directions which might guide future programs for educational change.

Much of the material in this chapter is transcribed from the discussion of the participants. Those quoted include Bill Caspary, Merrill Harmin, John Holt, Chuck Hosking, Marshall Rosenberg, Richard von Schmertzing, and Gus Seelig.

M. B. R.

CHANGES CHANGE AGENTS WANT

The overall question to which the Conference of Educational Change Agents addressed itself was "In what ways can we most productively work to bring about the educational changes that we want to effect?"[1]

One of the most immediate answers to that question was "We can establish alternative schools." Three of the conference participants (Richard, Chuck, and Gus) came from the LEAP (Lower Eastside Action Project) School in New York City. The problems of the New York City public schools had led the LEAP founders to search for an alternative. At LEAP they work with 12- to 16-year-old students from the ghetto area. Their focus is to meet the student on his ground and work with him in the hope of "turning him on" to learning again.

The LEAP staff came armed with some frustrations from their efforts to sustain an alternative to public education and also with some wants for which they hoped to get support from others at the conference. What follows are excerpts from the conference discussion.

RICHARD: One thing which I think this conference kind of exemplifies is the fragmentation in the alternative school and alternative education. We really have gotten it together in New York City and now have a number of alternative schools and a committee of community schools which is a beginning of a power base for the alternative school movement. But it bothers me that you had forty people on the invitation list to this conference and this number shows up. People are kind of scattered around doing their own thing and it leaves us powerless in the face of very powerful school systems all over the country.

[1] A Report of the Conference of Educational Change Agents, St. Louis, Missouri, April 3-4, 1971.

One of the things we have been pushing for for a couple of years now is the idea of an alternative board of education which would utilize resources of people who are not directly involved in alternative schools but who are interested in alternatives for education. We want to set up some sort of cover board for the country which would provide the basis for unifying the movement. People keep talking about movements and there ain't no movement! We'd really like to see people get together to clear the field. I really don't personally believe in educational reform. I believe in the complete turn around of the present educational system. I don't think you can do this through reform. My way to get at it is to form a power base which can kind of clear away the obstructions to creating alternatives. We don't need things like laws and regulations, the Board of Regents, and three bubbly fountains on the third floor before you can get a charter. If we can eliminate these restrictions, we can really get into creating a free field for many kinds of alternatives and then people can select from among the choices. I'm worried that we can't do that here because we obviously have too small a group. Maybe if people agree with my idea, maybe we can carry it back and try to work on it in our own way.

JOHN: Before we go any farther, I have to say I don't want that. I think we have got a movement and I don't think it has to be united under a single board in order to be effective.

RICHARD: I think that we probably agree on what needs to be done, at least to a certain extent. I hear a lot of points of agreement—deschooling, for example (considering some other forms of education than going to school). We are all saying that public education isn't working. What has been done to solve that problem is that a few people in a few places are creating alternative schools. Some people are going around trying to bring about reform inside the public schools. Other people are theorizing and writing books about how education could change if we ever had a place where that could come about. Other people are trying to train teachers

396

in new ways. I really feel that these are all disconnected or loosely connected activities that by themselves have a minimum amount of impact because they are not brought together and connected to form a base for some larger push against what's bad in education or for what's good in education.

For example, because it's loosely connected, it doesn't "bring down" the public school system in New York City. There are alternatives there; there are people theorizing; there are teachers who are teaching in new ways and yet the public school system in New York goes on and on and on. If we could get together and become very active and if we know what we want, like the end of compulsory attendance, for instance, we can become a threat to the system. We will be a power group.

BILL: I guess I tend to think in terms of very concrete objectives. For example, to get where you want to go would mean making available a lot of alternatives to education whether they be free schools or lofts or store fronts or whatever. You need a lot of places like this and you need to make them visible. But this seems to me an activity that can be done in a very decentralized way. When George Dennison writes a book, THE LIVES OF CHILDREN, even though he is a part of a movement he seems to be withdrawing more and more from talking to people. Yet everybody who is in one of those lofts or living rooms is reading his book. So it really is a direct working relationship.

RICHARD: And George Dennison—because he didn't hook up, the First Street School lasted 1 year. Did it even last a year?

JOHN: Two years.

RICHARD: And so many free schools are marks, one-shot deals.

MERRILL: You're not emphasizing, Bill, that the school failed, but that a guy wrote a book which is an important contribution.

RICHARD: And my feeling is that doing a 2-year deal and then writing a book which other people read is an example of our power-lessness.

JOHN: I don't feel powerless nor do I feel that I have any need except for about 48 more hours a day to do things worth doing. I've got no hangups about my work. I don't know the future. I change my mind each month as to what's tactically an effective thing to do, but by and large there is not much dissonance in me. Most of the time I'm pretty close to doing what looks to me like the best thing for me to do.

MARSHALL: I'm worried as I'm listening to you, Richard, that a good deal of your powerlessness comes because of your own problem-solving abilities. More specifically, when you use language like "bring down" I start wondering. If I was a member of a public school system I would start to feel threatened by you in reaction to your language. Now, Bill is on your side, but I don't see your interaction with him as open. My interpretation is that you're competing with Bill rather than trying to learn from him, which would make me worry that as an ally you wouldn't be easy to work with. These are things I would see you having the ability to control. As I see it, our power as a group, this group that is right here right now, is directly related to how we relate to one another.

RICHARD: I'd like to respond to what you said, Marshall. I hear what you're saying but I think that the language that I would use if I were to speak to public school people might be different. I also think that there are differences in style and my style comes from my hostility toward a lot of things. I have some very strong feelings and I'm very impatient because I feel the urgency of the problems, but I do hear what you're saying. I think that I can get past that. I think, too, that there's a problem of reference point. I feel that "power" is one of those words or reference points. There are probably a lot of negative things that people attach to the word "power," which I would not attach, and I am making the assumption that other people have the same reference point about the word that I do. Obviously that's not true. If we understand each other, words like "power" won't sound negative.

BILL: I think that there are some functions that are naturally centralized and some that are not. For example, I think of alternative education as basically a decentralized process. A certain number of people with a certain amount of energy get together and start a school in a specific place. The existence of some overall coordinating agency doesn't help that much in my mind. If that agency could raise money, that's great! That's a specific function that I might support.

RICHARD: I wanted to establish the need for some sense of unity, rather than decide the specific things that this organization could do once it was established. I say this partly because I don't have the answer. I think the organization would help solve problems. One function could be to assist in getting money, either through voucher systems or through hustling corporations. Another thing, and perhaps to my way of thinking the biggest problem they could help with, would be to help remove the legal codes which are obstructions to the establishment of alternative schools. These really have to be met and dealt with and changed.

MARSHALL: What you're saying now has an entirely different ring to me. Now I hear you saying you're seeing an organization which has as its purpose to help alternatives survive. It sounded before as if you were going to take over and decide how people should be. When you start talking about how these alternatives can survive, I can much better appreciate the organization.

JOHN: It brings me very quickly to the thought that the alternative school movement is defining itself as a bunch of good guys who are going to protect kids from all those other bad guys out there. If we get into defining ourselves in this way, I think we're making a terrible mistake. There are a lot of reasons why I think that, not least of all the immediate one that people would be jealous if we provided a free school experience for kids on a wide scale. There are a lot of people who would think, "Dammit, I didn't have these goodies. I had to go through that rat race and I stood it so why can't these kids stand it." Because of this very real fact of jealousy I find myself thinking more and more that as we discover the experiences that are really life-enhancing and growth-making, we've got to make them available to everybody and not just to people defined as kids. Tactically, that's very difficult. Resources are limited and we've got to start somewhere but I think we should keep that in mind.

CHUCK: The national board we're thinking of could be something similar to our LEAP board of directors for our own protection and our needs, providing political muscle or occupancy for a building—that sort of thing. When we need money in an emergency we can go to our connections to get it. A national board would not have to deal with individual schools and how they operate. For individual schools, the power they would have would come from what people felt they wanted to give them because the school was a good, necessary thing.

We still need to be diversified in our outlook. I don't know if you all know much about Harlem Prep. That's a school in Harlem whose goal is really to get people into college. I don't think that's a goal that I would support, but I think it's necessary to have a school that does that. At the same time, it's good to have a hundred different alternatives. They all need protection and we're going to have to be united to provide that protection.

GUS: Even if we create no alternatives, there's still a need, I think, to do away with an institution as harmful as the public school system. My options are limited. My brothers are both in school and I've got friends in prisons. It's clear to me that I'm going to have to shut schools and prisons down right away. It's hard for me to distinguish the two in New York. I have to build what I can in terms of alternative schools like LEAP.

RICHARD: LEAP is not the only type of school. We're 100 percent in agreement with having every range of possibility. That's what alternative means to me—to have many kinds of schools.

GUS: If we had one alternative to the public school, it wouldn't be an alternative. We've got to have a bunch in terms of the politics of the movement.

JOHN: In the last few years I've been impressed with what can happen if I'm not associated with anything and I can just follow my own design. I can see what needs to be done and with my own autonomy I can go and do it. However, I've become increasingly frustrated because I see the enormity of the task and I begin to wonder if I would be more effective getting out and trying to coordinate politically. I have trouble with organizations because there seems to me to be, within firmly established organizations, a kind of life cycle where the organization really isn't serving the mutual purposes of the people who put it together. It dies but doesn't disappear; it just stands there—a kind of corruption. The organization becomes its own reason for being. This is an exceedingly difficult thing to avoid. So I have a real paranoia about institutions. I don't work well with other people. I guess I am open to the possibility of new ways of coordinating so that one can have the kind of political power that I hear you talking about without getting into spending most of our time deciding which bureaucratic game to play. Our discussion has helped me clarify this conflict within myself.

RICHARD: If I gave the impression that I am looking for some marvelous bureaucracy that agrees upon everything a school should be, then I gave an entirely wrong impression. For me it gets into the concept of power—by what power could the organization survive? If the power we want is legal power, then I'm worried about getting into the same bind we're in with the public schools.

MARSHALL: When we start talking about keeping alternatives alive, I'm for that goal. When we start getting into the mechanics of it, whether it be a charter or whatever, I start to get concerned. Not so much the charter itself, but on what basis are we going to set up a charter? What kind of power do we want the organization to have? One of the things that I really didn't want in San Francisco when I started working with the schools there was a position within the school system. The only power that I wanted to have was the power of my ideas and my ability to communicate them to other people. I didn't want any legal, coercive power. It was at the point that I started to hear that you wanted a kind of credential power that seemed coercive to me that I got turned off.

GUS: The whole thing about a charter, at least as I'm thinking of it, is not a super board—a national board of alternative schools which would be as didactic as public school boards across the country are. It's more a legitimacy thing which I could see just growing out of a general desire for visibility. A sort of social acceptability might grow up among people, especially if the voucher system were to go through and if there were some structure that they could relate to rather than individual alternative schools. Parents would be able to talk with this organization about what specific alternative would be best for their child: The organization would be able to coordinate. A parent might be given a voucher for his or her child or the vouchers could be given to children by the age of 10 or 11 if that was when the child was ready to choose his own structure.

JOHN: Either you charter everybody and nobody pays attention or you start being selective and then you're back in the bag of approving of some and not of others.

RICHARD: When I said an alternative board might go around and charter schools I thought of it as an action against the absurdity of a group like a board of regents who has the power to charter schools on the basis of some absolutely ridiculous things. Things like three fountains on the third floor, a course on the evils of alcohol, the doors all opening in instead of out, celebrate national wildlife day— requirements like that. You never get a course in New York public schools on the evils of alcoholism but when you're an alternative school trying to get a charter, the law becomes important. We had to throw out two architects to meet the codes. We had to get exactly within the letter of the law.

Another thing, foundations are more likely to give money to an overall organization than to twelve different groups. The organization would then have to decide which group to give the money to.

JOHN: There would still be competition for the money. I think that education should be a consumer kind of thing with all doors open. If a 6-year-old is ready, he should make the choice of the school he wants and then go to it. I don't think the choice should be made by his parents.

MARSHALL: I think we do have a consumer thing now but only a very small percentage of people can afford it.

RICHARD: What we'd like to see is everybody having that choice.

[The discussion shifted here from the concern for some kind of coordinating organization for alternative education as a whole to some of the specific issues in individual schools.]

RICHARD: I know a lot of schools in New York are into having parents being a part of the program. We're not really interested in having parents as part of the program, but we do want older people, community people.

JOHN: I have something in mind—a conversation I had with the man who runs a school in Vermont called Shaker Mountain School. It sounds good from his description of what goes on there. He was talking about a camp they have in the country where kids can go to get away from their problems, which may be their families, and get a fresh outlook on things. It raised a question which I raise all the time. These experiences are important. Is there some way that this could be made available to people who are older? Would there be any way that an adult could have access to this kind of experience? He said, "Frankly, no. Most adults are so screwed up because of their experiences that they can't be around younger people without kind of pushing them around. We have to keep them out." For now I can think, fair enough, but I do want everyone included in the future.

RICHARD: Most of the alternative schools in the country that I know about are struggling every day for survival. We work with a minimal staff who has a maximum amount of hustling to do just to keep our doors open, just to make these alternatives available. I really think that what we need is an effort of the kind that you're apparently comfortable with, Marshall—an effort of people who can think of new ways of organization.

I don't want to talk about failures, or take things from history that are failure-set and put them on what I want for schools. Talking failure makes me very impatient. I'm interested in creating a clear ground where spontaneous creative communities which happen to be learning communities, or socialization communities, or whatever (I'm avoiding the use of the word school) can emerge and live and breathe. I think that this really needs and deserves a lot of energy from people who do have organizational abilities as I think you do.

CHUCK: I'd like to explain about our "hustling" thing. At the beginning of our school year we spent 2½ weeks in the country during which time we planned how we were going to structure our school year. We went under the assumption that everyone was interested in doing that and would make decisions, which were hard ones to make. We decided exactly what was going to happen, what times the school would be open, how we would take care of all the things we needed to take care of. We didn't want to have people telling us what to do about administrative things so we had to do them ourselves.

We broke up into what we called systems groups. One system was for hustling. This meant a group that could go out and get the materials we needed donated to us to build our building. We hustled doors, floor tile, plumbing facilities. All these things were hustled by people approaching various companies, telling them who we were and explaining what we needed. Out of this retreat, which we called LEAPfrog, we developed a hustling committee which consisted of about eight people. Both Gus and Richard were members. I happened to be in charge of maintenance.

In addition, we spent a lot of time getting to know one another through group "raps" and through some role playing. We worked on problem-solving, using situations such as the taxi strike in New York where the fares weren't high enough to support the cabs but people didn't like the poor service they were getting. We divided into groups to discuss problems like that. Through the group sessions we got out gripes and got to know one another.

A second answer to the question, "What can we do to produce effective educational change?" was, "We can train teachers in new ways to teach in new ways." One of the participants at the conference described the program for teacher training which he directs at a university. (See Chapter 11, "A Model for Teacher Training" by Merrill Harmin for details of this program.) The program aims primarily at training teachers for the public schools with emphasis on providing opportunities for self-directed, yet inter-dependent, learning. We report here some of the discussion:

RICHARD: I just really find it hard to relate to solving the prob-lems in education by changing the teachers that we have now be-cause I'm beginning to believe that a certain type of person goes into teaching as it's presently defined—you know, everybody knows what a teacher is because everybody's been taught. I find it really hard to relate to that general type of person. My feeling is that we have to generate other kinds of role models in public schools through the alternative schools where we have different types of teachers, or through the open schools where you have people going out relating to business. This would really almost flip over teacher education because you won't be working with the same people and you certainly won't be working with those who have been doing it for the past 10 years. One of the problems in New York is that they've taken a lot of "liberal" teachers from all around the public schools and put them in a "school without walls" essentially, and I just don't think it's going to work because the teachers still have a whole set of ideas and mind sets and interactional forms that I don't believe can be broken down. They are so strongly a part of who those teachers are and who they've been and what kinds of things they can relate to.

MERRILL: From my experiences, 55 percent of the teachers may be willing to change, but only a little bit. More like 5 percent are open to substantial change.

JOHN: It took me a long time to get from where I started as a teacher to where I was when I wrote HOW CHILDREN FAIL. That was a 6-year journey for me. When I started teaching I was absolutely conventional except that I liked kids and didn't want silent classrooms.

RICHARD: The thing that concerns me is that a lot of teachers will show up at conferences on alternative education who agree that the public schools are not good but that's as far as it goes. I guess a small change is better than no change at all, but I really feel that piecemeal reform is a finger-in-the-dike kind of thing. The few energetic, dynamic people in every school system would really just be batting their heads against a brick wall if they tried to shake off that enormous dead weight of the rest of the people and the curriculum and the bureaucracy and red tape.

MERRILL: Are you saying that my job of trying to change teachers, to help them step by step, is not going to pay off and I might better just try to help alternative schools develop?

RICHARD: No, what I'm saying is that I think we need other kinds of teachers for the new schools, and I think your job might be to find out what kinds of teachers are needed for the alternative schools and to modify your teacher training procedures so that you produce teachers for all kinds of schools rather than just for the public schools.

MARSHALL: In other words, you're saying it might be easier to start with people who are not teachers now and train them to be effective teachers?

RICHARD: Yes.

MARSHALL: I've tried it both ways, and my frustration is that I run into the same problem when I go in that direction. I find that the kinds of people who are not public school teachers are just as addicted to their way of thinking in trying to teach teachers because they've been through the public education.

407

MERRILL: I think you'd have an easier time working with non-teachers presently in that people who have not already started teaching, even though they have already gone through the public school system and have an idea what a teacher is, are still some-what more open.

MARSHALL: They don't have quite as much vested interest.

MERRILL: Not just vested interest, but the experience of having taught would have meant that they would have had to go through changes.

RICHARD: As alternative schools, we have some very specific needs in terms of teachers. To be more concrete, we need people who are decision-makers, who aren't afraid to control their own destiny. They need to be the kind of role model that students can relate to in terms of decision-making and problem-solving. My feeling is that the kind of people who are effective in teaching, as it's presently defined, will never make those decisions and will never present those role models. We have two kinds of people who show up at LEAP wanting to teach—people who are interested in doing their own thing without defining what that thing is, and people who have the attitude that they're there to do us a service and there's nothing really in it for them. I have a friend who was working with store front clubs and was also working at an outside job to keep the store fronts going, and the people (who happened in this case to be Puerto Rican) could really relate to the idea that she was doing something else—that was a good role model. They find very suspect the idea that some 23-year-old girl from Long Island would come in and teach at a ghetto school because she wanted to donate her life to the good of young people or something like that. They just can't relate to that at all.

MARSHALL: From my observation of your program at SIU, Merrill, I have a feeling you are training people who could go into this role and get the job done. What I'm wondering is how you find the people that you get into your program?

MERRILL: We kept selecting on things like strength and imagination—strength is a critical thing. Then we train them essentially by putting them into a LEAP type experience. It would not be impossible for us to float a school in various parts of the country to train alternative and free school staff, either on a long-term or short-term basis. Just the selective process we provide could be helpful.

RICHARD: If people knew what kind of person you're looking for—strong people who are into decision-making and who like to control their own lives, they would gravitate toward your teacher-training program and toward the alternative schools. With all that energy and strength in the alternative school movement and the weakness in the public schools, the result is obvious to me.

MERRILL: I wonder if I could go to the chancellor and say, "How about setting up a department of free school education?" I don't know how many times I'm asked, "Where can I go to school where I don't have to be dehumanized? I want to teach but I don't want to go through the present system." It's very hard, though, to actualize new programs at a university—the thing that made it real for me in the past was that I had a lot of money from Washington and could hire my own staff. And part of the problem is the credit question.

RICHARD: If you want to teach in a free school, you don't need credit.

MERRILL: There's a school in Seattle which has a program that may be interesting to us in lots of ways, as a prototype school. The director has been trying for some time to get help to get the school accredited in the state of Washington as a teacher-training institution. She's run into all kinds of roadblocks but now there's a real possibility of jumping state lines that's interesting. She's working with a college in California so that those students may go to her school for a year to intern, for which they will get a California certificate which can then be used in a lot of other places. It's interesting to me that a school in Washington can be a training resource for a California college.

MARSHALL: Another thing—I'd like to see you issue a certificate of competence rather than a certificate of accreditation. I'd like a certificate in which the student and faculty jointly agree as to what competence this person demonstrates.

MERRILL: That's essentially what we do now in the program at SIU.

MARSHALL: Actually it's becoming almost irrelevant. Think of all the people who have certificates now who don't have jobs, so you can't say you've got to have one in order to get a job. Maybe you say, "We'll teach you how to live on hunger!" I would like to see a large part of the training be in community organization skills so that people in the program would not believe they are going into programs that are already established but would think that part of teaching in this way requires setting it up yourself. We could start right off in college with the idea that we want people who are courageous enough to go out and set up their own jobs. John told me last night that he would like to see the kind of situation in which learners hired teachers. That way a teacher would make sure he had something to offer.

———

Another, and perhaps the most extensively discussed, answer to "How can we bring about the changes we want in education?" was, "We can learn to communicate our ideas and wants effectively." Incidents of misunderstanding and problems of semantics among the conferees themselves emphasized the importance of communication among those working for change as well as between them and people presently opposed to change. In connection with the

410

discussion on communication, the issue of "affective" versus "intellectual" approaches to education was raised, and a suggestion for a third, more inclusive, approach was offered. The dialogue which follows begins with a discussion of the importance of feelings in messages. John is describing two dinners he had recently attended.

JOHN: Both were small dinner gatherings. The first group was enormously committed to affective education, to openness and to always talking about feelings. The second group was made up of people who talk at what might be called the intellectual level. The feeling tone of the second evening, where people were dealing at what might be called the level of ideas, was much more friendly, relaxed, open, and human. At least, that was my perception.

MARSHALL: I just get terribly frustrated because I want your ideas but I find that I have so much trouble getting to them because they don't come at the level I'm comfortable with.

JOHN: Now in my own mind, and this may be my hangup, I can't separate my ideas from my feelings at a level of definition of words. I don't experience these two parts of my life differently.

MARSHALL: When I'm really functioning, I don't think I do either. I don't think there's a separation of them.

JOHN: I think of meetings I've had with teachers. Granted, the teachers have come to the meeting where I'm talking, so in some ways it's preselected and they have some interest in what I'm saying, so perhaps they're not representative or comparable to some of the groups you talk to. You may have many more opponents. But I think of a seminar that we had at Berkeley once where I was a resource person and we just sat in a room on the floor and I said, "Let's just talk back and forth in all directions and I'll chip in when I can or when people want to ask me questions." O.K., the thing started out on a very trivial level, or on a level of rather specific information type questions such as what to do when a kid can't add two and two. I took each question at face value and answered it as directly as I could. It was extraordinarily interesting to see how rapidly this discussion moved to a discussion of people's feelings of fallibility as teachers, of their weakness, of their fears of student rejection. In other words, we got into a level of very deep feelings without anybody ever suggesting that we ought to do it. That's not the only way, but at any rate it is the way I've been used to. My rather limited experience with the affective education people, or at least with those who have gone to conferences I've attended, is that it never gets to genuine feeling.

MARSHALL: I guess I just want to share with you my own agreement with what you're saying except for my frustration that I haven't been able to communicate to you that I think there's another possibility beside the affective domain as talked about by the people you describe. What I mean when I'm talking about the sharing of one's position is to start by grounding in where I am at the moment. John, I think I could learn more about your ideas if I just kind of heard more about your present feelings and thoughts and less about things that have happened in the past. But I was afraid that that would be imposing on you my desires for communication. I didn't want to put you in that bind so that you'd feel pressured to communicate in my way. So I'm just sharing with you my frustration.

———

The conversation then moved to a discussion of the previous night and how incidents of that night reflected the value of expressing feelings.

JOHN: Last night I really wanted help on that cab driver incident I had told you about.

MARSHALL: I'll fill the rest of you in. John got into a cab yesterday and the cab driver said, "What do you think about Calley?"

John tried to answer and the man said, "He was ordered to do it." So John was asking how to deal with an issue like that. But, John, if I had known from the very beginning that you had that much respect for my communication skills and that that's why you were bringing the incident up, if you had grounded that in where you were, it would have really significantly altered for me the whole course of things.

JOHN: I wanted to talk about communication, but in the context of that very specific event. My feelings were churning as I rode along in that cab. I felt fear of my own dislike of the cab driver and distrust of him—fear of my own perception of him as some kind of Nazi and disappointment in what I sense as a weakness of my own character.

MARSHALL: If I had known that last night—I'm not saying if you had *said* it,—but if I had been more sensitive to it, then I would really have wanted to give you an awful lot, but from my standpoint of not really knowing your feelings and of just hearing, "How would you have handled that?" I was just frustrated.

JOHN: As it was, I did get something. I didn't go home from last night's conversation feeling frustrated or with a lot of unmet needs.

MARSHALL: I'm just learning again how important feelings are to me. As it looked to me, all John wanted was some factual information, and the whole feeling part of that which I didn't pick up was what would really have made the difference for me.

BILL: The other side of the coin is your failure to share your own feelings, Marshall. It might have been different if you had shared the fact that you were feeling afraid to do your communication thing because that might really bother John. Instead of sharing that you just pulled away from it.

413

MARSHALL: My problem wasn't that, Bill, my problem was that I hadn't empathized before. I kind of purposely didn't express my feelings because I thought that John would see that as an intrusion, an imposing on him. I guess what I had heard John say in the past about affective education people got me worried about being lumped under that heading of someone who immediately starts to impose feelings on a discussion, so I chose not to share my feelings. I wasn't afraid to, I just chose not to. I was afraid John would see me as taking the position that the quest for any kind of intellectual clarification, for ideas, is bad, that if you're intellectualizing you're not being a real person. I was afraid of being put in that affective education category and that's frightening to me because I'm just as averse to their way of communicating as John is. But I do believe strongly that, to the degree I could have known John's feelings and desires as well as his thoughts, I could have done a better job of sharing information with him.

JOHN: Now I understand what you mean when you talk about feelings, desires, and thoughts, but my problem is that somebody else would say, "That's opinion," or "That's thought"—I don't know how to use these as criteria.

MARSHALL: I don't think I have understood John in the past. I think that what John has been expecting from me in the past is clarification about when feelings are really helpful, when they're constructive in communication and education. I think that what I heard until now was, "Hands off, I just want to talk about things that are very intellectual." Now I'm hearing him say, "Look, I don't like being put in binds, I don't like communicating about feelings if that means I have to give up any kind of quest for intelligence," but I don't hear him saying, "Hands off."

JOHN: That's accurate. What's even more important is the confusion that starts in some hypothetical situation if people were to say, O.K., now we're just going to talk about our feelings for awhile; I simply don't know what to say because I don't know how to draw the line in my own mind and experience. There's obviously a clear line for some people which I don't have.

MARSHALL: Part of my frustration is that there are times when I don't think that it makes much difference whether I report verbally what my emotions are or not, there are other times when it seems very important. I think part of the reason I've left you hanging on this in the past is that I'm not clear about when it's important and when it isn't. I don't know that if I want to know what time it is that I want to know anything about your feeling.

BILL: I think that one word that's missing there is needs or desires, that part of the thing that Marshall was looking for last night falls in the category of desire rather than feeling.

JOHN: Yes, I wanted to learn from him.

MARSHALL: I'm bursting to share some intellectual clarification. I like to have conversations grounded in feeling, but once they're grounded that way it isn't as important to me that the next messages always include them. It serves the same purpose as a transition sentence in an English theme. When a person shifts from one thing to another it just helps me to stay interested in it if I know their wants and feelings, so had you grounded the message last night in your feelings and desires, the whole subsequent course of our ideas would have been different for me.

JOHN: I think this is crucial. It's a thing I think about all the time. In connection with the affective education, whether sensitivity groups, or encounter groups, or the whole human development movement, this is one of the key issues and problems of our times. How do people get the barriers down, how do they get out of the boxes they've got themselves shut up into? I sense an enormous number of people working, struggling, groping in this area, I

think some very damagingly and dangerously and others construc-
tively. Most of the explorers with whom I've come into contact
seem to me to be quite frankly exploiters who are discovering ways
of dominating rather than freeing people.

MARSHALL: You're saying that if we want to help people we not
only have to present ideas for them to understand, but we also have
to find ways to release them from their own emotional ties?

JOHN: No, it's not ties. It's people building defenses up in all directions so they can't move. How do these come down, how do
people get so they can move, how do they get less afraid? Certainly
this has been a large part of my own personal history. I'm very
much more at ease in my skin and in my work than I was 20 years
ago. I've had a lot of luck because I found work that I liked and
in the course of my work I found all kinds of friends and all kinds
of options and space to move that a lot of hard-pressed people just
plain don't have. My job isn't like some teacher in a public school
with a job he hates. I've had some 20 years of pretty happy life
experiences in which to get rid of some of my armor, but I sense
that we've got to find faster processes that will work for most people. This partial cure is not widely available, so I'm concerned
about it. And there's a tremendously strong reaction in certain
quarters against talking about feelings. People who might be roughly
termed right-wing get really furious and angry when they hear about
teachers and children in schools having discussions of feelings. They
think the business of the schools is to teach facts.

MARSHALL: When I'm with people who have that view I say,
"That really aggravates you to think that what's going on in schools
now is not getting down to brass tacks," and they'll say, "You're
damn right." They know I've heard them, even though what I'm
doing is getting in touch with their feelings. They get expression
of feelings all mixed up with the acting on them and they think you
can't do that without avoiding intellect.

416

JOHN: You've unquestionably persuaded me that there's an important process of change that I've got to embark on but I still think it's going to be a very slow process. This is not something that I feel I could be taught to do.

MARSHALL: But I think that to make this an absolute and to say that you have to do it in every situation whether you feel comfortable in it or not is not what I mean. I'm all for people saying, "I chose not to be honest with you about my feelings in that situation because I was afraid," as long as that's the reason, rather than, "The other person couldn't handle it." If that's the reason, that other people would resent it, I would not like not expressing my feelings. If they don't want me to do it, then I want them to tell me that, rather than my making the assumption that everybody is going to be angry with my feelings.

RICHARD: But supposing that someone comes up to you, and this is a real problem for me, and says something like, "You have a Communist on your board of directors." It's really hard for me to get past a certain defensiveness. When I'm trying to empathize with somebody else and I'm feeling very emotional about what I'm saying, it's really hard. So if they said, "I think it would be really helpful if we switched roles and you tried to understand where I'm coming from," I go, "What! I'm feeling like yelling and screaming and you want me to turn around and be the person I feel like yelling and screaming at? It's impossible!" I don't know how to break out of that. Do you understand my dilemma? I don't know how to get out of my own caught feelings.

MARSHALL: When you've got really strong feelings of your own, at that moment how do you put yourself in the other position?

RICHARD: Yes.

MARSHALL: When I'm mad, I say just that. I say to the man, "Right now I'm just so angry and so frightened by what you're saying that I'm having real trouble understanding what you mean by it." If I don't want to empathize then I try to be honest about that because there's nothing that bothers me more than seeing another person really dying to say something but instead feeding back. To me it's important that whenever a person does empathize with me I can trust that he feels more interested at that moment in understanding me than in doing anything else. If it's more important to him to say what he's feeling, then I want him to do that. That's a check I frequently have to do on myself. If I catch myself really wanting to race on ahead when I'm trying to paraphrase, then what I'd really rather do is say my thing and let him be angry at me because I didn't understand him and let him say that. I know for myself that when I'm listening to another person and paraphrasing his message, it's really important that I really am at that moment trying to understand. I'd like to role play the situation you mentioned with you, Richard.

RICHARD: O.K.

MARSHALL: If you've said, "There's a Communist on your staff," and I've expressed my anger and fear and you come back with your original statement, I'd say (role playing) "I'm really frustrated now because I wanted so much to have you hear what I just said, that it's just really hard for me to deal with that question."

RICHARD: (role playing) "You're damn right, it's hard! You've got a Communist plot working in this country and you're part of it, no wonder it's hard! You're trying to take over the whole country, subvert our kids—what's the matter with you?"

MARSHALL: (role playing) "I think I've got my feelings under control now. I'd really like to see if I got that. You're angry right now because of what you see the Communists wanting to do in this country and you think that I'm in that with them."

RICHARD: (role playing) "Do you have a Communist on your board of directors or not?"

MARSHALL: (role playing) "I don't know of any but I'm worried that no matter what I say . . . ."

RICHARD: (role playing) "Well, everybody knows that John is a Communist!"

MARSHALL: (role playing) "If he is, I wasn't aware of it. I don't know how you define Communist, but if he is, I don't know about it."

RICHARD: (role playing) "Well, he goes around advocating that kids just be turned loose on the streets and not have to go to school and run around and have no authority over them. That's a plot to take over the country. He's probably getting paid by Mao-what's-his-name!"

MARSHALL: (role playing) "So, in other words, what makes you associate him with Communisim is the fact that you see him trying to subvert the young by teaching them to just do their own thing and disregard our social standards."

RICHARD: (role playing) "You're damn right he's subverting."

MARSHALL: (role playing) "I'm very anxious to share with you that I see what you say in a different way and I'd like to try to clarify what I hear you say. I guess I'm fearful right now that you're so angry with me that you don't want to do that."

RICHARD: (role playing) "That's kind of true."

MARSHALL: (role playing) "I'd really like to know what you mean by Communist. Do you mean some kind of anarchist who believes that you don't have to do anything you don't want to do? I agree partly—I do believe in children making their own decisions but I also believe in their being held responsible for the consequences of those decisions. I'm saying that I don't see what good it does to tell kids what to do, because they're going to do what they want anyway. But I want to make it quite clear that I'm not saying that I wouldn't like people in a position on the board to be very explicit about what they believe in. My experience is that the more I can get away from telling people what to do, the more interested they seem to be in what I'm saying. When I make a demand, I give them just two choices, to submit or rebel, and sometimes they do both."

RICHARD: (role playing) "But this letting kids run around and have all this freedom is what gets them out on the street marching against their country and burning their flag and disgracing our boys in Vietnam and bombing buildings."

MARSHALL: (role playing) "I'm really anxious to share that I don't want to assume responsibility for that because I don't see it that way at all. I said before that when you tell people what to do you give them two choices, to submit or rebel. I really think that those who are rebelling are rebelling against being told what to do in a way that they consider unfair. In our school we offer another alternative. We try to teach kids that there's a third way in addition to submit or rebel. There's a way to work cooperatively to bring about change, without violating other people."

RICHARD: (role playing) "All these fancy words are O.K. for you, but I don't know what you're talking about. All I know is that the kinds of schools that you people are talking about produce these long-haired hippies who go around and want to tear down the universities and the public school systems and burn and destroy everything. What they need is a good structured classroom where they learn to appreciate authority and to do as they're told! The public schools these days are just not strict enough. Probably the trouble

420

is that the public school people are listening to people like you and not being as tough as they should be. That's why those people are the way they are. It's the permissive society."

MARSHALL: (role playing) "Right now I'm just feeling a sense of despair because I see myself being judged, and I just feel there's no way that I'll be able to share with you what I really feel. And that gives me a kind of despair because I really get scared about what's going to happen to this country if people like you and me are unable to communicate with each other. I'm also personally frightened because I guess I have real fear that if your boss were to tell you to get rid of all the Rosenbergs in the world, from what you just said about authority I'd be scared that you'd so it without question."

RICHARD: People could come back on something like that and say, "You're damn right, my boss is the good Lord and I'll do whatever I feel is right—if that means doing away with all you dirty Jew commies and niggers, I'll do that too."

MARSHALL: All I can do is just repeat what I said—I just despair because I really think I have something to offer there. I try to express my feelings as a human being and I'm trying to understand his feelings as a human being. If I think I've got to change him, I make it much harder for change to occur. I think we have another practical example of the crucial importance of communication with the newspaper Gus was telling us about. [editor's note: The paper referred to was to be a collection of news contributed by high school students in New York City which would then be edited by Gus and distributed to area students.] It's great that those people should communicate with each other and share frustrations of their different situations, but I'm also interested in the fact that teachers and administrators are going to pick those papers up and read them and I'm worried that the language will create more barriers than already exist.

RICHARD: Some people are very angry and want to talk about pigs and that kind of thing—that's where their heads are and they wouldn't want any editor trying to tone down what they want to say. If somebody else wants to come out and do a soft rap that he hopes people will hear, that's cool, too.

GUS: In terms of the paper, I want people to know the kind of thing that's happening. Yesterday there was a girl—she's diabetic—who was about to give herself an insulin injection. Some school authority saw her, assumed it was heroin, and she was arrested and is now in the hospital really sick because of not getting the insulin. It's pretty hard to worry about your language with that kind of stupid thing going on. It's pretty hard not to think of yourself as being at war with the public schools.

MARSHALL: I can understand the rage, but I'm bothered by the way it's expressed. Even if you say that you would only say it that way with friends in here, it bothers me that you think in terms of "pigs" or "stupid." I can't really join a group and be actively committed unless they want to provide a more meaningful way, a more loving alternative.

RICHARD: O.K. Marshall, to say to me that I should really be interested in providing a loving alternative when I'm spending 16 or 17 hours a day working in a school which is a loving alternative means nothing to me. I feel I'm doing that and my anger still burns.

MARSHALL: I'm frustrated because I didn't really get to my point. I think that people's thinking shapes their subsequent behavior. When we even start thinking of being at war with public schools, that way of thinking alters our subsequent activity. My suggestion is that I would be more comfortable with some other way of thinking because that could lead one in different directions.

RICHARD: Let me ask you this. Does it disturb you more when Gus or I say that we're going to be at war with public schools than it does when John says he's at war with public schools?

JOHN: Except it's a metaphor I never use. I'm confused and worried when I hear war with public schools, because I just don't know what that means. Maybe it means things I 100 percent approve of, such as starting schools like LEAP. But it may mean things I disapprove of, like calling teachers "pigs," or it may mean things that I would absolutely disapprove of, like setting fire to a building when there were a lot of people in it. I don't know what you mean.

RICHARD: What I mean, personally, is the abolition of the public schools. The reason that I want to see them abolished is that I feel we need rapid change, we don't need piecemeal older forms, we don't need stop-gap methods. We really need some way of bringing about rapid change and I think we share a sense of urgency in that need.

MARSHALL: We do share that but in the past when I've been really impatient I have engaged in a lot of name calling and have been very self-destructive for my own goals. When I start using metaphors like, "we have to go to war with the public schools, we have to get rid of them," I go more in the direction of attacking in my speeches and my activities. Even if I'm just thinking out loud, my language infuriates other people I'm with. Even my colleagues tell me they get turned off—and if people who are really for me get that way I know how it affects those who don't agree with me. So it's because of my impatience for real change that I'm impatient with the language.

CHUCK: Marshall, if I agreed that your way would be faster and more effective, I'd do it. I'd force myself to do that, but in talking with Gus and Richard and other people at LEAP I really feel that Gus and his paper will not be talking primarily to the public school teacher or administrator with whom he would have to use loving terms. He'll be talking more to the student, and if he's going to use loving terms as far as the public schools go, that's really going to confuse his readers.

MARSHALL: Let me indicate what I mean by loving terms. He said before, and I'm just catching a couple of words out of context here, "Now that's stupid." I would have been much happier if he'd said, "When I see things like that, I get enraged."

JOHN: It really might not have been stupid from the viewpoint of the teacher. It might have been the only logical thing to do and once you judge it as stupid someone who is behaving in his perception logically is separated from you. I think the way to start is to understand where they are and help them move from there. There are a lot of things you can do feeling your rage, and yet start where they are.

CHUCK: But what I hear Marshall saying is that if you want to be effective you need a loving approach to convert people to that way of thinking. I disagree if you're talking to students.

MARSHALL: I would say that when I'm talking with students I feel an even more strong responsibility for not making value judgments in the form of facts. I'm concerned with how many students have been taught by the public school people to think in categorical terms that things are stupid or not stupid, absurd or not absurd, that there's a single one right answer and somebody in authority knows it. I'm upset with that whole way of thinking, whether I'm thinking that and sharing those thoughts with groups of angry students, or whether I'm sharing thoughts with a group of people within the school systems. I'm reluctant and fearful of the consequences of not just being open and honest about my own feelings but talking in terms like, "that's absurd."

CHUCK: In other words, rather than editorializing on what the facts are, just present the facts?

MARSHALL: Rather than confusing my own opinion with facts, I would want to make clear that all I'm sharing is my own feelings. I don't mean to say that when I go into public schools now I talk nice sweet language, but rather than coming in and using words such as, "The practices that you're now engaging in are absurd," I say, "I'm just full of despair when I see that happening." I don't say, "What's happening in the public schools is wrong." I'm not saying, "You've got to stop doing this." I say, "I want you to do something else." How I communicate makes a big difference in how people respond.

CHUCK: I would agree with you on that, but what I'm asking is whether you would say that exact same thing to students.

MARSHALL: Exactly. My language would not be different for students. The vocabulary might, but the process wouldn't.

CHUCK: O.K., I wouldn't come up to a student and say, "That scares me that they arrested someone."

MARSHALL: Let me show you the difference. To the student I might say, "I'm hip to that." With a faculty member I'd say, "I'm comfortable with that."

CHUCK: Well, I think that if a newspaper is going to speak to students you can probably start with a language more like antipublic school and translate it into pro-alternative schools, which is not just softening or euphemizing but changing from a negative to a positive pole. And when speaking with teachers you can probably start not with the antipublic school thing but with a pro-alternative school and show that that means necessarily that public schools will have to be abolished.

MARSHALL: I think we're getting closer to understanding one another except that I'm not just for talking about positives as opposed to negatives. I have nothing against talking about being aghast at the public school system. I'm just afraid to use an establishment language when we're talking about a thing that the establishment is not doing. For me, establishment language is that there are good guys and bad guys. I'm for strong, vehement language, but in terms of the newspaper I would like to see something other than judgments. My despair is that I see young students resort to doing the same thing the schools do, using the same words, the same tactics, judging the system. They know that they don't like it, but they don't even say that they don't like it. They say that the system is sick; they say that they're oppressed. They don't say they're feeling powerless and angry.

CHUCK: I don't think that anyone would say that that's where you stop. You have to go from there to a positive position.

MARSHALL: Here's my distrust of that. My observation is that I don't see people shifting after awhile. I see them thinking in a kind of worrying way about where do they go, and the mentality is oriented toward knocking the system. When that happens they get out of touch with themselves. They just get in the track of always saying what's wrong with the system and that we have to get rid of it, which is, for me, a much easier thing to do than to start by saying where I want to go in relation to that.

JOHN: My communication problem is close to yours although not quite the same. I'm very troubled, frightened, as well as confused, by abstract language. I think, for example, that things like My Lai begin when you start talking about people as slobs or bodies or something like that. It's one of the reasons why I really press for specifics, why, for example, I quibble with Richard on "war" as different from "abolish." I'm partly confused that if somebody were to say to me later, "Oh, you were at that conference when they talked about abolishing the public schools.

What did they mean?" I'd have to say I don't know. I feel strongly
unwilling at the moment to be part of an organization that stands
for the abolition of schools, if when people ask, "What does abolish
mean?" I don't know the answer. It might mean that schools will
not be compulsory, in which case I understand, or it might mean
that the state shall be forbidden to be in the school business, which
is something else. That might be what you mean but isn't what I
mean. Are we saying that the state should be forbidden from being
in the school business? I think there's a very good case to be made
if we're saying that the state wants to run schools, so let's let them
do it but nobody has to go unless he wants to. That's something
else. We may mean both. If a student who has been in the system
for 10 or 12 years were here talking about abolishing the public
schools it means a whole different thing to him. It means freedom
and after awhile it means a lack of something. For a teacher it
means a whole threatening of security and it means a total void.
It means recycling your energy whether you were satisfied with
what you were doing or not; it means going through a whole lot of
changes. I think that's the difference in the way I would approach
teachers and students when I talk about abolishing schools.

RICHARD: What I hear from what you say, Marshall, is that you
don't mind people being angry, you don't mind people saying bad
things about the public school system, but you want to say them
in personal terms rather than in some kind of abstract and rhetorical
terms.

CHUCK: I'm not going to hook into this business of saying it in a
loving way because the public schools never did anything for me
that would make me love them.

MARSHALL: I'm not asking you to do it because of anything
they did for you. I want you to do it because I want you to do it.
I'm not trying to convert you but I'm telling you I want you to
change. If you tell me right now, "Man, I don't want to change,"

427

I accept that. But when you say you don't want to change because they haven't given you anything, I want you to know that there's another possibility. You can change because I want you to and I think I've got good reasons for wanting. I just want you to consider that.

———————

One of the approaches suggested as a means of producing changes in education was that of changing the value system of the community in which the education occurs. This approach is related to that of effective communication, in that that communication is the means by which the change in value system is brought about. The discussion which follows describes the process in more detail.

MARSHALL: I believe that one answer might be to try to educate a community first of all to look at its present value structure, at what they would like their value structure to be, what they believe in. Then if they look at their institutions to see if they're consistent with their values my guess is that change will be much easier. Once people start to really get clear about what they want out of this world it becomes easier for them to destroy those institutions which are inconsistent with their values.

MERRILL: So that's a road toward changing the schools, really. Show people the inconsistencies between what they really want and need and the school institution.

MARSHALL: What I find is that when I really communicate with people that I think fall into a pattern that I don't particularly like, that I'm tempted to call somewhat conservative or reactionary, I find that we have the same values. When it becomes evident to them that their behavior is inconsistent with their own values I hear them hungrily saying to me, "What other alternatives are there?" I find that when they discover the inconsistencies, they say to me, "We have to change the schools, because they're certainly not set up to do what we agree is important." If I were to go to these

428

people and my opening statement was, "I think we ought to do away with compulsory education," I not only don't think I would get much understanding, I would probably get a fantastic amount of opposition. John Gardner says in RECOVERY OF CONFIDENCE that now is not the time to come with a new value system; now is the time to get people to act in a way that is consistent with the values they've had all along. The people in this country are committed to a certain value system, but they've been raised themselves according to people who've been raised by a divine right value system, and they're caught there. They don't know any other way, but when they see the inconsistencies they're hungry to learn new alternatives.

MERRILL: Let me go back for a moment. Suppose you've got a group of teachers who now say, "Yes, we really want to accomplish what we're talking about," what is your next step?

MARSHALL: My second step is to give them an alternative—to show them cognitively a way of behaving in a way that would be consistent with their values. But just getting cognitively some alternatives is far from living them.

MERRILL: And what is the cognitive alternative you give them?

MARSHALL: I teach them how to relate in a different way. I have it broken down into two skills that we've already talked about—how to share yourself, which I can break down into three components of self-focus, reporting on present feelings, thoughts, and wants, and reporting in relative rather than absolute terms. The second skill is empathy, which involves an other-focus, an acknowledgment of the other person's feelings, thoughts, and wants, and understanding the other person's viewpoint in a relative rather than an absolute way. A third skill that follows from those two is nonviolent conflict resolution. I can teach teachers and others these skills in workshops cognitively, I can get them to know, but that doesn't mean they're going to be able to do it. The next thing then is experiencing, sometimes for the first time in their lives, what it's like to relate to each other in this way. At that point things become powerful. Once they realize that there is another way of life, we've made a start. The next phase I get to in my workshops is to point out that the reality of life is that you're not only going to be in relationships where everybody is trying to learn, you're also going to be in relationships where you're going to be misunderstood and attacked. I try then to teach them how to relate in this way even when people put them in the worst imaginable binds. Then I try to find support groups to meet to keep them moving in this direction.

———————

This chapter has pointed out some of the directions in which people attempting to bring about educational change are focusing their efforts. Although some participants were identified with a particular reform tendency, the conference reveals a common commitment not only to looking for specific approaches but also to looking beyond them and to expressing a humanistic vision of social change and individual growth. The conference reveals also a common—and perhaps uncommon—urgency that more and more people keep moving in that direction.

INDEX